WYOMING'S WEALTH
A History of Wyoming

By Bill Bragg

Edited by Amir Sancher

In cooperation with:
Alan G. Wheeler
Hattie C. Burnstad
Karol L. Burrell

Paintings and Illustrations
Courtesy of

R.E. Carothers
Shell, WY

Harold Hopkinson
Byron, WY

Glen Hopkinson
Cody, WY

Photographs Courtesy
Wyoming State Historical Archives
Cheyenne, Wyoming

R. E. Carothers

"And Hanna prayed and said, My heart rejoiceth in the LORD, mine horn is exalted in the LORD, my mouth is enlarged over mine enemies because I rejoice in thy salvation." 1:Samuel 2:1

WYOMING'S WEALTH
A History of Wyoming

Second Printing
Library of Congress Number 76-47108
International Standard Book Number 0-89100-001-1
Big Horn Publishers, Basin, Wyoming 82410
©1976 by Bill Bragg. All Rights Reserved
Printed in the United States of America

Cover Bronze: ''Ex-Rider''
by R. E. Carothers
Shell, Wyoming

''Dedicated to the memory of all the Riders who lost their lives in any and all ways.'' 1975

Available from:
Big Horn Book Company
211 So. 4th Street
Basin, Wyoming 82410
(307) 568-2413

About the Author

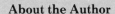

William F. (Bill) Bragg, Jr., was born in Wyoming. His family were Territorial pioneers of the state. Following his service in the U.S. Marines during World War II, he received a B.A. and M.A. degree in history from the University of Wyoming.

A teacher, Historian for the U.S. National Park Service at Fort Laramie, a member of the Wyoming Travel Commission, Executive Secretary for The Dude Rancher's Association, worked for the Jackson Hole Fine Arts Foundation, a sporting goods salesman. Bragg has also served as the Executive Secretary of the Wyoming Republican Party.

During those years, and up to the present time he wrote scripts for, or acted in a number of television commercials, and documentary motion pictures. He also created and narrated over 200 radio stories which have been aired over a wide number of Wyoming radio stations.

Most recently, he wrote the script for, and then narrated a 30 minute documentary motion picture based upon Wyoming's history.

Also, a number of his stories of Wyoming have been recently published by a Norwegian publishing house.

He is an active member of the Wyoming Writers, and the Western Writers of America, Inc. He is the public information officer at Casper College, and teaches Wyoming history at the same school.

PREFACE

I wrote this book because as a teacher of Wyoming history I couldn't find just exactly the right kind of textbook from which to base my courses. Many other teachers in Wyoming schools have told me they had the same problem.

So I sincerely hope they find this a useful text.

As for the students who read this book, I sincerely hope they find it anything but tedious remembering it is a broad look at the color and the action of Wyoming's past. The book is not intended as an indepth look at Wyoming's economics, its politics, or past social events.

The book is aimed at an enjoyable and interesting way of discovering—*Wyoming's Wealth*—which is of course its heritage.

To the many teachers at Casper College who helped me past anxious moments, I owe a debt of gratitude. In particular, I'd like to thank Dr. Peter K. Simpson and Dr. Cecil (Scott) Jones as well as the Goodstein Foundation Library director Gordon Hargraves and his entire staff.

My friends at Natrona County Library were invaluable in their help too, and I'd like to thank them. Also, the Archives section of the University of Wyoming, the State Historian, and the State Department of Education were outstanding in their advice, photographs, and research material.

My dear friend and constant advisor Dr. T.A. Larson never faltered once in helping me surmount the toughest difficulty, and I'll always be grateful to him.

The staff and board of the Wyoming Industrial Development Corporation were staunch in their belief that I could write this book. To them, my thanks for their patience and belief in this work.

James and Richard Kost, the publishers, plugged right along with me, and to them, I owe a special thanks for making all this possible.

And, finally my family and my wife remained loyal at all times to me and this work. Their devotion gave me the time to do the work, and the energy to finish it.

TABLE OF CONTENTS

Dedicated to the memory of my father,
William F. Bragg, Sr.,
whose enduring and lasting love of Wyoming
inspired me to write this book

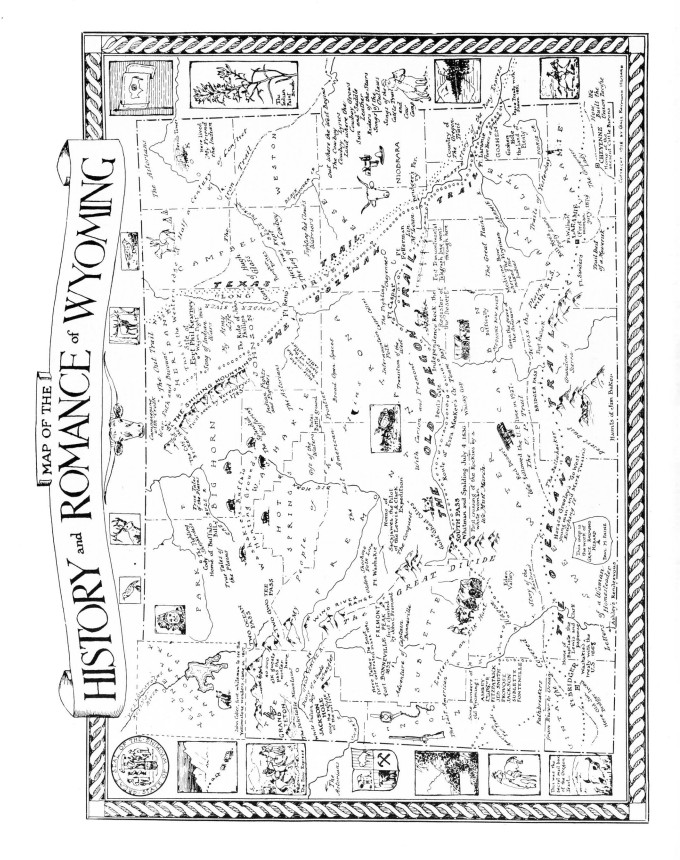

MAP OF THE HISTORY and ROMANCE of WYOMING

"Wyoming – A Mapmaker's Delight."

The map-maker who sets out to work with Wyoming has a rather easy starting point. He needs four straight lines, with the east-west lines about three inches to the north-south two inches, or multiples thereof. The southern boundary is very slightly longer than the northern because of the natural contour of the earth. The first thing to locate on the map is Yellowstone National Park in the northwest corner, and then he will never turn his map upside down.

He would then trace the spiney backbone of America, the Continental Divide, from the northwest corner slanting southward and leaving the state about halfway between the east and west borders and on into Colorado.

Using the Continental Divide as a guide, he next starts placing some of Wyoming's more important mountain ranges. Starting in the Yellowstone Park area north and east of the Divide and running into Montana would be the Absaroka, Carter, the Owl Creek turning east about a third of

the way down; below Yellowstone along the western boundary, the Tetons; then the Gros Ventre; then on both sides of the Divide more than half way down the state, the mighty Wind River Range. Still along the western border are the Bear Tooth, Bear River, and Salt River Mountains. About midway in the northern border, the Big Horns come out of Montana, move southeast and then turn west to converge with the Owl Creek to enclose the Big Horn Basin. The far northeast corner is occupied by the Black Hills. Slightly east of the center in the south are the Sierra Madres and then the Laramie, while closer to the center of the state are the lesser (in altitude) Rattlesnake, Green, and Seminoe.

With the mountains located, the map-maker turns his attention to the rivers. Tributaries of three great river systems rise in Wyoming. Again the map-maker starts in the west with the Snake rising in Yellowstone Park, flowing south about one-third of the length of the state, then bending

2

west and leaving the state through its beautiful Grand Canyon.

Starting on the west side of the Divide, high in the Wind River Mountains, the Green winds southward and out of the state at Flaming Gorge.

The Tributaries of the Missouri-Mississippi are many. The North Platte enters the state from Colorado in the area of the Sierra Madres, makes a great loop up to the center of the state, turns southeast and leaves the state along the lower eastern border to cross most of Nebraska before joining the Missouri. Flowing north, out of Wyoming is the Yellowstone which feeds out of Yellowstone Lake, cuts through the famous Yellowstone Grand Canyon and into Montana. The Wind, which rises east of the Divide, flows southeast for about a hundred miles, turns north, cuts through Wind River Canyon in the Owl Creek Mountains and comes out as the Big Horn to flow north into Montana and join the Yellowstone at Miles City. The Powder and the Belle Fourche also flow north to the Yellowstone in eastern Wyoming.

Several of these rivers have fertile valleys that the map-maker may put on his map because they are important to the population—such as Big Horn Basin, Platte Valley, and Green Valley.

The Red Desert in southwestern Wyoming must be labeled as well as the Great Basin.

Sandstone Formation, Red Buttes

Because the state is one of the Rocky Mountain states and has such variations of altitude, mountain peaks and passes are more important than in many states. Some of these could be

The "Tetons" from Cottonwood - 1901

Gannett, Fremont, Grand Teton and Cloud Peaks and Togwotee, Teton, Powder River Passes and The Summit. Natural lakes such as Yellowstone, Jackson, Jenny, Lewis, and Shoshone in the western part of the state are put on next by the map-maker.

Then he may decide to add the reservoirs that have been built in this century—Buffalo Bill,

Alcova Canyon, Natrona County, WY

Pathfinder, Seminoe, Alcova, Boysen, Glendo, Guernsey, Fontenelle, Yellowtail, and so on.

If the map-maker wishes to include Wyoming's political facts, the first location, of course, is Cheyenne in the southeast corner of the state. The next step would be adding county lines, realizing there are twenty-three counties, ranging in size from 10,000-square-mile Sweetwater to 2,000-square-mile Hot Springs. The county seat may be located in each county.

The National Forests and Reservoirs with their controlling dams show many interesting developments.

The addition of leading highways also shows the influence of mountains and mountain passes upon our population locations. Tourist attractions and large airports bring out some more challenging growth patterns.

3

CHAPTER I

GEOGRAPHIC WYOMING

Only two states in the Union are shaped like rectangles— and Wyoming is one of them. With an area of 97,914 square miles, Wyoming ranks ninth in size. It lies in the heart of the Rocky Mountain West between 41 degrees north latitude and 45 degrees north latitude, and its longitude is between 104 degrees 3 minutes and 111 degrees 3 minutes west.

Since the Continental Divide runs almost the entire width of the state north to south, streams rising in Wyoming eventually flow into all three of the great western river systems—the Columbia, Colorado, and Missouri. Water, its source, quantity, and use have always been of prime concern to Wyomingites and was even covered in an article of the state constitution. Conservation and reclamation have long been of concern with the first dam, Buffalo Bill, being constructed in 1910 followed immediately by Pathfinder. At the present time, most of the rivers are included in large overall power reclamation and recreation projects such as Missouri Valley, Platte Valley, Jim Bridger, etc.

Wyoming has 17.3 million acre-feet of water which comes from rain, snow, sleet, hail, and mist, with a little flowing in from other states. At present, only about 15 percent of this surface water is used; the remaining 85 percent flows out of Wyoming and is used in other states. Wyoming has a vast amount of subterranean water, although no one knows exactly how much there is. Some of this water is being used for irrigation in southeastern Wyoming. These enormous reserves are being submitted to a very careful study before being allotted for increased agricultural or industrial uses. Caution is being used, because no one knows yet how much water from precipitation would be needed to replace the underground water used or how long the replacement would take. Once that is known, underground water may be used in many ways.

Gros Ventre River, WY

Because of the vast mountainous regions we have many national forests. The first national forest was established in northwest Wyoming in 1902 and was then called Yellowstone Forest Reserve. Presently that area is part of the Shoshone National Forest. Other National Forests wholly or partly in Wyoming include Bridger, Big Horn, Medicine Bow, Black Hills, Teton, Caribou, Wasatch, and Targhee. Within the forests are areas called "Wilderness Areas" where there are no roads or accommodations and vehicles are not allowed to go. These are to be kept virgin just as nature made them, and people only hike and backpack into these areas.

It is easy to see why Wyoming calls tourism—the encouragement and guidance of tourists—one of its important industries. The two main tourist attractions are Yellowstone National Park and Grand Teton National Park. Yellowstone, which is the home of stupendous waterfalls, great lakes, a variety of wildlife, matchless geysers, and "paint pots," was America's first national park, founded in 1872. Only a few miles south, the more recently created Grand Teton National Park has millions of visitors each season.

Old Faithful Inn, Yellowstone Park

The towering Tetons are often compared to the Alps of Europe although Wyoming's highest peaks are not here but are Gannett and Fremont in the Wind River Range. Among Wyoming's other tourist attractions must be included such things as Devils Tower, hunting and fishing, camping, rodeos, dude ranching, and many other things.

Wyoming's longest established industry is agriculture with cattle and sheep ranching, dry and irrigated farming all contributing to the income of the state.

Jackson Lake, Jackson, WY

Sheep—One Of Wyomings Oldest Industries

Another industry important to Wyoming's enconomy is based upon the recovery of minerals such as coal, oil, gas, uranium, iron ore, bentonite, trona, gypsum and even sand and gravel.

Wyoming ranks as the fifth largest producer of oil. Nearly every county produces oil or gas. Wyoming ranks seventh in the nation in natural gas production.

Wyoming is one of the largest coal producers in the nation. It is estimated that Wyoming has approximately 445 billion tons of coal in reserve. Historically, coal was first used as fuel for railroads. Today, coal is produced mainly for power in coal-fired power generating plants. While Wyoming consumes a portion of this coal, much of it is exported to other states.

Wyoming's low-sulphur coal is found so close to the surface that in many cases the thick seams can be easily mined. Because this coal has a low sulphur emission which, in turn, reduces air pollution, Wyoming coal is in great demand.

These three properties of Wyoming's coal—low in sulphur content, ease of mining, and huge amounts—have caused Wyoming's labor force to swell enormously in the past few years.

Wyoming coal production, in the same manner as oil production and natural gas production, is helping the nation meet the energy crisis. The energy crisis has plagued the United States since the Arab demands for higher crude oil prices rocked the world in 1973. With oil in great demand, oil rigs drill at near capacity. By 1974, well over 100 rigs were drilling in Wyoming. This is the highest count in the Rocky Mountain region.

An outcome of the coal boom, Wyoming is now experiencing the planning of three new coal-fired power generating plants. These are in addition to the new 400-million-dollar plant at Rock Springs now under construction.

Power plants at Kemmerer, Glenrock, and Gillette are already using Wyoming coal. Demands for Wyoming coal will continue and will result in a rich future for coal mining in Wyoming.

Coal Mine Located In Big Horn County, WY

Uranium was first found in Wyoming near Lusk in 1918. Since that date, uranium mining has grown rapidly, and now Wyoming is ranked second only to New Mexico in uranium production. Nearly forty percent of the national supply of that mineral is found in Wyoming.

Iron ore, at present, is mined only in Platte and Fremont counties. The mine at Sunrise in Platte County has been mining iron ore since 1900 and is probably the oldest operating mine in Wyoming's history.

Bentonite, an all-purpose ore, is found in large quantity in northern Wyoming. By 1973 nearly a million and a half tons of the clay-like bentonite had been exported to overseas buyers or used in the domestic market. Because it can bind small particles together, bentonite is used to form pellets of the tiny iron ore fragments found in the Atlantic City, Wyoming, iron mine. This cuts down the cost and difficulty of shipping the fine taconite iron ore. Bentonite is also used in drilling oil wells, in heavy construction, and in foundry work. It is "the ore of a thousand uses."

Trona is mined in the Green River area in southwest Wyoming. One source said, "The high-grade trona ore is mined, refined, and calcined into 99.98% pure sodium carbonate. Almost all of the baking soda used in the western United States is produced at Green River."

Oil shale, ballast, gypsum, sulphur, sand, gravel, rock, and limestone are other mining ores that will be, or are now being, mined and refined in Wyoming. Clearly, Wyoming's economic future seems to be on the upswing.

Wyoming's Wealth Includes Wood And Wood
Products Such As The Lodge Pole Pines

Timber is another natural resource found in Wyoming, with nearly one sixth of the state covered by lumber trees, or over eight and a half million acres of forest land directly under the supervision of the U. S. Forest Service. More than half of Wyoming's trees are classed as lodge-pole pine. The rest of the trees valued for timber are Douglas fir, Engleman spruce, and aspen. Wood and wood products are the third largest industry in the state. Another beautiful tree is the cottonwood, Wyoming's state tree, growing in profusion along rivers and streams. Cedar and juniper cover some of the mountains, giving them their "black" appearance.

The climate in Wyoming is dry and cool. While an occasional snowstorm may cover the state in September or October, *Fall* is considered one of the better seasons for visiting Wyoming. The heaviest winter storms occur from February through May.

Rainfall averages 15.8 inches per year. The growing season in Wyoming varies from thirty days at higher altitudes to one hundred fifty days in the lower river basins, or valleys.

The temperature has ranged from a 1933 reading in Yellowstone National Park of 66° below zero to 114° above, in Basin in 1900. Winter temperatures range from one extreme to another, depending upon the location within Wyoming. It has been 20° below zero in Casper and 20° above, at Lander at the same time on the very same day.

Probably the worst storms occur *after* the snow has finished falling, when a strong surface wind will cause the snow to string out in a blinding "ground blizzard." This condition is not only a traffic hazard, but it causes the temperature to drop drastically according to "wind chill" measurement. Thus, a current temperature of 20° above zero can mean, in terms of a wind chill, as much as 24° below zero on the human body in a 50 mile per hour wind. That same 20° weather can drop to a minus 9° below zero when a wind races over 20 miles per hour across frozen snowfields. Wyoming drivers and ranchers have learned to govern their driving habits and ranching chores in the winter according to the strength of the wind and the degrees of temperature.

From prehistoric times to the present, Wyoming has been the habitat for a wild, often exotic array of animals, reptiles, birds, and fishes. Fossil hunters and scientific expeditions have carted off tons and tons of skeletal remains of prehistoric habitants of Wyoming. Today these treasures can be seen in college, university, and natural history museums all over the world, as well as in private collections.

Moisture in Wyoming Averages
15.8 Inches Per Year

8

Modern times have seen the animal kingdom of Wyoming well taken care of by the hard working and dedicated members of the Wyoming Game and Fish Commission. The annual big game harvest in Wyoming, during which thousands of out-of-state hunters occupy the state, helps keep the levels of the herds in balance with nature and, at the same time, keeps the herds young and strong.

Elk do not inhabit the plains as they once did, but they still provide a major hunting attraction in Wyoming each season. Wyoming's elk herds are among the most numerous in the United States today.

Grizzly bear are not so plentiful as they were during the "mountain man" period of the 1800's, but they can still be found in Wyoming today in the Dubois, Pinedale, Jackson, Cody, and Yellowstone regions. The more common brown and black bear can be found in nearly every forested region of Wyoming today.

Bighorn sheep once lived along the banks of rivers in the plains but are found today living in the higher rugged mountains. They too can be hunted in Wyoming during a designated hunting season.

Moose are hunted in the state and ordinarily can be found in most major mountain drainage areas along the western side of the state. Some moose, however, have been transplanted by the Wyoming Game and Fish Commission to other forested and mountainous areas of the state.

The most commonly hunted big game animal in Wyoming is the black-tailed mule deer, characterized by its big mule-like ears. As the herds increase each year, whitetail deer hunting is also growing more popular.

Wyoming is the home of the world's largest herd of North American pronghorn antelope. These speedy animals have provided many interesting hunts for thousands of hunters over the years. The pronghorn, not considered a true antelope by zoologists, is noted for its keen eyesight and speed.

Hunting jackrabbit and cottontail is a popular sport in Wyoming, as is hunting such predators as bobcat, mountain lion, and coyote.

Sage grouse are plentiful—in fact, Wyoming is the "sage grouse capital" of the United States. Chukar, pheasant, duck, and geese provide from good to excellent hunting, too. While not located all over Wyoming, fine wild turkey is found along the eastern edge of the state.

For the fisherman, Wyoming is truly a heroic sport-fishing state. Here sportsmen can take

advantage of nearly every kind of fishing except, of course, saltwater fishing. At high altitudes the classy golden trout can be caught, as well as the mackinaw, brown, cutthroat, rainbow, and brook trout. Occasionally the ardent fisherman can find the grayling an excellent fighter.

All over Wyoming the thousands of miles of fishing streams and hundreds of acres of surface water also offer walleye, bass, crappie, perch, sauger, channel catfish, and bluegill. And if the time is right, the rare ling can be caught through the ice in the Lander- Shoshoni-Dubois-Riverton region.

Animals such as elk, bighorn sheep, and grizzly bear changed their habitat from the plains to high country when white men moved to Wyoming in large numbers.

But even with the people and the mining and the agriculture and the tourists, Wyoming has wide expanses of land where there are no people at all. These vast, "empty" areas give the viewer a sort of "big" feeling and show us plainly that there is plenty of elbow room left in Wyoming.

And while Wyoming citizens' feelings may be divided as to the use and development of the state's vast array of resources, they all stand solidly together in their love of their native or adopted State of Wyoming.

" Prehistoric Bison Hunt At Casper "

The ancient hunters clutch their stone weapons at their sides this morning, listening to the big herd of buffalo across the river. They wait patiently for the buffalo to cross the North Platte, though they cannot see them through the fog and mist rising from the river.

The hunters wait silently. They know the herd will follow the trail which leads from the river bottom to the area they have chosen to trap and kill the animals. They had watched the herd last night and had seen several old bull buffalo, the leaders, cross the river and bed down for the night. The hunters knew then that the rest of the herd would come across the river this morning, and they selected their kill site. Here a well-worn buffalo trail leads into a long, narrow sandbank filled with deep, loose soil. When the herd move through it, slowed down by the heavy sand, the hunters will begin their kill. When the great beasts try to climb up and out of the trap, the hunters will hurl their spears.

The women, children, and old ones wait in the rear. They carry the hides, heavy with more spears and hammerstones and skinning tools.

When the kill starts, those in the rear will join the hunters, forming a ring around the herd.

This is a vital kill. Soon the sky will fill with snow, and the rivers will freeze. Now is the time when the hunters must find their cliff caves and try to outlast the winter ahead. The meat and hides won here today will provide food and cover until the green grass of spring appears, signaling the end of one more winter.

Several young scouts slip back to their stations. This indicates the herd is on the move. The wind has not shifted, coming steadily into their faces. That is good; smell of man would have excited the herd, turning them away at the last moment.

Now the hunters can hear the chug-chugging of the labored breathing of the big buffalo, as they climb slowly up the steep river terrace to the grassfields hiding the hunters and their sand trap.

As the morning breeze parts the ground fog, the big brutes emerge from the gray sheets of fog and file slowly into the trap. The hunters hold their breath, waiting for just the right moment to spring the trap.

Now! The hunt leader rises. He shouts and throws his spear into the side of a fat cow buffalo. The rest of the hunters follow his lead, each picking out a good target and hurling his spears into it.

Meanwhile, the women, children, and old ones rush up to join the hunters and hand out more spears and hammerstones to the laboring men. Everyone is shouting excitedly, and the buffalo are bellowing as the kill progresses. The strong hunters knock down those who are frantically trying to climb the wall of the trap to safety.

The kill is all over in a few minutes. The exhausted hunters sink to their haunches as they watch the women and others slide down into the sandbank, full of the slaughtered beasts. Then they join them, and the job of butchering the successful kill begins.

This story is based upon evidence found by State Archeologist George C. Frison, while digging near Casper in May and June 1971. Deep in the bed of an ancient sandbank spear heads were found among the fossil remains of over one hundred now-extinct bison—or buffalo, as we usually call them.

These remains, dated with a radioactive carbon test, are thought to be 10,000 years old. And while, certainly, there are no living witnesses to this bison hunt, according to Dr. Frison's evidence—it could have happened that way!

Artifacts Provide Clues of Paleo-Indian Existence

CHAPTER II

ANCIENT MAN IN WYOMING

The most ancient man in Wyoming has been the subject of intensive search for over fifty years. A whole array of scientists, including *anthropologists* (those who study the relics and remains of the past), *geologists* (those who study the earth, especially its rocks and minerals), and *paleontologists* (those studying the fossils found in ancient geological formations), have pooled their efforts in trying to piece together the story of ancient man. But, so far, the results of these efforts have been mighty slim.

These scientists are especially happy when they find *artifacts*—what is left of simple tools, weapons, pottery—that prove there was once some sort of civilization in the area. Artifacts tell a story, often an interesting one, of a people of long ago.

But *Paleo-Indian* (*paleo* means "old," and this is what Wyoming's prehistoric man is called) has proved to be elusive to this army of scientific detectives because he has left very few artifacts, no real account of his history: where he came from, how he lived, how long ago he was here.

Among the few clues we have that this Indian even existed are crude pictures carved and drawn on cave walls and cliffs in Wyoming—the carvings and drawings are called petroglyphs and picto-

Petroglyphs and Pictographs Are Evidence
Of Early Paleo-Indian Life

Mummified Pygmy Discovered in the Pedro
Mountains Located 65 Miles From Casper; WY.
October 1932

graphs. As yet, we have no way of dating these simple pictures.

The fact is, very little is known about Paleo-Indian in Wyoming—or anywhere else in the Western Hemisphere. We do not know just what this early man looked like because, as far as is known, his skeleton has never turned up in an excavation. No one is absolutely certain, either, how he got to this area or where he went when he left. No one knows if Paleo-Indian brought cultural equipment to this area and, if he did, how he used his tools.

As a matter of fact, no one can say for sure whether Paleo-Indian originated in the New World or just migrated here from across the sea.

A Mastodon Hunter

About all that is really known is that Paleo-Indian was a hunter—Wyoming's first real big game hunter. That is definite. His "projectile points" have been found *in situ* (meaning "close by" or "in the original position") with the fossil remains of huge, now extinct, prehistoric mam-

mals that roamed the hills and plains of Wyoming thousands of years ago.

This proves that Paleo-Indian was here when the towering mastodon, an elephant that stood as much as fourteen feet high at the shoulder, died near Worland. Paleo-Indian projectile points were found in the remains, or *"in situ"* with the remains, of that ancient behemoth. A carbon age-dating fixes the date of that mastodon at 11,200 years before the present time!

Excavation discoveries

It is also known that Paleo-Indian roamed near Casper, because his projectile points were found among the fossil remains and bones of buffalo killed in a sand trap. Again, a carbon dating produced the date of those buffalo at 10,000 years before the present!

So: from these and other scientific excavations, it is now known that an ancient big game hunter lived in Wyoming and elsewhere on the High Plains of the West as much as 25,000 years ago, even earlier. And it is known from the fossil

13

Fossilized Animals Give Archaelogists An Insight
Into Prehistoric Environment Throughout
Wyoming

remains of the animals living in those times that Wyoming was a prehistoric big-game-hunting paradise. As many varieties of big game existed in Wyoming then as exist in Africa today: giant sloth, horses, camels, mastodon, and the hairy mammoth (another type of elephant) lived all over what is now Wyoming.

One of the favorite targets of the Paleo-Indian was the bison. They were larger than those we now have in America. Often when the bones of this extinct animal are exposed after an "archaeo-oological dig," fine leaf-shaped flint points of Paleo-Indian are found, still embedded in the fossil bones.

Bering Strait Bridge

Thus, over the years, Paleo-Indian has left an artifactual trail documented by digs all over America. The trail of chipped flint and well-designed artifacts seems to back up the current theory that this ancient nomadic hunter came to the New World from Asia on a land bridge between the tip of Siberia and Alaska.

Once, when the northern half of North America was covered with a huge shield of ice, a bridge about 50 miles long surfaced between the two continents at Bering Strait. Various animals crossed this bridge, traveling in both directions, followed by ancient big game hunters. Over a great span of time, tribe after tribe or band after band of hunters followed the animals as they sought food, into the land of the New World.

The sleuths of time, our geologists, say that somewhere during this period of Paleo-Indian migration, an ice-free corridor appeared along the eastern flanks of the mighty Rocky Mountains, which would include the states of Montana, Wyoming, Colorado, New Mexico and extend south into Mexico.

The animals naturally followed this corridor and were funneled into what is now Wyoming, bringing Paleo-Indian with them. Evidence of these animals and the flint projectile points of their hunters range all the way through the High Plains states, where the ice-free corridor appeared. It is there where most of the evidence of early man in the New World is being found.

As Paleo-Indian arrived, he brought with him flint-tipped spears and an atlatl. Atlatl is an Aztec word for a throwing-stick. This tool, or weapon, preceded the bow and arrow. By use of the throwing-stick, or atlatl, a spear or dart-like weapon could be thrown harder and for much longer distances than by hand. Properly used, an atlatl can cast a spear with as much force as a powerful bow can send an arrow. The atlatl, acting as an extension of the arm, helped early man meet the challenge of the huge animals he hunted on foot.

Age-dating methods

For years archaeologists began counting the history of ancient man in North America from the time of Coronado's expedition into southwestern United States about 1541 AD. Anything before that would be hard to age-date, since no real way of determining age had been accepted other than *stratigraphy;* digging down into the earth, where each layer or strata reached is older than the one just passed. The lowest strata is assumed to be the oldest.

That is stratigraphy, and it provided a sort of chronology for early archaeologists.

In 1838, a projectile point was found in Missouri near the fossil remains of a mammoth. The age could not be determined by stratigraphy. Similar circumstances were recorded. Each one may have satisfied the finder as to its age but not the skeptic in Europe or the eastern part of America. What was needed was an ancient artifact in situ with fossil remains of an extinct animal—which had not been touched or moved by an over-anxious digger or collector.

Finally, in 1926, that evidence was found in tiny Folsom, New Mexico. A beautiful fluted projectile point was found in situ with the bones of a type of bison known to have been extinct for thousands of years. The work was carried on by a thoroughly competent archaeologist. Even when he announced the find, it took three years of digging and more in situ evidence before the find was authenticated. Then the announcement was made that ancient man had, indeed, lived in North America long before the time of Christ.

Still the problem of accurate age-dating remained. Since 1926, however, and aside from stratigraphy and the geological answers to soils laid down over the ages, new methods have come to the front:

One of them was "dendrochronology," which involves counting tree rings in ancient trees. A wide ring was formed during a wet year and a narrow ring during a dry one. The scientist just had to find a date of a dry or wet year in history and then count the rings of a tree, stump, or chunk of wood at the archaeological site of an excavation. This method could not be used, of course, when wood could not be found, so more work was continued on the hunt for an easier solution to the problem of age-dating.

15

Carbon Dating Discovered

Then, a scientific breakthrough announced that carbon gave off a certain amount of energy at a known calibrated measure of time which was tested against ancient, but known, historic dates in Egypt and Israel. Thus, the Carbon-14 age-dating device was discovered and used. All that was needed was carbon from a campfire, and the time element backwards into time and the dim past could be counted with some degree of accuracy.

However, no test is perfect, so the scientists have continued to experiment and develop the other types of tests mentioned, although C-14 is still widely used and fairly dependable. This means of age-dating has been improved upon since its early arrival, and with it have come other radical changes and means of dating the past.

It was found, for example, through protein chemistry that animal acids change with time and temperature, establishing a new method of dating. Another new method was found in "paleomagnetism"—analyzing the changes that have occurred in a magnetic field over the ages. "Thermal luminescence," based upon heating a mineral and measuring the effect, is also now used in dating.

So, while ancient man has proved to be an elusive target over the years, the scientists have been working on means and ways to establish, beyond any doubt, the antiquity of substances— bones, projectile points, seeds, etc.—found in the animal traps of Paleo-Indian. Applying these new age-dating devices to the tools used, or to bones left behind, or to seeds found in the traps, or to the camps left behind by ancient man where he cooked his food or butchered his kills—testing all of these findings has certainly increased the knowledge we now have of Paleo-Indian in Wyoming. New discoveries are continually being made at new sites where various age-dating techniques are being applied to the evidence gathered by the archeologists.

Much of the information we've received about ancient man in Wyoming can be traced directly to the work of Dr. W. T. Mulloy of the University of Wyoming. In more recent times State Archaeologist Dr. George C. Frison, also of the University of Wyoming, has added much to Wyoming's growing wealth of information about Paleo-Indian. These two professors have been instrumental in preserving Wyoming's oldest natural resource, the history of man. However, they have not done this alone; hundreds of rockhounds, arrowhead collectors, and amateur archaeologists have tipped off Mulloy and Frison to promising finds.

At Casper, several residents found evidence of what they felt was Paleo-Indian's presence near that city. Dr. Frison examined their evidence and found that it was good enough to excavate during May and June 1971. The results disclosed a site where buffalo had been slaughtered by Paleo-Indian over 10,000 years ago.

More recently, another Wyoming resident, Donald Colby, asked Dr. Frison to check into a clue he had found near Worland. The results were an excavation which produced projectile points in close association with the extinct mastodon. A positive age-dating indicated that the site was used 11,200 years ago!

Since it is most important to record everything possible about an artifact at the time it is found, these projectile points have been described in detail—and even given names for identification.

PROJECTILE POINTS OF HISTORY

First found in New Mexico. From 2 to 4 inches in length, with long parallel sides. It is somewhat roughly flaked; notched on one side, producing one "shoulder." Older than *Folson,* it may approach the age of 25,000 years.

SANDIA

Sometimes called *Plainview,* has been found at Yuma, Arizona; Eden Valley, Wyoming; and Scottsbluff, Nebraska, to name only a few places. Well flaked, fine pressure ribbon-like flakes. One to 5 inches long. 7,000 to 10,000 years old.

YUMA

First found in Folsom, New Mexico, in 1926. About 2 inches long, leaf-shaped, with ear-like "tangs," and a deep-channel flute and concave base. Possibly 10,000 to 13,000 years ago.

FOLSOM

Named after Hell Gap which is near Guernsey, Wyoming. Leaf-shaped, these points have an extra long tang for jab or thrust. Found also at Casper, Wyoming, at a bison kill site, they were from 2 inches to 5-1/2 inches in length. 10,000 years old, perhaps older.

HELL GAP

A *Clovis,* New Mexico, find, and it, like the Folsom, has a channel groove. Average size is 3 inches, but it has been found up to 5 inches in length. From 10,000 to 13,000 years old.

CLOVIS

Deep concave bases with a channel flute. Running up to 4 inches in length, these have pronounced rounded basal ears and are reminiscent of the *Clovis.* Radio carbon dated at 11,200 years before the present time.

COLBY

If you, as an arrowhead hunter—or an amateur archaeologist—find a spear point that you feel may be extremely old, here are a few simple rules to follow:

1. Take a photograph of the find *before* you remove it, or before any of the ground or earth near the find is disturbed by movement, footprints, etc. Lay some object like a pocketknife, a watch, or a coin beside it so as to give the find a true size in relation to the object it is photographed with.

2. Mark the spot so you can return to it—and maybe it would be a good idea to push some brush over it. Leave it alone until you have contacted the local archaeological society, a competent geologist, or the State Archaeologist.

These rules are simple and easy to follow. Use them. Bide your time until you have heard about your find from authorities. You will be doing yourself and your state a service in helping to preserve a small slice of prehistoric time in Wyoming.

VIGNETTE:

"The Casper Kill - A Study In Cooperation"

Two couples, Mr. and Mrs. Egolff and Mr. and Mrs. Laird, were arrowhead hunting when they found a fluted projectile point near the newly constructed Control Data computer plant near the city of Casper. They immediately placed that information in responsible hands.

Dr. George C. Frison arrived soon and determined that this could possibly be a site worth excavating.

The problem was that the site was right next to the plant parking lot, and less than fifty yards away was the constant stream of highway traffic on Interstate 25. Also, the site overlooked Casper, a city with more than 40,000 people living in it.

If Frison was going to dig, he would have to have protection for the site and help in his work. An army of spectators could slow down the dig, which could certainly create problems in the painstakingly slow method of excavating and digging a site—much care must be taken, you know, in recording each layer of soil as it is removed.

The wind was bad, so snow fences were put up to halt the constant shifting of the loose soil. The State Highway Department allowed patrolmen to assist Frison.

Natrona County Commissioners and the Casper Police Department also helped, as did others in the Casper city government.

A local geologist who is also an acknowledged archaeologist, John Albanese, helped by mapping and surveying the area for Frison. Members of the State Archaeological Society who lived in Casper helped Frison, as well as college students interested in anthropology.

The owner of the land surrounding the plant was Mr. H. O. English, who, with his wife, aided Frison when he could. Also, the gracious management of Control Data, the computer plant, assisted Frison, having given permission for the excavation.

All of these efforts paid off. Frison praised the Casper couples who had made the original discovery of the site when he said, "...full credit must be accorded to them in recognition of their restraint and concern. Any other course of action on their part could have resulted in a serious loss to Paleo-Indian studies.''

In his book *The Casper Site, a Hell Gap Bison Kill on the High Plains,* Frison reported, ''The Casper Site consisted of a steep-sided trap formed by the wings and leeward end of a parabolic sand dune, into which bison of a form now extinct were driven and killed. The animals were subsequently butchered and parts saved were removed to another area for further processing.''

Hell Gap was a Paleo-Indian site discovered near Guernsey. The name was given in 1961 to a stylized projectile point found there, and points found in Casper were of this same type; hence the name Hell Gap.

The really thrilling evidence to hundreds of arrowhead hunters, rockhounds, and amateur archaeologists were the sixteen perfect projectile points found, along with eleven others which were in just two pieces. A total of sixty separate projectile points were recovered from the Casper site.

Some hunters of the gem-like projectile points and other artifacts look all their lives for just **one** Paleo-Indian point, hoping it will be perfect. Frison and his workers excavated and found sixty at one site!

When Frison made a complete report on the dig, he pinpointed its age at 10,000 years before the present time.

There are many, many sites in Wyoming that have been found, examined, excavated, and reported. And while the Casper site is not the only one, it is a classic example of Wyoming at its best, as government and local residents joined together to preserve and amplify Wyoming's ancient heritage.

Indian Woman And Travois

"Pedestrian To Dog To Horse"

Ancient man in Wyoming did not have the dog with him to assist in carrying supplies when he struggled across the Bering Strait and finally arrived here, nor did he have the horse to ride on. No remains of anything resembling either have yet been found in any of the camps, kill sites, or butchering stations unearthed by archaeologists who are relentlessly on Paleo-Indian's trail.

Thus it is plain to see that Paleo-Indian was a pedestrian as well as a hunter. On foot, and constantly on the hunt, he found the High Plains—and Wyoming, in particular, with its endless variety of big game—a suitable place to live. It was here he could find and kill the hairy mammoth, the huge mastodon, the giant bison, and camel, sloth, and other animals that provided tools, food, clothing, and shelter.

He transported everything he and his tribe owned. Thus, when the dog did arrive, it was made into a beast of burden. Very likely a *travois* was attached to the dog for hauling. This method of using parallel sticks with a hide stretched between them for the equipment loaded and lashed down onto it, was seen in 1541 AD by members of Coronado's expedition in the Southwest.

Paleo-Indian who kept to the High Plains were first seen by Coronado's Spanish conquistadores. At that point in time, another important event took place in the life-style of the Indian—the appearance of the horse, ridden by the Spanish explorers. History shows that the Indians were astounded by this beast and showed fear and excitement that man could ride upon it. Within a very short period, however, the Indian found that man on horseback was no immortal, as he first had thought: both the man and the horse could be killed. And it didn't take the Indian too long to convert the horse into a means of transportation for himself. This added a new way to go to war, to hunt, or to move a camp—the three uses the Indian made of the horse. And by 1740 the horse had changed the life and style of many Indian tribes.

Up until that time the Arapaho, Gros Ventre, Cheyenne, Crow, and Sioux were semi-sedentary tribes, content to settle and remain more or less in one area, moving only as the quest for food or intrusion of enemy tribes made it necessary. But the arrival of the horse changed them virtually overnight. And, when they had learned to master the horse, they became relentless warriors and nomadic buffalo hunters on the High Plains.

The Sioux had been pursued by the Ojibwa for many years, shoved out of the lush woodlands of Iowa-Wisconsin-Minnesota westward onto the more arid plains of the Dakotas and Nebraska. But when the Sioux got the horse, they halted their westward movement, held their hunting ground, and pushed the Ojibwa back to the east while taking command of their own tribal territory.

The horse was an animal which thrived on the plains. Good grass, plenty of water, and hundreds of thousands of square miles of range helped the stray, stolen, and lost horses of the early Spanish to multiply rapidly. The so-called wild horse is really a ''feral'' horse, a domestic horse which has been freed or strayed. His offspring are denoted as wild, even though the parents had been domestic horses.

As long as there were vast herds of buffalo to hunt and live off of, the Indians were nearly indestructible; the U. S. Army discovered this in the battles and wars they fought with the Indians. The Indian was a fierce warrior, and on horseback, as he defended his land and people and hunted the buffalo, he was an outstanding example of the finest light cavalry ever to appear in the world.

Many of those famous fighting tribes of indians hunted and fought in Wyoming. We remember them as Arapaho, Cheyenne, Crow, Commanche, Bannock, Blackfoot, Shoshone, Sioux, and Ute Indians.

A number of Shoshone and Arapaho Indians still live in Wyoming, many on the huge Wind River Indian Reservation. The reservation contains nearly three million acres and is located in the triangle between Lander, Riverton, and Dubois.

This reservation was first assigned by treaty to the Indian Chief Washakie's Shoshones and also some Bannock Indians in 1863. That treaty was modified in 1869. By 1877, after the Bannock decided to move back to Idaho, the Arapaho were placed on the reservation. The last count taken in 1974 shows that there were approximately two thousand Shoshone and three thousand Arapaho Indians living there.

Many Indians, however, have taken their place in modern society, living and working and studying side by side with the other people of various backgrounds who make up today's American citizen.

CHAPTER III

INDIAN WYOMING

The early colonists in America, we know, found Indians in every area of the New World that they penetrated. It seems apparent that the Indian was often willing to befriend these strange white men and share their knowledge and even the land. But language, customs, and the early settlers' great need of farm land were such barriers that before many decades passed, the two groups were enemies. Indians had no true concept of the meaning of boundaries—they came to this land and roamed and hunted where they would. When the white man did the same, the Indians took exception to his claiming specified areas as his own, where he felled trees and built buildings and cut roads, upsetting the habitation of the game animals.

True, the white man paid money, in many instances, for the land he claimed. But he didn't understand the loose structure of the tribes—the chiefs and *sachems* did not have complete control of the comings and goings of those considered to be under them, even if the chiefs themselves should understand the meaning of limited boundaries—which they seldom did.

Too, the widespread practise of scalping, torture, and sometimes taking young captives as slaves certainly made it unlikely that the white man would have an objective, live-and-let-live attitude toward the Indian.

All of this resulted in a relationship that, at best, was an uneasy one between white man and Indian and proved to be disastrous to the Indian, himself. He was pushed farther and farther west, forced into a way of life totally different from that that he was bred to, and consequently struck back at times in bloody warfare.

While war was a way of life with many of the tribes, and their experience and knowledge of the terrain made them a formidable foe, the white cavalry succeeded in driving them westward.

It was a distressing problem, and in 1828 Supreme Court Justice Joseph Story of Massachusetts wrote,

> What can be more melancholy than their history? [Referring to the plight of the Indians]. By a law of their nature, they seem destined to a slow but sure extinction. Everywhere, at the approach of white man, they fade away. We hear the rustling of their footsteps, like that of withered leaves in autumn, and they are gone forever. They pass mournfully by us, and they return no more.

Early Arapahoe Home Located On Shoshone Reservation

Reservation System

In Congress there seemed to be a feeling that the disappearance of the Indian was loss of a national asset. There were those in Washington who felt that if the Indian could be *excluded* from white man's society by means of *seclusion,* the Indian might be saved. They were worried that disease, whiskey, and bad habits learned from white men had thinned the ranks of the Indians. Excluding the Indians and secluding them meant only one thing—a reservation system.

That solution was a hopeful one, because the West seemed ideal for the Indian. But it was impossible to keep the white man off the reservation land, and it certainly meant little to the Plains Indians, who had no concept of land boundaries.

The Army was responsible for carrying out the policies that were set up, as well as enforcing the rules and regulations from Washington. And most of the military establishment had the same problem the policy makers had—they never really distinguished one race or tribe of Indians from another. The tactics learned among the woodland Indians in the French and Indian Wars were certainly not useable against the High Plains Indians who roamed everywhere from the Canadian border area in North Dakota and Montana south to Mexico.

If ever there was a race of men and women born free, it was the horseback hunter of the High

Pictured Above—Chief Buffalo Wallow

24

supply of weapons. He was generally a very handy man around an Indian camp, because he could usually repair a broken rifle, construct a good knife, fix a trap, and work with iron. He could also be counted upon to have trade goods at his disposal.

The invasion of the West was begun by the mountain man. The occasional explorer had been a curiosity to the Indian. Now, trading posts began to appear, as beaver were trapped and traded. The rendezvous system (yearly gatherings of traders and trappers) helped intitiate a chain reaction of change in the West.

Concept of Manifest Destiny

Behind all this westward activity was the theme of *Manifest Destiny,* the absolute certainty that Americans must press on, clear to the western sea. Nothing could turn them away from that dream. And, sadly enough, the Indians were in the way.

Pictured Above Are Cornelius Vanderbuilt and Wife [Arapahoe] Depicts Formal Dress of That Tribe

Plains. He had come into his own when the horse made its appearance. By 1750 most the the tribes fighting in the bitter Indian wars on the Plains were fast becoming masters of horsemanship. Reverting from their semi-agricultural patterns, they became fierce, warlike, nomadic hunters of buffalo.

Mountain Men

The mountain man came to know the Plains Indian first. Reports from early explorers tried to tell the differences between the tribes, but little was learned from these reports. The mountain man came to Wyoming and to the West to live. This was where his business was—where the beaver were most numerous. Many a mountain man lived with a tribe of Indians, was often adopted as a ''brother'' by some small chief, took an Indian wife, and raised Indian children (he was known as a squawman by his fellow trappers). While the mountain man may have fought with various tribes, he usually had found one tribe to his liking.

Now that the mountain man was ''kinfolks'' with an indian tribe, he helped them fight their enemies and went with them on their hunts, where his guns were a welcome addition to their

Emigrants Move West

With the discovery of the relative ease of crossing the Rockies by way of South Pass, the emigrants began to trickle out to Oregon Territory on the Pacific in ever-increasing numbers. Soon

THE BULLETIN OF THE PLAINS.

Mormons Trek To Utah

they were joined by the Church of Latter Day Saints, or Mormons, as Brigham Young led them to a "promised land" near the Great Salt Lake in Utah. Almost on their heels, the greatest wave of emigration in America's young history took place, with the discovery of gold in California. Many thousands of frenzied gold seekers were added to the group that took to the westward trail in the next few years.

In 1849, soldiers were placed at Fort Laramie to preserve peace, and in 1851 the Great Council was convened there. This was the largest gathering of Plains Indians ever held in one place, and the Indians were reassured that the white men were not after their hunting ground. They agreed to allow him to go his way undisturbed.

However, within a very few years the damage to grass and the departure of the buffalo became obvious, and the Indians grew uneasy. As a result, there were an increasing number of skirmishes and loss of life along the trail.

The period of the 1860's and 1870's saw much strife between the red and white men, several changes of people and policy in the Indian Bureau, victories and defeats for both Indians and Army, and much suffering, finally ending in the campaign of 1876 and the compulsory residency on reservations for the Indians. It had taken nearly twenty years for the Indian to resign himself to the overpowering strength of the United States Government and the inevitability of the reservation policy. During that time, Indians decreased greatly in number.

Wyoming Indian

The most numerous and probably the most fierce Indians on the High Plains were the Teton Sioux. From the Sioux tribes came chiefs and leaders like Sitting Bull, Red Cloud, Crazy Horse, Old-Man-Afraid-of-His-Horses, American Horse, and others equally famous.

The entire Sioux nation was made up of three mighty groups: the eastern, or Santee; the Yankton, or middle group, including the Asiniboin in the north; and the Teton Sioux in the west, which included seven distinct tribes: the Brule (Burnt Thighs); the Ogalala (Bad Faces); the Hunkpapa (Campers at the End of the Camping Circle); the Minniconzou (Those Who Plant by the Water); the Itazipka (Without Bows) the Sihasapa (Black Feet—not to be confused with the Blackfoot in Montana); and, the Ohenonpa (Two Kettle) tribe.

The Sioux had fought a number of battles with the Northern Cheyenne but, after 1850, became allied with them and agreed to fight their common enemies. The Northern Cheyenne like the Sioux were also divided into seven distinct tribes.

Finally the Northern Arapaho were allies to both of these powerful nations. The sub-tribe of this third powerful force of Indians were the Gros Ventre, confederates of the Northern Cheyenne.

When the Teton Sioux first hunted in the buffalo-rich Powder River country in Wyoming, they found the Crow Indians already there. The Crow called themselves Absaroke, or "Bird People." For years they had hunted the tributaries to the Yellowstone River; they had followed buffalo up and down the Powder River, Tongue River, the Rosebud River and the Big Horn River.

In fact, the Crow had almost exclusive hunting rights in the Big Horn River and Wind River sections of Wyoming, having hunted in all these regions undisturbed. But now they found competition from the Teton Sioux and Northern Cheyenne in the Powder River region and from the Shoshone Indians in the Wind River and Big Horn River areas, and in 1866 Chief Washakie of the Shoshones had fought the Crow for the territory and won. The Wind River country became exclusively Shoshone hunting country from that date.

At first, the Shoshone people, called Snake Indians, had not been equal to the fierce Sioux or Crow. But, under the wise leadership of Chief Washakie, these Indians grew in strength. After

Chief Washakie Of Shoshone Tribe

a few skirmishes with white men, these tribes then became the ears and eyes of the Army, or scouts on many occasions. Thus, as friends to the white men, the Shoshone Indians were able to survive the Plains Wars better than most tribes.

The Shoshone had a close relation, in language, in the Comanche Indians; they were never great friends and seldom fought together as allies. The Comanche had come to Wyoming and found the southern middle border area to their liking, but they never really made any serious attempt to take and hold that territory as their own hunting country.

Other relatives of the Shoshones were the Utes and Bannocks.

The Nez Perce came to Wyoming from the East in order to hunt but, like the Comanche, they made no real attempt to stay. The famous Nez Perce Chief Joseph traveled through parts of Wyoming on his historic flight from the Army in 1877.

From all these Indians came the sounds of war. Having guns, now, at their command and horses and with an intimate knowledge of the terrain, they presented a formidable problem to the Army. General Phil Sheridan had only a relatively small group—less than sixteen thousand officers and men—to police the High Plains. This unit was required to supervise every state west of the Missouri River, including Texas. (California, Nevada, Idaho, Oregon, and Washington were not then a part of the Sheridan command.) So at all times the Army was stretched very thin as it tried its best to carry out government policy. Sheridan reported that his military division had within its boundaries in 1882 ninety-nine Indian tribes "...aggregating about one hundred and seventy-five thousand persons scattered over an area of more than one million square miles of frontier country."

VIGNETTE:

INDIAN COLOR

To the Plains Indians, various colors meant certain things. For instance, green was the color used to depict growing things which meant life. Green colors were usually made from dried water plants, algae, boiled rotten wood, and from earth which, we have since learned, contained copper ore.

Yellow meant perfection and could have been derived from yellow grass, or cured grass, which was fed to the Indians' horses. It also signified the sun. To make the color yellow, they mixed clay with ground-up buffalo gall stones, pine tree moss, and certain selected vine roots.

The Indians produced black color from charcoal which was ground up and mixed with inner bark of trees called **bast** and then roasted. Black meant death—not growing, not glowing.

White bespoke of action, blurred movement. This came from a chalk-like dirt and clay mixed with what we now know as kaolin, or aluminum silicate.

Blue came from blue mud. We call it bentonite. Some kinds of boiled roots were used for blue, also. Blue meant the sky, long life, or serenity.

Red stood for warmth, the tipi, home, and Wyoming's red hills. In fact, red came from those very hills. Oxidation of iron helps turn the hills red-colored, so iron was the chief ingredient in the red dye.

Mixing these colors created other colors, each having their own meanings. The Indians smeared their bodies with buffalo fat before painting to prevent the paint from running. Paint was applied with a finger or the tip of a feather. The various designs and the manner in which paint was applied also had definite meanings.

When white men brought commercial colors west, the Indians responded to them in absolute delight. And the mirrors which the white men brought helped them apply their own paint, instead of relying upon another to daub their features and bodies for religious ceremonies, dances, or battle.

Generally speaking, women did the painting. They had to belong to a paint guild before they could qualify to find the sources of paint, mix it, and apply it. Other guilds women belonged to were the quilling guild, feathercraft guild, and cornstalk guild.

The quilling guild obtained porcupine quills, colored them, and then braided them or sewed them on clothing, shields, moccasions, horse trappings, and other Indian regalia. Like all the guilds, the quilling guild was rigidly controlled; if a woman was accepted as a member, she had to serve her time as an apprentice as she slowly learned the secrets of all aspects of quilling.

Among the men various societies developed. Some were based upon warfare, some upon horsemanship, some upon hunting, and all carried religious overtones. Governed usually by a sort of self-perpetuating group of headmen who had served long periods in the society, these headmen generally had the last and final word on any action an individual or even the whole tribe might wish to take.

Headmen conducted the tribal ceremonies. When one of them died, another was chosen from the ranks of the societies prevalent in that tribe. Some of the more common societies were Dog Men (often called Dog Soldiers), Wolf, Crazy, Hoof Rattlers, Red Shields, and Buffalo Societies. Boys, at the age of puberty, were sponsored or chosen to join whichever society they desired.

Camps or villages were governed by the decisions of the societies, or sometimes by religious cults. No fracas, argument, or fight could be settled without cult or society referees.

Since Plains Indians were nomadic, it was a society that made the decision to move camp. It ordered the people to strike their tipi lodges, laid out the line of march, provided guards along the trail, and made certain that young and old were taken care of as the whole village moved to another location. It also scouted ahead for water, fuel, and food. Finally, the society was the one to order a halt and to pick out the new location of the village.

Punishment for an offense could result in the loss of a finger, a hand, an arm, or one or both eyes. The worst punishment was being banished, cast out from the village and tribe.

Camp security was provided by a society. It also provided a sort of town crier who rode up and down the village streets loudly announcing all events. A birth, a forthcoming dance, a hunt being organized, a horse raid, and other ceremonies were some of the events proclaimed by the town crier.

Competition among the cults and societies was fierce. It was from these arrow shooting contests, lance throwing, horseback riding, and other contests that young braves learned their skills as warriors.

Young warriors raced up and down the streets of their villages in that day and age, much as boys and young men tear up and down the streets of their towns today with their hot rods or motorcycles. So a cult had the job of protecting pedestrians and taking care of traffic control just as modern police do in towns today.

The Plains Indian tribal society was a compact, well-organized, and well run unit, inhabited by a proud people. Their life and style of living had developed over thousands of years of nomadic living on the High Plains. And, as it turned out, Wyoming became the battleground for a good share of the Indian wars, fought to uphold a way of life against the encroachment of enemy tribes and, finally, of white men.

EPIC:

"Grizzly Bear"

James Clyman was one of the hardy young men with the Ashley-Henry 1822 Expedition to the Rockies. He appears to have served as clerk because he was better able to write than most of the party. In later years, his account of the expedition was widely published. The incident described here is well-known and is supposed to have occured near the Wyoming-South Dakota border in mid-October 1823.

Clyman's personal account of what happened, complete with his own brand of spelling and style, follows:

While passing through a Brushy bottom a large Grssely came down the vally we being in single file men on foot leding pack horses he struck us about the center then thrning paralel to our line Capt. smith being in the advanc he ran to the open ground and as he immerged from the thicket he and the bear met face to face Grissly did not hesitate a moment but sprung on the capt taking him by the head first pitcing [him] sprawling on the earth he gave him a grab by the middle fortunately cathing him by the ball pouch [a pouch which held the 1/2-ounce lead rifle balls] and Butcher Kife which he broke but breaking several of his ribs and cutting his head badly none of us having any surgical Knowledge what was to be done one Said come take hold and he wuld say why not you so it went around I asked the Capt what was best he said one or 2 [go] for water and if you have a needle and thread git it out and sew up my wounds around my head which was bleeding freely I got a pair of sissors and cut off his hair and then began my first Job of dessing wounds upon examination I [found] the bear had taken nearly all of his head in his capacious mouth close to his left eye on one side and clos to his right ear on the other and lad the skull bare to near the crown of the head leaving a white streak whare his teeth passed one of his ears was torn from his head out to the outer rim after stitching all the other wounds in the best way I was capabl and according to the captains directions the ear being the last I told him I could do nothing for his Eare O you must try to stich up some way or other he said then I put my needly stiching it through and through and over and over laying the lacerated parts togather as nice as I could with my hands water was found in about a mille when we all moved down and encamped the captain being ale to mount his horse and ride to camp whare we pitched a tent the onley one we had and made him as confortable as circumstances would permit this gave us a lisson on the character of the grissly Baare which we did not forget....

That was one experience, as Clyman stated, that they wouldn't forget. As for Jed Smith, he stayed down for a couple of days and then, with marks on his face and minus an eyebrow the rest of his life (he let his hair grow to hide his mutilated ear) got up and led the way west, deeper and deeper into Wyoming.

Smith traveled all over the West, going as far as San Diego and Los Angeles and up to Oregon in 1827-1828. He walked and rode horses across most of the Rocky Mountain region, as well as the West Coast. For many he was known as the ''Buckskin Knight,'' carrying his Bible in one hand and his Hawken rifle in the other. He died in 1831, after being attacked by Comanche Indians while leading a wagon train to Santa Fe.

MOUNTAIN MAN WYOMING

As far as we know, the first white men to enter Wyoming were the French Canadian brothers named de la Verendrye at the head of a small expedition exploring the West. From records left behind, this small group saw the "Shining Mountains," which we believe were the Big Horn Mountains, in January 1743 from a point between Gillette and Sheridan before turning back.

Then, with the completion of the Louisiana Purchase, it remained for explorers and mountain men employed by fur traders to fill in the blank spaces on the huge $15,000,000 tract of largely unexplored land. This comprised at least a part of the area we now call Louisiana, Arkansas, Missouri, Oklahoma, Kansas, Iowa, Nebraska, South Dakota, Minnesota, North Dakota, Montana, Idaho, and Wyoming.

Seeking the elusive route to the Orient had been one of the reasons President Thomas Jefferson initiated the Louisiana Purchase. In addition to nearly doubling the size of America, Jefferson

33

also was buying the right to free navigation on the Mississippi River. The President was curious, too, as to the source of the Missouri River. Knowing that England and France controlled the fur trade in the upper Missouri River regions, he considered all of those factors in making the decision to send Meriweather Lewis and William Clark on their epic exploration to the Pacific Ocean and back in 1804-1807.

Once this famous Corps of Discovery had returned and Lewis and Clark had made their reports on the successful trip, the door was officially open to American fur trading ventures in that region.

Lewis and Clark Expedition

Although Lewis and Clark did not enter Wyoming, two of its members played important roles in the history of Wyoming. One of them was the young Shoshone girl Sacajawea, who carried her baby son, Baptiste, to the West Coast and back. Kidnapped by the Minnataree Indians when she was eleven, Sacajawea had been sold by them as a slave to a French Canadian trapper named Toussaint Charbonneau. Later she became Charbonneau's wife when she was seventeen, and accompanied him along with the Lewis and Clark Expedition from Fort Mandan, North Dakota to the Pacific Ocean and back. Charbonneau was an official interpreter to the Corps of Discovery. Two theories are prominent today about Sacajawea's later life: one, that she lived to nearly 100 years of age, and died at Fort Washakie; and, the other that she died on December 20, 1812 at Fort Manuel Lisa in what is now South Dakota. Neither theory is important as we consider her every bit as much a heroine on the trip West, as we consider each and every member of the Lewis and Clark Expedition a hero!

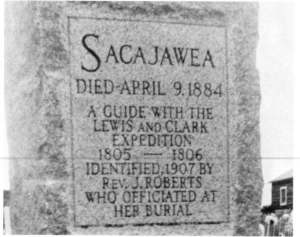

Sacajewea Monument

John Colter Hired

The other member of the Lewis and Clark expedition who left his imprint on Wyoming was John Colter. He was hired by fur trader Manuel Lisa in 1807 to guide members of the Lisa organization on a fur trading trip into the Yellowstone region. From a post built at the mouth of the Big Horn River where it joins the Yellowstone, Colter spent the better part of 1808 traveling through what we now call Yellowstone Park and Jackson Hole and over the towering Teton mountains into Pierre's Hole in Idaho. Accounts of this trip gave the name Colter's Hell to the region of Yellowstone because of the boiling springs, steam rising from the ground, bubbling mud pots, and erupting geysers.

The men now entering this region were intent upon securing beaver pelts, or plews, as they called the prime skins. These pelts were sent east, with the bulk being exported to England, France, and other nations of the world which had for nearly two hundred years used this skin in making hats.

Trading Companies Emerge

The famous North West Company and Hudson's Bay Company in Canada had sent thousands of beaver skins to Europe. Of course, other skins were tanned and became items of trade as well, but hatters wanted beaver skins, and during the years of the mountain men in the West, over 100,000 plews a year were sent east and on to Europe. There they were converted into the familiar tricorn hat, the cocked hat for the military, the tall top hat favored by the more stylish men, and finally into the broad brimmed hat with a much lower crown worn by the clergy, western men, and several religious sects.

Women liked beaver fur, too. Muffs, coat collars, elegant gowns with fur trimmings, slippers, and mittens as well as their smart little hats were decorated with the celebrated American beaver fur.

Since fur trapping had been developed to a fine art in the Great Lakes region, it became an economic tool for traders who found many adventurous young men who had the urge to see the West and the Rocky Mountains.

They literally paid their way West by becoming company fur trappers as they either worked for a wage or for shares. Others were free trappers who trapped and sold to the company offering the best price. In nearly every instance, however, the trapper worked for a fur company in the early stages and then became independent, free to work on his own.

It did not take a great deal of capital to equip a trapper, so a young man anxious to start on his own could usually furnish his own gun and clothing and possibly his horse. If he signed up with a trader, the company supplied the traps, supplies, trade goods, and horse if needed.

Life As A Trapper

We would think the life of a trapper as hard and lonely. Each man went off to his particular area alone or occasionally with a partner, built himself a small cabin or shelter by a stream and started setting his traps as soon as the weather became cold—that was when the fur was thickest and most beautiful. The traps had to be checked every day or so, regardless of weather, or the pelts were ruined. After each check the beaver had to be skinned and scraped and the plew stretched on a hoop made from a small willow to dry.

In the spring the trapper packed his catch and traveled to the nearest trading post or back to Saint Louis to do his trading. After 1824 this was made easier by the holding of the rendezvous, the meeting place where trappers could sell their furs to the traders and buy supplies for the coming season.

A trapper, if he survived the cold, the hostile Indians, and various accidents, often joined with an Indian tribe, and very soon the Indians were also actively taking part in the fur trade and entering into the activities of the rendezvous.

Trapping Expands

American fur traders were ready to follow the route taken by the Lewis and Clark expedition and claim the trapping grounds. Manuel Lisa and Pierre Chateau, Jr., moved into the upper Missouri River area, but by far the most ambitious venture was that of John Jacob Astor of New York. His destination was the mouth of the Columbia River, at which site the first trading post of his Pacific Fur Company would be built. He divided his expedition, sending part of it by ship around South America and up the Pacific coast. The other part, under the command of Wilson Price Hunt, moved out of Saint Louis in the spring of 1811 and was met by angry Indians—and rumors of more angry Indians. Hunt changed his plans and route of travel, several times using boats, canoes, horses, and finally having to go on foot. He crossed northern Wyoming, traveling along the Powder, then west over the Big Horn mountains near No Wood. South again to the Wind River near Shoshoni. Up the Wind River past present Dubois and over Union Pass—and there Hunt saw for the first time the "Pilot Knobs," as the Tetons were called, most important landmarks. Eventually they arrived at the Columbia.

Hunt's party, too, included a young Indian woman, an Iowan called Aioe. Known later as Marie, she underwent all the hardships of the tortuous journey to be with her husband, a Sioux interpreter and hunter for the Astorians. This nineteen year old girl had given birth to her third child on December 29, 1811, in the deepest wilds

of Idaho. This baby was the first to be born on the original Oregon Trail.

Once the party had made contact with the ship at Astoria, the name of the post on the Columbia, it was decided to send an overland party back to Astor in New York with a report of their efforts.

Stuart Builds First Cabin

Young Robert Stuart, one of the men arriving on the ship, was chosen to lead the party back to New York. Just a year after Hunt was at Jackson Hole, Stuart was back, leading some of Hunt's men. They continued eastward, crossing in the South Pass area of the continental Divide.

Since winter was coming on, the Stuart party built a cabin at Bessemer Bend on the North Platte and proceeded to lay in a supply of meat. They were able to sleep, rest, eat, and hunt and slowly regain their strength (Stuart called the cabin the Chateau of Indolence). Their time of rest came to an abrupt end, however, one morning early in December. They were rudely awakened by a war party of twenty-three Arapaho Indians, searching for a party of Crows who had stolen their horses.

The Indians stayed with them for two days and ate up almost all their meat supply. And when they left, the Arapaho let the white men know that they would be back—and when they came back, they would want to trade for guns, powder, and lead.

Stuart had other ideas, for he didn't relish meeting the warriors again. So on December 13, 1812, Stuart and his men deserted their "Chateau" and headed downstream. That cabin, incidentally, is said to have been the first one built in Wyoming.

Blazing The Oregon Trail

Stuart actually blazed the Oregon Trail, since he followed it across Wyoming, with only a couple of detours. Robert Stuart and Wilson Price Hunt thereby proved that migration to the West could be achieved on foot and on horseback. And, it should be noted, Stuart actually had found South Pass, although he did not recognize it for what it was—an easy crossing of the Continental Divide. The Pass received no publicity until the Ashley-Henry men used it.

More Expeditions

During this time America was at war with the British, and Western exploration received little notice. In 1822, however, another expedition was being outfitted which would lead to Wyoming.

An advertisement appearing in the Saint Louis *Missouri Gazette& Public Advertizer* on February 13, 1822, read,

> To Enterpising Young Men: The subscriber wished to engage One Hundred Men, to ascend the Missouri to its source, there to be employed for one, two, or three years. For particulars enquire of Major Andrew Henry, near the Lead Mines in the County of Washington, (who will ascend with the party) or to the subscriber at St. Louis.
> William H. Ashley

Among those who joined the company of Ashley and Henry were men whose names have become landmarks on rivers, mountains, forests throughout the West: Jim Bridger, James Clyman, Jedediah Smith, Tom Fitzpatrick, Mike Fink, David Jackson, William L. Sublette, Daniel Potts, Hugh Glass, Zacharias Ham, Jim Beckwourth.

First Mountain Men

This was the "core" of the mountain men. Though many followed the trade over the years, it was this group who provided the central fiber of the American mountain man movement as they trapped and traded their way up and down every river system, from Taos, New Mexico, to British Columbia, and from the Pacific Ocean to the muddy Missouri River.

Ashley and Henry were making a major effort at capturing a large share of the beaver trade that year. They loaded twenty-five tons (50,000 pounds) of every conceivable type of trade item on two keelboats and headed up the Missouri. The first year was spent in fighting hostile Indians and getting located. So it really was not until 1823 that they sent their brigades of trappers south from the Yellowstone River region into what is now Wyoming.

Jim Bridger In Wyoming

Entering Powder River country, one member of the expedition, probably the famed Jim Bridger, found a petrified forest near Buffalo. The story of its discovery met with such skepticism that over the years it grew into the well-known tale of the "petrified bird on the petrified branch singing a petrified melody."

Part of the late fall and early winter was spent with Crow Indians in the Dubois area. The leather-clad band of white men joined the Crow hunters in a grand buffalo hunt near Dubois that fall. Then in February 1824 they tried to pass over the Continental Divide at Union Pass. Because the snow was too deep, they were forced to skirt the Wind River mountains, going past both Riverton and Lander to what is now South Pass.

Leaving the warm comfort of the Dubois country, these men, clad in buckskin, wearing homemade blanket overcoats, legs wrapped in strips of blanket, trying to start fires with flint and steel in the windy wastes of South Pass in March, were caught up in one of the worst winter storms that man has yet recorded.

They cached part of their saddles, bridles, traps, and trade items and split up, planning to meet each other in early June on the Big Sandy.

Meeting On The Green

There they would meet and then try to haul what furs they had obtained, by trade or by trapping, back to Saint Louis in the summer. Actually, the meeting on the Big Sandy could be called the first *rendezvous*, a pre-planned meeting place. However, the word rendezvous (from the French words meaning "present yourselves") came to have a more particular meaning for the Western fur traders.

During this time William Ashley was putting together a long line of pack mules and horses in preparation for an overland trip back to the Green River area of Wyoming where he hoped to meet with his men, bringing them much needed supplies and receiving the furs they had trapped. Ashley headed northwest and crossed the Laramie

Plains in March, arriving at the Green by mid-April 1825. He built skin boats and floated down to Henry's Fork where he set July 1 as the date of the rendezvous. He broke his party into units and sent them out to find trappers and friendly Indians and announce the meeting.

Then, he climbed into his flimsy boats and sailed down the Green River. This was not the peaceful voyage that it sounds like—Ashley could not swim and had been injured by a fall in early April. Still suffering from broken ribs, he was taking a chance.

He learned this as his water-borne expedition slid into and out of the towering chasms and bucked and rolled in the tumbling white water. Half a dozen times Ashley had to be rescued and pulled to safety before drowning.

At one point he left his name inscribed upon the walls of a canyon—ASHLEY - 1825—proving that he had been there. The doughty man kept to his course, going around the worst of the white foaming rapids, slipping along on placid waters in the cool canyons until he finally called a halt, realizing he would have to turn back to the rendezvous. He had traveled hundreds of miles downriver and had followed the Green into Colorado as it curled snakelike to its meeting with the mighty Colorado River.

Back at Henry's Fork, nearly one hundred and twenty-five men met for the exchange of beaver pelts for trade items sorely needed. Thirty of these men were deserters from the Hudson's Bay Company; the rest were Ashley's men. Few Indians had come, so the mountain men loaded up supplies, planning to visit friendly tribes that fall and carry goods to trade for beaver, otter, fox, and buffalo hides.

An example of what was taken by one mountain man is seen in this list, which has been preserved:

28 pounds of tobacco
35 pounds of coffee
9 pounds of sugar
6 fire steels
3 dozen knives
3 gross of assorted buttons
3 dozen fish hooks
5 dozen awls
9 dozen assorted iron finger rings
7 pairs of scissors
2 dozen combs
7 dozen flints
32 pounds of gunpowder

This man was Johnson Gardner, whose name was misspelled years later by explorers in the Yellowstone. In giving his name to a valley and its river in Yellowstone, they spelled it **Gardiner.**

The well-known Kit Carson traded only $53.75 worth of beaver for a like amount of goods. He received eighteen pounds of coffee, eighteen pounds of sugar, three knives, five pounds of assorted beads, a dozen iron finger rings, one and a half yards of cloth—at $9.00—and three dozen assorted buttons.

"Rendezvous" Complete Success

The trade fair was a complete success, and Ashley set out for the journey home the next day. He left with all his men, heading north across South Pass, and then uncovered a cache of beaver pelts he had hidden the previous year about ten miles south of Lander. There he was attacked by a yelling, snarling band of Blackfeet who drove off all but two of their horses.

Half of his party had gone on to the mouth of the Wind River Canyon and were waiting for him there when an "express or courier" arrived to tell them of Ashley's plight. By the time they had turned and got back to their leader, a band of Crow Indians had attacked him.

Bridger Floats "Bad Pass"

But, Ashley and his men won both battles and continued north through the Big Horn Basin. At the treacherous Big Horn Canyon Jim Bridger proved himself as a river pilot, as he rafted the fur packs down the river and through the dangerous canyon to a point where the Big Horn River joined the swift-moving Yellowstone. At twenty-one years of age, Bridger was the first white man to float that canyon, often called "Bad Pass" by both mountain men and Indians.

Rendezvous Yearly Event

The whole affair—the trip out, the rendezvous, and the trip back—was a success. So Ashley spent the entire fall of that year getting ready to return. He had set another rendezvous date, and he wanted to be there in plenty of time.

In the meantime, Ashley's men had divided into several semi-military units and fanned out across the Rocky Mountains. Each unit, or brigade, was headed up by a captain. In turn the captain had several lieutenants who transmitted his orders to the pairs of trappers who worked, ate, and traveled together with a larger unit of ten to twelve men.

A brigade traveled through mountain valleys long regarded as personal property of one Indian tribe or another. The Indians fought them, stole from them, and, when they got the chance, ran off their horses or killed one or two trappers as they waded in beaver ponds or other isolated places.

The brigade functioned in a military manner, as an organized means to prevent attack and loss of beaver, or worse—loss of life. Every morning before dawn the horse guards would check each ravine, gully, or other likely hiding places for Indians. Meanwhile, the leaders of the caravan would be eating their breakfast, saddling horses, and preparing to move out. When they pulled ahead in the lead, the second unit would eat, saddle up, and then follow. Other units would follow suit.

Guards ahead, on the flank, and in the rear kept the brigade captain constantly advised as the long string of horses, mules, and men pushed deeper into beaver country.

Jim Bridger acquired the name Gabe when he was a lieutenant to Jed Smith, a brigade captain. Smith was noted for carrying his Bible and quoting from it. Since he used young Bridger to communicate his orders to the mountain men, as the Lord Jehovah used the Angel Gabriel to communicate His desires, the mountain men called young Bridger Gabriel. That name was soon shortened to the nickname Gabe, which Bridger carried with him all his life.

Profitable Meetings

The rendezvous of 1826 was held near Hiram, Utah. Once again Ashley found it a success. He was able to take back one hundred twenty-five packs of beaver skins to Saint Louis, realizing nearly $60,000 in the Saint Louis market and showing a good profit.

Thus it was at the peak of success that Ashley then sold out to Jed Smith, William Sublette, and David Jackson. Ashley would continue to bring trade goods to the rendezvous, and they would carry on with the business of trading with the Indians and catching beaver.

Ecology Minded Trappers

Ashley had warned his men earlier about trapping one area too much, fearing that the beaver would soon be trapped out. This word and warning of early day management and conservation was heeded at first, but other trapping firms coming into the Rockies, such as the Hudson's Bay Company, the North West Company, and others, continued to trap over waters already trapped. In a few years trapping beaver became difficult as beaver became more and more scarce.

Trading A Way Of Life

The third rendezvous was held at Bear Lake, which straddles the border between Idaho and Utah. Enroute to the rendezvous, a small four-pound cannon was hauled over South Pass and became the first device with wheels to cross the Continental Divide.

The fourth rendezvous was also held at Bear Lake, but in 1829 the rendezvous was held at a place called Oil Springs on the Popo Agie River about ten miles southeast of Lander. Popo Agie (pronounced poe-poe-azyuh) means headwater in the Crow Indian language. The Popo Agie is the one of the headwaters of the Wind River.

Captain Benjamin L.E. Bonneville Teamed Up With Nathaniel Wyeth To Form A New Trading Company.

Rocky Mountain Fur Company

Thereafter a rendezvous was planned for each year, either on the Green River, the Popo Agie, or in Idaho, many of them memorable for one cause or another. In 1830, William Sublette brought ten canvas-topped freight wagons to the Popo Agie, the first to come that far west. They also observed the Fourth of July at a huge, grey boulder rising out of the Sweetwater flats and gave it the name it still bears, Independence Rock. This was the year that Thomas Fitzpatrick, Milton Sublette, Henry Fraeb, Jean Baptise Gervais, and Jim Bridger, calling themselves the Rocky Mountain Fur Company, bought the Ashley business.

Historic Mix-up

A mix-up left the trappers without a summer meeting in 1831. Henry Fraeb—Old Frappe, as they called him—finally brought supplies to the trappers in November. Then, at the Pierre's Hole, Idaho, meeting the next year, several changes came about. In the first place, new faces, new competition, with the arrival of Captain Benjamin

L. E. Bonneville and Nathaniel Wyeth. Then, this rendezvous was followed by the Battle of Pierre's Hole, a skirmish with a Blackfoot war party in which Andrew Sinclair was killed. William Sublette was wounded and was cared for by Dr. Jacob Wyeth.

The next year the American Fur Company dogged the steps of the Rocky Mountain men, spying on them and attempting to acquire their best trapping grounds. Bridger led his men on week-long tramps, packing into and out of regions, hardly stopping, and fighting bad weather and angry Indians as he tried to shake off his dogged followers and competitors. Thus, no one really prospered that year.

At the time of the 1834 rendezvous on the Green River, William Sublette and Robert Campbell constructed a trading post where the Laramie and North Platte rivers came together, calling the post Fort William. This was far east of the rendezvous site but on the trail which led to it, and soon it became an important stopover. Jason Lee stopped there that year with a party of missionaries he was taking to Oregon. An important advocate of settlement in Oregon, Lee,

Fort Laramie in History

a Methodist minister, returned several times on missions in the east to secure more missionaries and settlers for the Pacific coast area. Later on, the post at Fort William changed names, finding its way into the pages of history books as Fort Laramie, because of its location on the Laramie River. (*Laramie* had been name for Jacques La Ramie, a French Canadian fur trapper killed on the river in 1820's.)

The rendezvous meetings continued and became more and more popular with the Indians, as well. They would come, bringing whole families along, with their best horses, best furs, and dressed in their finest beaded buckskin regalia. Nothing like it has ever been repeated in American history for color, as the Crow, Nez Perce, Bannock, Shoshone, Ute, and Flathead tribes paraded their savage and multi-hued costumes before white men—who were themselves a colorful lot of men, as one can imagine. "I'll meet you on the Green," was a common saying as the period of trading came to an end for another year. Horse racing, foot races, wrestling matches, shooting exhibitions, knife throwing, and gambling were common, and the use of rum and whiskey sparked wild celebrations and dances that lasted far into the nights.

Furs were not the only items bartered. A good horse was worth many beaver plews, as was a good rifle or a well-balanced throwing knife. And sometimes the Indians got so carried away at an event that they would actually put up a member of their family in wagering on the outcome. It was not uncommon for a mountain man actually to "win" an Indian wife at a rendezvous.

Remembering that the mountain man had lived with death literally lurking in each valley and along each stream all year long, it is easy to see why they would relax completely as they met friend and foe alike at this neutral ground of the rendezvous. More than once a mountain man talked quietly with an Indian who had tried his best to kill the same man during the year. The wonder of it all was the few really bad fights and killings took place at the rendezvous. In fact, the rendezvous became a sort of armistice period during which the participants forgot their cares and troubles, their blood enemies, and language problems as they traded for the next year's supplies of "necessaries"—tobacco, flints, powder, lead, coffee, sugar, and the like.

The lure of the West and the rendezvous drew others to the meetings who were not directly connected with trapping and trading.

Sir William Drummond Stewart, a Scottish nobleman from Great Britain, was a visitor to the rendezvous. He had fought Napoleon, and in 1833

Fort Laramie, WY In 1836

he came West to the rendezvous, bringing young Benjamin Harrison with him. (Harrison was the son of William Henry Harrison, soon to become ninth President of the United States. His nephew, also named Benjamin, would be the twenty-third President.)

Stewart came back year after year to visit the rendezvous, to mix with the colorful lot of mountain men whom he deeply admired, and to drink in the glory of the Wind River Mountains.

Stewart's famous trip in 1839 was an important one to the world of culture, because Stewart brought with him a young artist named Alfred Jacob Miller. No one had yet painted the great scenes Stewart had seen, and he wanted them captured on canvas. Then, when back in his baronial castles in England and Scotland, he would be able to savor those memories of glory and excitement that he had tasted as he traveled with Bridger, Fitzpatrick, Sublette, and various tribes of Indians.

Women In Wyoming

Miller sketched and painted his way all across Nebraska and Wyoming to the Wind River Mountains. His works, once forgotten for a time, are classic works of art and have become priceless, as valuable portrayals of the early West.

For the next three years the rendezvous was held at the previous site on the Green River near where Daniel is today. Dr. Marcus Whitman and Reverend Samuel Parker were on hand in 1835, and Dr. Whitman had occasion to operate on Jim Bridger's back, extracting an iron arrowhead which had been left there three years before by an angry Blackfoot. (Captain Stewart slipped it into his pocket as a memento of the event.)

The 1837 rendezvous saw the Presbyterians, Marcus Whitman and H.H. Spalding, with their wives stopping on their way to Oregon. The two women were the first white women to cross South Pass, and both were the first white women many of the mountain men had seen for a long time. For the Indians it was a strange sight and one which caused the redmen and their women great wonder at the pale texture of their skin.

By 1833, the American Fur Company had absorbed the Rocky Mountain Fur Company. And that year the famous pioneer, John A. Sutter, came through on his way to California.

Kit Carson Signs On

Jim Bridger was in Saint Louis when the pack left there for the 1839 rendezvous. In fact, many of the mountain men were off on other pursuits, trying to find a way of life that would support them in the Rockies. Kit Carson became a scout and finally found fame as a brigadier general. Stewart had assumed his position as a lord in faraway Murthly Castle in Scotland. Bridger was contemplating a trading post with Louis Vasquez, who already had run one.

Campbell and Sublette and their post on the North Platte took the play away from the rendezvous now. Their post became the Rocky Mountain center of trade. The rendezvous was being replaced by posts and fortifications!

Original Trading Post of Jim Bridger

JIM BRIDGER

Of all the notable mountain men who made the history of Wyoming and the nation for nearly three-quarters of a century, Jim Bridger has to top the list!

As he lived in the West, mostly Wyoming, he was able to meet each change of mood and times and yet emerge as a leader. He was a blacksmith when needed; he was a river pilot when needed; he was advisor to the emigrants and military when needed; and, he helped Wyoming take shape and become, finally, a territory. He was also an

explorer, hunter, trapper, scout, guide—and a good husband and father.

Bridger discovered the Great Salt Lake and built the first post for emigrants on the Oregon Trail who needed help, supplies, advice, or directions to their various destinations—Utah or Oregon or California.

When Army engineers needed a guide to help them survey the vast regions that Bridger was acquainted with, they turned to Bridger for help. When the Army needed a chief scout in their

Famous Explorer, Trapper, Scout and Frontiersman, Jim Bridger

military campaigns, it was Jim Bridger, in many cases, that they hired.

Bridger had a reputation for fanciful stories, which came about when his listeners simply couldn't believe the stories he told about geysers shooting up into the air and petrified forests he had seen and the mountain of obsidian that surely looked like glass....He became disgusted with their disbelief, and in retaliation, embellished his stories, many of which have become a part of American folklore.

Bridger was born in Richmond, Virginia, in 1804. In 1812 his family moved to St. Louis, gateway to the wild frontier. During the next few years he was an apprentice Missouri River pilot and blacksmith.

In 1822 he joined the Ashely-Henry expedition as a hunter-trapper, and at eighteen years of age he went west. By the time he was thirty years old he had crossed South Pass on the old Indian trail which became the route of the emigrants and the Oregon Trail. He discovered the Great Salt Lake, found Two Ocean Pass, made reliable reports on the wonders of the Yellowstone regions, was the first white man to raft down the treacherous Big Horn Canyon, and was part owner of a fur trading company.

Bridger never missed a summer rendezvous of fur traders. Over the years it was to him that mountain men turned for advice, as their trade began to dwindle.

Major General Greenville Mellen Dodge

44

As a father, Jim Bridger made every effort to see that his children, who were half Indian, were given the chance for an education. He sent them to areas where there were proper schools, since there were no schools in Wyoming at that time.

The grand old Mountain Man died at Westport, Missouri, in 1881, at the age of seventy-four years. Some years later, General Grenville Dodge saw to it that a monument was erected honoring Jim Bridger. At the dedication of the monument, Dodge was the featured speaker. He said,

I found Bridger a very companionable man. In person, he was over six feet tall, spare, straight as an arrow, agile, rawboned, and of powerful frame; eyes gray, hair brown and abundant, even in his old age; expression mild, manners agreeable. He was hospitable and generous, and was always trusted and respected. He possessed in high degree, the confidence of the Indians....Naturally shrewd, and possessing keen faculties of observation, he became one of the most expert hunters and trappers in the mountains.

Unquestionably Bridger's claim to remembrance rests upon the extraordinary part he bore in the explorations in the West. As a Guide he was without equal, and this is the testimony of everyone who ever employed him. He was a born topographer; the whole West was mapped out in his mind, and such was his instinctive sense of locality and direction that it was said of him that he could smell his way where he could not see it.

He was the complete master of plains and woodcraft....In all my experience I never saw Bridger...meet an obstacle he could not overcome. He could make a map of any country he had ever traveled over, mark out its streams, mountains and obstacles correctly....He was a good judge of human nature. His comments upon people that he had met and been with were always intelligent, and seldom critical. He always spoke of their good parts, and was universally respected by the mountain men, and looked upon as a leader. He was careful never to give his word without fulfilling it....He felt very keenly any loss of

confidence on his judgment....And when he struck a country or trail he was not familiar with, he would frankly say so....So remarkable a man should not be lost to history.

EPIC:

"Indians Come To Fort Laramie"

Francis Parkman visited Wyoming and spent some time at Fort Laramie in the summer of 1846. Out of those experiences came his book *The Oregon Trail.* Like a good reporter, Parkman was a keen observer of all detail and gave a vivid picture of life in and around the fort which was owned by the American Fur Company. The following is his account of a band of Sioux Indians coming to the fort to visit and to trade.

May was telling a curious story about the traveler Catlin, when an ugly, diminutive Indian, wretchedly mounted, came up to a gallop and rode by us into the fort. On being questioned, he said Smoke's village was close at hand. Accordingly, only a few minutes elapsed before the hills beyond the river were covered with a disorderly swarm of savages, on horseback and on foot. Walked down to the bank. The stream was wide, and was then between three and four feet deep, with a swift current. For several rods, the water was alive with dogs, horses, and Indians. The long poles used in pitching the lodges were carried by the horses, fastened by the heavier end, two or three on each side, to a rude sort of pack-saddle, while the other end drags on the ground. About a foot behind the horse, a kind of large basket or pannier is suspended between the poles, and firmly lashed in its place. On the back of the horse are piled various articles of luggage; the basket also is well filled with domestic utensils, or, quite as often, with a litter of puppies, a brood of small children, or a superannuated old man. Numbers of these curious vehicles, traineaux, or, as the Canadians call them, travois, were now splashing together through the stream. Among them swam countless dogs, often burdened with a miniature traineaux; and dashing forward on horseback through the throng came the warriors, the slender figure of some lynx-eyed boy clinging fast behind them. The women sat perched on the pack-saddles, adding not a little to the load of the already over-burdened horses. The confusion was prodigious. The dogs yelled and howled in chorus; the puppies in the travois set up a dismal whine as the water invaded their comfortable retreat; the little black-eyed children, from one year of age upward, clung fast with both hands to the edge of their basket, and looked over in alarm at the water rushing so near them, sputtering and making wry mouths as it splashed against their faces. Some of the dogs encumbered by their load, were carried down by the current, yelping piteously; and the old squaws would rush into the water, seize their favorites by the neck, and drag them out. As each horse gained the bank, he scrambled up as he could. Stray horses and colts came among the rest, often breaking away at full speed through the crowd, followed by the old hags, screaming after their fashion on all occasions of excitement. Buxom young squaws, blooming in all the charms of vermillion, stood here and there on the bank, holding aloft their master's lance, as a signal to collect the scattered portions of his household. In a few moments the crowd melted away; each family with its horses and equipage, filing off the plain at the rear of the fort; and here, in the space of a half an hour, arose sixty to seventy of their tapering lodges. Their horses were feeding by the hundreds over the surrounding prairie, and their dogs were roaming everywhere. The fort was full of warriors, and the children were whooping and yelling incessantly under the walls.

Parkman had been talking with William F. May, a Kentucky born mountain man who had served among the Mandan Indians on the Upper Missouri River in 1822. Then May went to Santa Fe and worked along that trail. When he died, he was buried in Salt Lake City in 1855.

The much traveled Catlin was undoubtedly George Catlin, an artist who captured much of the flavor of the West in the early days of the fur trade. Like Miller, Catlin traveled among the Indians at a time when photography was not available and was able to catch on canvas the mountain men and Indians.

Smoke was an Oglala Sioux chief, and a friend of Parkman's.

CHAPTER V

EMIGRANT WYOMING

Leather In Demand

Although the silk hat replaced the beaver hat, there was still a demand for otter and fox furs as well as an increasing need for leather. One reason that Fort Laramie (as Fort William was now called) survived the decline in the beaver market was the increased demand for leather from buffalo hides—the post was located in the heart of buffalo country.

Buffalo-Restaurant Of Plains

The shaggy beast, roving the plains by the thousands, had been a walking commissary for the Plains Indian, providing him with food, shelter, fuel, clothing, toys, religious fetishes, weapons, and was an object of his religious worship.

To the white man, the buffalo was the source of good tough leather for boots, traveling bags, straps for the springs of stagecoaches, hinges on doors, gloves, and guard's helmets. Buffalo horns and bones were used for knife handles, buttons, and powder horns, and in later years buffalo bones were used for fertilizer.

Both the red man and the white considered the buffalo meat excellent food. A little later on, buffalo meat would feed a whole army of men laying iron rails across the face of the nation.

When Fort William was built in 1834 it was intended to be the trading center of the fur industry. Campbell and Sublette planned to have a supply of "necessaries" there the year round so the mountain man could come in to trade and meet with his friends, both red and white. As it turned out, when the beaver business fell off the fort was still able to do a remarkable business in buffalo robes.

Indians Came to Trade

The most important reason for Fort Laramie's survival was its location on the Oregon Trail. Only when the "Big Medicine Trail," as the Indians called it, was replaced by the railroad did Fort Laramie's importance decline.

Indians that inhabited the area close to the fort were tribes of the Sioux. In 1835 the Oglala came to trade with the "yellowhides," as they called the white men, and other Sioux tribes who appeared later were the Brule, Teton, Sans Arc, Hunkpapa, and Minniconjou. Allies of the Sioux, the Arapaho and Cheyenne, came often to trade, while occasionally the Comanche and Crow showed up and, upon rare occasions, the Shoshone.

More Posts Established

Other posts to accommodate the fur trade were appearing on the scene. Fort Hall in Idaho and Fort Davy Crockett on the Lower Green had already been established, and soon several forts appeared on the South Platte in competition with Fort Laramie—Saint Vrain, Lupton, Jackson, and Vasquez. Only the first two survived any length of time, and even they did little business after migration along the Oregon Trail increased.

Around 1840 a new post was built near Fort Laramie. It was enough to cause the American Fur Company, who now owned the post, to rebuild. Sun-dried mud bricks, or adobe bricks as they were called, were used to do the job. When it was completed the post was re-named, being called Fort John, probably after a member of the company named John Sarpy. Nevertheless, the name Fort Laramie hung on.

The new trading post near Fort Laramie was named Fort Platte by its builder, Lancaster P. Lupton, a former Army officer now engaged in the fur trade. But Fort Platte declined after a few years under the weight of competition with the bigger post and the powerful American Fur Company.

Fort Bridger Started

When the first canvas-covered-wagon caravan pulled into Fort Laramie in 1841, they saw a sparkling new settlement, nearly white with its new adobe walls. It was a happy sight for the travel-worn wayfarers.

The historian for that caravan was John Bidwell. Part of the group were on their way to California and part of them would go to Oregon. Their guide was the old mountain man, Thomas Fitzpatrick, better known to all as Broken Hand. Leading an emigrant wagon train was a new role for Fitzpatrick, who had come to Wyoming in 1823 as a mountain man with Ashley. But the wise mountain-man guide had the caravan stop at the fort, repair their wagons, and take a deep breath before heading west across the wide expanse of Wyoming. There were eighty persons in that party that paused at Fort Laramie.

However, it was not just Fort Laramie that drew them that way, but the Oregon Trail. All the way from the Missouri to the Big Sandy over South Pass the trail was a natural highway for their passage west.

Several hundred miles along the trail to the West, Jim Bridger and his partner, Louis Vasquez, were building a post. Both men had visited Saint Louis and had stopped at other posts and forts. They saw what was going to happen, so it wasn't accidental that this post was built for the use of emigrants. In fact, Bridger, who had been an apprentice blacksmith in his youth, had hauled, all the way from Saint Louis, the necessary equipment to set up a blacksmith shop at the post. This was another first for Bridger, in the annals of Wyoming history.

The blacksmith shop had a forge, anvils, hammers, bellows, and shoes for horses, mules, and oxen. A good supply of iron tires was available, too, to the trail-weary travelers as they arrived at Fort Bridger where Old Gabe made them welcome.

Stewart's Historic Trip

In the meantime Jim Bridger received an invitation to join Sir William Drummond Stewart in 1843 on a long and lavish trip into the Wind River and Green River areas that Stewart loved so much. But Bridger could not accept, since he was going trapping for beaver in the Milk River country of Montana.

Bridger missed the trip of a lifetime—Stewart's long train was brimful of colorful guests. One writer said, "There were bugg ketchers, lawyers, botanists, and doctors..." as well as some of Stewart's old mountain men cronies. Each evening they dined off tables set with white linen, ate off china plates with matched silverware, and drank fine Rhine wine from sparkling crystal glasses. The nobleman had sold one of his castles in Scotland and meant to have one last royal fling in Wyoming before assuming his duties as a lord.

Emigrants still trickled up the Oregon Trail that year, and all that remained to start a mass migration west was some sort of nation-wide inducement. It could be a religious movement or some sort of well-publicized slogan which might direct Americans with an itch to travel to stream west and use the Oregon Trail.

The Mexican War

In 1846 a national crisis did occur. It was the Mexican War. This war cleared title to the land in Wyoming where Fort Bridger was located, set up the Southwest as part of the United States, and gave Americans the area on the West Coast called California. The Mexican War also helped spur the Mormons on to Utah, as part of them paid their way to "Zion" as soldiers in the war. The leaders helped form a Mormon battalion that fought well

"Manifest Destiny"

in the Mexican War; the pay those soldiers received was sent to the Mormons to help them finance their trip to the Great Salt Lake.

Of course, the idea of Manifest Destiny played its share in the growing emigration to the West, as politicians in the East claimed that it was the fate of Americans to inhabit and control all the land from the Atlantic to the Pacific.

"Fifty-Four Forty Or Fight!"

The Argument with the British over Oregon had resulted in the slogan Fifty-four Forty or Fight—referring to the Fifty-fourth Parallel, as a boundary line. That slogan, the idea of Manifest Destiny, and the Mexican War all helped focus attention on the Oregon Trail and the West. And the Mormons were traveling on the other side of the North Platte from time to time, calling their trail the Mormon Trail.

Gold Discovered At Sutter's Mill

But what really riveted national attention on the West was the discovery of gold in the mill race at Sutter's Mill in California. The ex-Swiss Guard officer, Captain John Sutter, achieved immortality with that event.

News of the gold discovery in California raced around the world. In England, France, and all across Europe men bought passage to the fabulous goldfields in California. Chinese came across the Pacific and so did Australians and New Zealanders. But, the greatest tide of people that was to flood the Oregon Trail came from the American East.

Farmers, mechanics, tradesmen, lawyers, doctors, teachers, men of the cloth, and bankers dropped their ordinary pursuits and scurried around trying to buy freight wagons, of any sort, as gold fever hit them. Using mules, horses, and oxen to haul their wagons, they loaded on all their worldly possessions, their wives, their children, and dogs, and followed their own "Manifest Destiny."

By June of 1850 nearly 12,000 men had marched past Fort Laramie on the Oregon Trail, headed for California. Those men brought only a hundred women with them, and one hundred children. They came in three thousand wagons and used ten thousand horses, four thousand mules, and four thousand oxen to get them past Fort Laramie. They also brought two hundred cows with them. Before 1850 ended, records at Fort Laramie released figures showing that fifty-five thousand people had marched up the Oregon Trail. Even then, only four-fifths of them had taken the time to register.

In the span of a few short months the leisurely ways of a frontier folk at a far-flung trading post had been transformed into a traffic-congested crossroads. Where once the only loud noises had come from a thundering herd of buffalo stampeding across the plains, or from the stuttering brilliance of a summer electrical storm, and from the noisy gathering of red and white men at a rendezvous, now the air was filled with the noise of humanity crying, shouting, yelling, and creaking up the Oregon Trail. The tranquility of the West had been punctured, and from now on the noise of civilization would become a part of the color of the West—and Wyoming.

Debris was scattered for miles, as naive women had tried to lug heavy furniture, huge stoves, and other heavy objects to their new homes. The offending objects were discarded by anxious husbands and fathers, unloading wagons of all that was not absolutely necessary in order to keep their oxen, mule, or horse teams alive and strong enough to keep up with their wagon train.

Fort Laramie Purchased

By now Fort Laramie was the property of the United States Government, having been purchased for $4,000 in 1849. Only two companies of Mounted Rifles and one company of Infantry was stationed there. The purchase had been made in June of that year and directly following this the soldiers went to work sawing trees into lumber and finding sand and lime for concrete with which to construct new buildings.

When the area was first being explored by the white man, two companies of cavalry and one company of infantry would have been enough to maintain a lasting peace with the Indians along the Oregon Trail. The Sioux, Arapaho, and Cheyenne still came to the post to trade and meet with traders doing business near the post.

Indians Stopped Wagon Trains

The Indians also stopped wagon trains and were given coffee, powder, flints, lead, food of all descriptions, and cloth and trinkets; since it had been their custom to visit with a wagon train of traders, the Indians expected all the other wagons to stop, too. While some of the Indians asked the emigrants for these items, other Indians began to demand the food and trinkets. And there were some who simply moved their lodgings to the edge of the Oregon Trail and begged.

Changing World Of Indians

With all the hardship and struggle for survival that the Indians endured, the best of them were a proud people who had established and observed a disciplined, organized way of life. They were **of** the land, having worked out a successful way of living off its bounty. The Oregon Trail, now a mile-wide swath across the earth, was a grave foreshadowing of change. Grass was disappearing, and with it the buffalo, and even more ominous was the diminishing of the proud, independent spirit of the Indians.

Cholera Epidemic Of 1850

In Saint Louis in June of 1850 more than five thousand people died from cholera. Other cities also suffered from the epidemic of the dread disease. Since many emigrants outfitted at or near Saint Louis, cholera was picked up and carried along the Oregon Trail, resulting in hundreds of deaths. Cholera could be passed by food, by touch from person to person, and by drinking contaminated water.

It was a disease that played no favorites, taking its victims from the most robust as well as the weak and elderly. Major Cross, a quartermaster with the Mountain Rifles, told of his mule driver, Sam Miller, who fell ill one morning a few miles east of where Casper is today. By the time the cavalry officer got back to their camp on the North Platte, Miller had died. Worst of all, the tale was not uncommon, as hundreds of people wrote in their day-to-day diaries and letters back home of a friend or beloved member of their family's being buried at some lonely site on the Oregon Trail.

It is interesting to note that one group was able to avoid the illness, being led by an Englishman named Henry J. Coke, who carried a large amount of medicine in his wagon. Claiming to have a regular apothecary shop, he also prepared his food well and boiled his drinking water. All of his people made the trip in good shape and arrived in California alive.

Indians Struck By Cholera

In retrospect it is easy to say that the emigrants **should** have dipped their buckets and cups into the dirty brown North Platte which was still carrying melting snow water; because, unsightly though it was, it was safe to drink. Instead, they dug into the sand and drank the cool water that rose to the surface. Once this still surface water was contaminated, others who passed by helped themselves and also fell fatally ill from this disease. The Indians, too, suffered from cholera, brought west by the white man.

53

Bitter Winter Weather

Another problem the pioneers faced in traveling the Oregon Trail was crossing the Sierra Nevada range of mountains before winter storms closed off its passes. If they got caught in the icy grip of the huge snowfalls, a miserable death by starvation and privation befell the emigrants already worn out from the long trip.

The tragic story of the Donner Party caught in a blizzard in 1846 is common knowledge—out of a group of eighty-eight, only forty-two survived. Therefore, a well-organized wagon train tried very hard to hold to a schedule that would keep them ahead of the early fall storms.

CORRESPONDENT PAWNEE

News, any news, of what was occurring west of Saint Louis sold to the newspapers and got printed into handbooks. If the story was big enough, it became a full-size book. Newspapers, handbooks, and the larger books sold out rapidly as a news-hungry populace bought them and eagerly devoured each one.

Often newspapers hired correspondents to report by letter what was taking place in the West, how the emigrants were faring, and what Indian life was really like. The correspondents were ordered to keep the information coming. The paper would print it and the public would certainly buy it.

One such correspondent for the *Missouri Republican,* a Saint Louis newspaper, wrote all his reports from Fort Kearny on the North Platte. Everybody who went by also passed Fort Laramie, making correspondent ''Pawnee,'' as he called himself, interesting reading and giving an insight into the kind of people on the Oregon Trail. Here is a letter from Pawnee to his editor in May, 1849:

The ice is at last broken, and the inundation of gold diggers is upon us. The first specimen, with a large pick-axe over his shoulder, a long rifle in his hand, and two revolvers and a bowie knife stuck in his belt, made his appearance here a week ago last Sunday. He only had time to ask for a drink of buttermilk, a piece of gingerbread and how 'fur it was to Californy', and then halooing to his long-legged, slab-sided cattle drawing a diminutive yellow-top Yankee wagin, desappeared on the trail toward the gold 'diggins'. Since then wagons have been constantly passing. Up to this morning four hundred and seventy-six wagons have gone past this point; and this is but the advance guard.

Every state, and I presume almost every town and county in the United States, is now represented in this part of the world. Wagons of all patterns, sizes and descriptions, drawn by bulls, cows, oxen, jackasses, mules and horses, are seen daily rolling along towards the Pacific, guarded by walking arsenals. Arms of all kinds must certainly be scarce in the states, after such a drain as the emigrants must have made upon them. Not a man but has a gun and a revolver or two, and one fellow I saw, actually had not less than three bowie knives stuck in his belt. Many of the parties as originally formed in the states have had dissensions and are broken up. Each fellow is striking out for himself. This mode of life soon brings out a man in his true colors. No one knows a man and he does not know himself, until he is brought out in his true character—in the tented field, or on some such expedition as is now occupying so many of our citizens.

Such an emigration as is now passing over the plains, has not had its parallel in any age. Composed, as it mostly is of the best material of our land, the country that receives it must necessarily assume a commanding position. Many rascals, however, are along with this crowd, to give it a little wholesome (?) seasoning.

The last arrival from the frontiers is a solitary foot traveler, who says he has come all the way from Maine without the assistance of either railroad, stage, steamboat or telegraph wires. He is accompanied by a savage looking bull dog, has a long rifle over his shoulder, on the end of which he carries his baggage, consisting of a small bundle the size of your hat. He has not provisions but gets along pretty well by sponging on his fellow travelers....

One of the men with the Mormon mail, is just in from the 'diggins' in California, and is certainly a happy fellow, for he says that he has as much gold as he wants. He showed a stocking full as a specimen and as you may well suppose, the emigrants opened wide their eyes at the sight of the glittering mass.

If nothing else, the last paragraph probably excited enough readers in St. Louis to cause them to throw off their ordinary existence, sell out, and join the throng heading for the ''diggins'' in ''Californy''—maybe with a banjo on their knee!

It is fortunate for us in our study of history that Mark Twain came through Wyoming on his way to Nevada! He was traveling in a stagecoach in the summertime with his brother Bemis, who was on his way to Nevada Territory to serve as Territorial Secretary. This was in 1861. Enroute, Mark Twain came upon a pony express rider and later described his impressions in his book *Roughing It.* The following passage comes from this book:

In a little while all interest was taken up in stretching our necks and watching for the 'pony rider'—the fleet messenger who sped across the continent from St. Joe to Sacramento, carrying letters nineteen hundred miles in eight days! Think of that for perishable horse and human flesh to do! The pony-rider was usually a little bit of a man, brimful of spirit and endurance. No matter what time of day or night his watch came on, and no matter whether it was winter or summer, raining, snowing, hailing, or sleeting, or whether his 'beat' was a level straight road or a crazy trail over mountain crags and precipices, or whether it led through peaceful

EPIC:

"Pony Express"

regions or regions that swarmed with hostile Indians, he must always be ready to leap into the saddle and be off like the wind! There was no idling for a pony-rider on duty. He rode fifty miles without stopping, by daylight, or moonlight, starlight, or through the blackness or darkness— as it happened. He rode a splendid horse that was born for a racer and fed and lodged like a gentlemen; kept him at his utmost speed for ten miles, and then as he came crashing up to the station where stood two men holding fast a fresh impatient steed, the transfer of rider and mail-bag was made in the twinkling of an eye, and away flew the eager pair and were out

of sight before the spectator could get hardly the ghost of a look...The stagecoach traveled about a hundred to a hundred and twenty-five miles a day (twenty-four hours), the pony-rider about two hundred and fifty. There were about eighty pony riders in the saddle all the time, night and day, stretching in a long, scattering procession from Missiouri to California, forty flying eastward, and forty toward the west, and among them making four hundred gallant horses earn a stirring livelihood and seeing a deal of scenery every single day in the year.

We had a consuming desire, from the beginning, to see a pony-rider, but somehow or other all that passed us and all that met us managed to streak by in the night, and so we heard only a whiz and a hail, and the swift phantom of the desert was gone before we could get our heads out of the window. But now we were expecting one along every moment, and would see him in the broad daylight. Presently the driver exclaims:
'Here he comes!'

Every neck is stretched further, and every eye strained wider. Away across the endless dead level of the prairie a black speck appears against the sky, and it is plain it moves. Well, I should think so! In a second or two it becomes and horse and a rider, rising and falling, rising and falling—sweeping toward us nearer and nearer--growing more and more distinct, more and more sharply defined—nearer and still nearer, and the flutter of the hoofs comes faintly to our ear—another instant a whoop and a hurrah from our upper deck, a wave of the rider's hand, but no reply, and man and horse burst past our excited faces, and go swinging away like a belated fragment of a storm!

So sudden is it all, and so like a flash of unreal fancy, that but for the flake of white foam left quivering and perishable on a mail-sack after the vision had flashed by and disappeared, we might have doubted whether we had seen any actual horse and man at all, maybe.

At that time the speed of the express riders excited even the most staid onwatchers. They were able to carry the mail in just a little over a week from Missouri to California, while before the mail had taken over three weeks to travel as far. When Mark Twain was riding in that coach, the Civil War was in its infancy, and news—any news of the war—was eagerly awaited in the West and all along the Pony Express route.

Within 18 months, the news was given an *electrical* boost as it was flashed from coast to coast by means of the telegraph. That resulted in the slow but sure demise of the Pony Express.

Pony Express National
Pony Express Centennial Association
Trail Marker

COMMUNICATION AND TRANSPORTATION WYOMING

The various means of travel used by the Indians, mountain man, explorer, emigrant, soldier and the citizen are an important aspect of Western history.

"Shanks mare," or walking, trudging on foot, was one of the main ways of travel. A variety of horses, mules, burros, and oxen were used by most men and women after 1840, either to pull a vehicle or to be ridden. Often when using the wagons or other vehicles the people still walked many miles to save the animals for the hard and dangerous pulls.

Rubber Raft Introduced

Lt. John C. Fremont had introduced the inflated India rubber raft on the North platte, but boats of many kinds were used on the Missouri. Bull boats (made from buffalo hides) and flatboats or rafts were used extensively by the fur trappers while the Indians met the white man in their canoes often made from hollowed-out logs.

Caissons had been used to haul cannon over South Pass. They were a sort of two-wheeled carriage carrying field and mountain artillery and pulled by a span of horses or mules.

The prairie schooner, freight wagon, stage-coach, army ambulance, and the buckboard were the wagons most used in Wyoming from 1833 through 1868, when the railroad entered the picture. It was the Conestoga wagon and other types of prairie schooners that made all America into a nation that still drives on the righthand side of the road. The rule on the Oregon Trail and most other trails with heavy wagon and freighting traffic, was to keep to the right. It came from the simple act of man riding one horse of the team. He would choose the left-hand horse, because that one was easier to mount since that is the side always mounted. Likewise, it was easier to dismount on the left too. Thus, riding in that manner, the rider will guide to the right and pass right so he can observe any clearance needed.

Conestogas Lead The Way

The Conestoga wagon, built in Lancaster County, Pennsylvania, was huge, usually being from 24 to 26 feet long, standing 11 to 12 feet high and weighing almost 3,000 pounds. It was called "schooner of the prairies" because of its boat-like shape and was made of durable wood—oak or poplar. The beds and sides were so well fitted together on these wagons that many were caulked with pitch and floated across the river, the wheels having been taken off and strapped to schooner sides.

Underneath, very, very heavy oaken axles were used, and at first they squeaked and groaned so badly that emigrants spent a great deal of the time greasing them each night they stopped. As they crossed the sandy hills and plains of Nebraska, the sand stuck in the grease and acted like an emery board, cutting deeply into the axles so it was not unusual for the wheels to fall off. The emigrants soon learned to bear the groaning and squeaking of dry axles turning against the hubs.

The iron tires on the Conestoga wheels were

from two to four inches wide. The front wheels were 3 feet 6 inches in diameter and the rear wheels stood 4 feet 8 inches high. Felloes, the wooden parts of the wheel which were curved, were welded together with iron bolts, and then the iron tire fitted to the wheel. The whole affair was then ready for mounting on the axle by a wheelwright, the man who made wheels for a living. Linch pins which held the wheels to the axles, looked like extra-heavy or extra-large hairpins. Some folks used nuts, but the linch pins were common.

The wagon, when new, was usually red, white, and blue. The body was painted blue, the wheels and underneath, or running gear, were painted a bright red, the canvas top was a snowy white.

It took about three teams of horses to pull each Conestoga. The lead team was up front, the swing team in the middle, and the wheelers, the team closest to the wagon. Very large horses were needed to pull the heavy Conestoga, and they were costly. So many emigrants settled for oxen, while some used mules. Ten mules were required, however, to do the job that six big horses or six oxen could do.

On the left side of the Conestoga, in the front, was the long brake lever. Sometimes, rather than using the brakes, the wheels were deadlocked—a chain was run around the rims of the wheels from one wheel to another, stopping the wheels from turning. That way, the schooner would slide down the steep hill without gaining too much speed.

Later on, Conestoga and Studebaker manufacturers came out with a small version of the original prairie schooner. It was lighter, had a special iron axle and could carry about 6,500 pounds of freight. Mules could pull this wagon, and thus the trip west was hurried along from the usual 8 to 12 miles per day by oxen and the older, heavier wagon, to 20-25 miles a day with mules or horses drawing the new, light wagon.

In addition, instead of walking alongside this newer version of the prairie schooner and driving the team with a bull whip, the driver now could ride on top of a seat in front of the wagon. A woman could do the job, leaving the man to take care of loose stock, keep an eye out for raiding redskins, or help the teams up and down gullies.

Era Of The "Wagonmaster"

Prairie schooners usually traveled in units, and the size of the unit depended upon the size of the caravan. The Mormons called their units "battalions". All of them found a leader was necessary, and the leader was usually elected by the emigrants to be their captain, or wagonmaster. In turn, an experienced guide was hired. The guide usually charged by the wagon or by the person. If there were 500 people in a unit or wagon train he might charge a dollar a person, thus earning $500 for guiding that particular wagon train from Missouri to California. Many of the guides were former mountain men who started doing this when the beaver market fell off.

Each wagon train was really a small community on wheels. Someone was designated to perform marriages, to attend to burials, and to set fines for crimes. The wagonmaster usually took care of these duties, but he might name someone else to do the work.

Music and Sunday sermons were always in demand. At night when the wagons were corraled into a circle, bow and fiddle, banjo, mouth harp, or other musical instruments helped homesick travelers to keep up their spirits.

School wagons took care of the education of the children. Many men and women earned their way to California by holding daily classes inside one of the old slow-moving prairie schooners. And, when the three R's (reading, writing and arithmetic) were over for the day, youngsters sat spellbound while a real mountain man showed them how to set a trap, how to repair a rifle, or how to tell one tribe of Indians from another.

The order of march was important. After yoking-up, the wagon train would lurch forward at dawn. At noon the train halted and the oxen, horses or mules were turned loose to graze and rest while everyone ate a good noon meal. About an hour and a half later the yoking-up process was repeated and off the wagons went until late afternoon.

The "Wagon Circle"

Since each unit was divided into equal-sized sections, when it came time to circle up for the night, one unit went in one direction until it met the other unit coming from the opposite direction, forming a circle. Each wagon tongue would point out, while the wheels were locked with those of the neighboring wagons. Thus, overlapped as they were, it was nearly impossible for a herd of buffalo to stampede the chained wagons with guards posted each night at the entrances. Stock was driven past the entrances into the circle of wagons at night as the families retired.

Freighting units did not "corral up" the same way as the emigrants did, although they followed the pattern of turning into a circle. When they ended up, each wagon tongue pointed either in or out with each alternate wagon. When it came time to yoke up at dawn, speed was a factor and the bull whackers, or drivers, could move faster.

The ''Bullwhacker''

The bullwhacker got his title from the long leather whip he carried, occasionally cracking it, or ''whacking'' it over the heads of his oxen to guide them. A bullwhacker was never cruel to his teams, and if he was, the wagonmaster soon got rid of the man. The bullwhackers were very skillful in handling the oxen and were well paid.

If the trail was easy with no clogging sand or mud, two wagons were tied together and both teams yoked up pulling the double load. If the trail was extremely rugged, it might take two teams to haul a wagon up a hill or through a bog.

Each bull whacker had a helper called a ''swamper.'' If it was a jerkline outfit, the swamper rode in the wagon handling the brake and a ''jerkline.'' This jerkline was a single rein or line that ran to the forward team, where it was attached to the bit of the leader who was trained to respond to jerks while the other members of the pulling team followed his movements. The whacker walked beside his wagon.

Usually, freighting was done by professional contractors. The freight wagons were just a smaller version of the prairie schooner and were common in Wyoming from the Oregon Trail period until the 1920's when they were still being used to haul heavy oil field equipment and to pull huge loads of wool from the ranches to the railroad shipping points.

Arrival of the ''Stagecoach''

The most fascinating wagon was the stagecoach. It was imported from England and Europe, but when it arrived in the West, it was a much smaller and lighter version than its European cousin.

Usually, the stagecoach made in Concord, New Hampshire, weighed about 3,000 pounds and could haul 4,000 pounds using a four-horse team. It had steel axles, and the coach swung on leather thorough-braces of many thicknesses, which gave the occupant a feeling of swinging and swaying as the coach bumped along, taking the hard knocks and bad places in the road on its own coiled steel springs. It was not uncommon for a person unaccustomed to stagecoach travel to become ''seasick'' because of the swaying.

The Concord coach held three seats. Two faced

forwards and one faced to the rear. On top there was a large seat for the driver who sat on the right-hand side so he could also handle the brake. If the region and road was not subject to masked robbers or pesky Indians, then passengers might ride by the driver. Otherwise, a shotgun guard carrying a rifle, shotgun, and two revolvers rode beside the driver to protect the coach.

Around the top a metal guard held extra luggage and in the back, as well as the front, ''boots'', or leather-covered boxlike carriers, held passenger luggage, mail and small freight.

The route usually dictated the number of relay stations but normally a stagecoach had to change teams every 10 to 20 miles. Sometimes these places were called swing stations, and the eating houses were set far enough apart so a coach made a stop at noon and for the evening meal, where lodging for the night was also available. In the morning , after a hasty dawn breakfast, the fresh teams were harnessed and were off at top speed again. Some stagelines covering long distances carried on day and night.

One type of wagon seen in Wyoming for many years was the army ambulance. It grew out of the rough two-wheeled cart used to transport wounded men to hospitals. The cart was drawn by a single animal.

The ambulance cart evolved into a four-wheeled light wagon with good springs between the axles and the bed, which helped take care of the jolting and jarring of the wounded on their way to medical aid. This wagon became for the Army then what the jeep is today, the usual means of transportation, outside of the single rider on a single horse. This vehicle drawn by a team of horses or mules carried not only the sick and lame, but generals and their baggage, paymasters and their pay chests, women and their families, and if a non-commissioned officer or officer was transferred, into this small wagon his worldly possessions were piled along with his family and then the ambulance became a sort of moving van.

The bottom of the wagon, not the bed, arched up to a sort of well just behind the driver. This gave the front wheels more room to turn without rubbing against the body of the wagon, making the ambulance a highly maneuverable vehicle. The driver sat up front on the right side and had only a dashboard between himself and his team.

An oil cloth and waterproof cover was stretched across the top, and rolled up on the sides in fair weather. It was let down and tied to the wagon in foul weather. It also had a boot in back and a sort of chain-supported tailgate, which gave the ambulance the ability to carry extra luggage.

For the rancher, the commonly used wagon was the buckboard or buckwagon. The floor of this vehicle, which was built with one or two seats, was made of boards which were springy and tied down to bolsters just over the axles, giving it a sort of spring action as the wagon moved along.

The seats had springs which ran under them from side to side, and a small railing ran around the rear of the wagon for tying down luggage or ranch supplies hauled from the nearest town. In most cases the buckboard was open to the elements, having no cover over it. It became one of the most popular vehicles in the West and in Wyoming because it was easy to hitch a team to it, and it was easy to drive. It was light and seldom got mired down. If it did, a ten-foot pole could be used to lever and pry it out of any bog or chuck hole. It was the family wagon for the rancher, while the townsman used a similar type buggy usually with a roof covering it.

———————

VIGNETTE:

"Mark Twain describes South Pass"

Mark Twain wrote about "Black Jack" Slade, a renowned killer, but a highly efficient stage station manager. In an encounter with Slade, probably at Sweetwater Station, Twain writes:

In due time we rattled up a stage-station, and sat down to breakfast with a half-savage, half-civilized company of armed and bearded mountaineers, ranchmen and station employees. The most gentlemanly-appearing, quiet, and affable officer we had yet found along the road in the Overland Company's service was the person who sat at the head of the table, at my elbow. Never a youth stared and shivered as I did when I heard them call him SLADE!

Here was romance, and I was sitting face-to-face with it!—looking upon it—touching it—hob-nobbing with it, as it were! Here, right by my side, was the actual ogre who, in fights and brawls and various ways, had taken the lives of twenty-six human beings, or all men lied about him! I suppose I was the proudest stripling that ever traveled to see strange lands and wonderful people.

He was so friendly and so gentle-spoken that I warmed to him in spite of his awful history. It was hardly possible to realize that this pleasant person was the pitiless scourge of the outlaws, the raw-head-and-bloody-bones the nursing mothers of the mountains terrified their children with. And to this day I can remember nothing remarkable about him...The coffee ran out. At least it was reduced to one tin cupful, and Slade about to take it, when he saw that my cup was empty. He politely offered to fill it, but although I wanted it, I politely declined. I was afraid he had not killed anybody that morning, and might be needing diversion. But still with firm politeness he insisted on filling my cup, and said I had traveled all night and better deserved it than he—and while he talked he placidly poured the fluid, to the last drop. I thanked him and drank it, but it gave me no comfort, for I could not feel sure that he would not be sorry, presently, that he had given it away, and proceed to kill me to distract his thoughts from the loss. But nothing of the kind occurred. We left him with only twenty-six dead people to account for, and I felt a tranquil satisfaction in the thought that in so judiciously taking care of No. 1 at that breakfast table I had pleasantly escaped being No. 27.

Having "escaped" Slade, Mark Twain and his brother are next found at South Pass:

The hotel keeper, the postmaster, the blacksmith, the mayor, the constable, the city marshal, and the principal citizen and property-holder, all came out and greeted us cheerily, and we gave him a good day. He gave us a little Indian news and a little Rocky Mountain news, and we gave him some Plains information in return. He then retired to his lonely grandeur and we climbed on up among the bristling peaks and the ragged clouds. South Pass City consisted of four log cabins, one of which was unfinished, and the gentleman with all those offices and titles was the chiefest of the ten citizens of the place. Think of a hotelkeeper, postmaster, blacksmith, major, constable, city marshal and principal citizen all condensed into one person and crammed into one skin. Bemis (Twain's brother) said he was 'a perfect Allen's revolver of dignities.' And he said that if he were to die as postmaster or blacksmith, or as postmaster and blacksmith both, the people might stand it; but if he were to die all over, it would be a frightful loss to the community.

On that happy and humorous note, and with tongue in cheek, we lose sight of Mark Twain and his brother Bemis. They were on their way to Nevada and soon would tell other tall tales—like the Jumping Frog of Calaveras County—to the everlasting delight of all.

Joseph A "Jack" Slade Otherwise Known As "Blackjack" Slade Was A Highly Efficient Stage Station Manager And A Renown Killer. Born 1829 Died: March 10, 1864

Major General John C. Fremont

"Fremont floats the Platte"

In August 1842 Lieutenant John C. Fremont climbed into an India rubber craft and, with an exploration party, floated from the mouth of the Sweetwater through the "Firey Narrows," past the place which was to become Pathfinder Dam, in one single day.

Excerpts of his logged journal of that day are quoted in the following pages allowing the reader a glimpse of the kind of man Fremont was, and the chances he and his men took.

> August 24. We started before sunrise, intending to breakfast at Goat Island. I had directed the land party, in charge of Mr. Bernier, to proceed to this place...(he says his boat floats like a duck on the river here)...We were approaching a ridge, through which the river passed by a place called 'cannon', (pronounced kanyon) a Spanish word, signifying a piece of artillery, the barrel of a gun, or any kind of tube; and which, in this country, has been adopted to describe the passage of a river between perpendicular rocks of great height, which frequently approach each other

so closely overhead as to form a kind of tunnel over the stream, which foams along below, half choked up with fallen fragments. Between the mouth of the Sweet Water and Goat Island, there is probably a fall of 300 feet, and that was principally made in the canons before us...as we neared the ridge, the river made a sudden turn, and swept squarely down against one of the walls of the canyon with great velocity, and so steep a descent, that it had to the eye, the appearance of an inclined plane. When we launched into this, the men jumped overboard, to check the velocity of the boat, but were soon in water up to their necks, and our boat ran on; (here he stopped and checked ahead, but decided to risk it and shoved off). We all again embarked, and at first attempted to check the way of the boat; but the water swept through with such violence that we narrowly escaped being swamped...Had our boat been made of wood, in passing the narrows she would have been staved; but her elasticity preserved her unhurt to every shock, and we seemed fairly to leap over the falls...In this way we passed three cataracts in succession (then they came out on smooth water, and immediately plunged into a narrower and deeper chasm)...An ugly pass lay before us. We made fast to the stern of the boat a strong rope about fifty feet long; and three of the men clambered along among the rocks, and with this rope let her slowly through the pass (then the boat turned sideways, or broadside allowing saddlebags and sextant to be swept over the side, both of which were later recovered). We pushed off again; but, after making a little distance, the force of the current became too great for the men on shore, and two of them let go of the rope. Lajeunesse, the third man, hung on, and was jerked headforemost into the river from a rock twelve feet high; and down the boat shot like an arrow, Basil following us in the rapid current, and exerting all his strength to keep in mid-channel—his head only seen occasionally like a black spot in the white foam. (At an eddy the boat slowed down enough for all three men to rejoin their craft) I determined to take him (Basil) and the two others aboard, and trust to skill and fortune to reach the other end in safety. We placed ourselves on our knees, with the short paddles in our hands, the most skillful boatmen being in at the bow; and again we commenced our rapid descent. We cleared rock after rock, and shot past fall after fall, our little boat seeming to play with the cataracts. We became flushed with success, and familiar with danger; and, yielding to the excitement of the occasion, broke forth together into a Canadian boat song. Singing, or rather shouting, we dashed along; and were, I believe, in the midst of a chorus, when the boat struck a concealed rock immediately at the foot of a fall, which whirled her over in an instant. Three of my men could not swim, and my first feeling was to assist them and save some of our effects; but a sharp concussion or two convinced me that I had not yet saved myself...

No one drowned. All of their effects except one journal were found. Wet and cold, the party reached Goat Island and spent the night there in good spirits. The 29-year-old Fremont had floated the North Platte for the first time in a rubber boat and later earned the title of "Pathfinder" from the national press in America. That name was then given to the huge dam built in 1909 on the same river, in Fremont's exciting 'canon' area.

It had taken Fremont four days to travel from nearly the same place earlier that summer on his way west. On the return trip, using the rubber boat, it took one day to travel the same distance.

Gannet Peak

TOPOGRAPHICAL WYOMING

Bonneville Climbs Gannet Peak

In September 1833 Captain Benjamin E.L. Bonneville climbed the highest peak in Wyoming. As far as it is known, he was the first to record that climb of what we now call Gannett Peak, 13,785 feet above sea level.

Bonneville was a West Point graduate trained in map making and, while his fur ventures were not so successful as he hoped, his climb can be recorded as a Wyoming "first." The map, which he drew later on, could possibly be the first on-site map drawn of the Wind River Mountains from knowledge gained personally by the map maker himself. Bonneville was often referred to by that nickname — Mapmaker.

Fremont Exploration

Nearly ten years went by before another topographer, or mapmaker, came to Wyoming. That was Lt. John C. Fremont who arrived at Fort Laramie July 13, 1842. The Topographical Corps of the United States Army had ordered Fremont west to explore the region between the Missouri river and South Pass.

Fremont was the first of a number of topographical engineers in the Army to probe Wyoming and the West. Usually, those engineers took a cartographer with them, a man solely trained in the art of making maps. In some cases those topographical engineers took botanists, mineralogists, hydrographers, and other professional scientists. These men filled their journals with information on soil, minerals, water, climate, animal life, and plant life. They told, also, of the history of the Indians they encountered, as well as their attempts to understand the Indian languages and tongues.

On Fremont's journey, he had a German-born cartographer named Charles Pruess with him, although Fremont had been a topographer himself for a number of years. He took a hunter to supply his party, and his guide was mountain man Kit Carson. The rest of the party was made up of twenty Creole and Canadian voyageurs, all of whom were expert on river navigation and fur trading and understood the language of a number of Plains Indian tribes.

In Fremont's own duffle bag there was a homemade American Flag bearing 26 stars in the blue field, representing the number of States in the Union at that time. On August 15, 1841, Fremont was to unfurl the flag and plant it on top of a peak in Wyoming, reporting, "We mounted a barometer in the snow at the summit, unfurled the national flag to wave in the breeze where never flag waved before."

The flag had been made by Fremont's wife and

Platte Bridge Station

"The Pathfinder"

is now in the Southwest Museum in Los Angeles, California. It was the first national flag to fly from the top of the Wind River range, or for that matter, anywhere in Wyoming at that elevation (over 13,000 feet above sea level).

The next year, Fremont went west again. The United States was trying to establish claims to the West Coast, and Fremont's trip was intended to help.

When Fremont returned from the second trip in 1834-1844, he was called "Pathfinder" by the newspapers all over the country. While the title may have been presumptuous in light of the hundreds of men who had preceded him, it was well deserved, considering the valuable information he had accumulated and the light that information cast upon a section of America whose broad outlines had been mysterious and usually scoffed at as tales of men like Colter and Jim Bridger. Now those tall tales were beginning to be recognized as fact, and Fremont enabled Americans to learn more about their native land.

Fremont's father-in-law was U.S. Senator Benton of Missouri, the powerful chairman of the Armed Forces Committee in the Senate. Senator Benton made certain that Fremont's report got full attention in the Senate and in the House of Representatives.

Fremont's maps and those of Charles Pruess, the cartographer who accompanied Fremont on the trips, made a huge contribution to the knowledge of the West for the government and for the people of the nation.

Fremont served as major general in the U.S. Army, as Governor of California, and as U.S. Senator from California. He ran for President in 1856, but was defeated. Years later he served as Territorial Governor of Arizona from 1878 until 1882.

The Famous "Dragoons"

Colonel Stephen Watts Kearny and Captain Phillip St. George Cooke were also soldiers important to Wyoming's History. They led five companies of the First Dragoons to South Pass in 1845, to the Plains Indians an impressive display of military might. The 280-man unit—requiring 15 supply wagons pulled by six-mule teams, and two small mountain howitzers—also had a small herd of cattle and sheep moving along with them as a source of food, should the plains not be able to support them. Each Dragoon, considered the elite of the U.S. Army, carried a saber, carbine, and pistol.

Oregon Trail diaries record the passage of this splendidly uniformed column of soldiers mounted upon fine horses, and in nearly every case the diary reported relief at the sight of the soldiers. Emigrants were heartened to see them, representing, as they did, help in case they needed it; but, more important, representing a government that was taking an interest in the trail west and the people traveling on this trail.

Colonel Kearny led his men to Fort Laramie on June 14, 1845. Camping there, they visited Fort Platte as well. At Fort Laramie, Kearny seized the opportunity to address 1,200 Sioux Indians visiting and trading at the post, saying:

> Sioux: I am glad to see you. Your Great Father has learned much of his red children and has sent me with a few braves to visit you. I am going to the waters that flow to the setting sun. I shall return to this place and then march to the Arkansas and home. I am opening a road for the white people and your Great Father directs that his red children shall not attempt to close it. There are many whites now coming on the road, moving to the other side of the mountains. They take with them their women, children and cattle. They all go to bury their bones there and never return. You must not disturb them in their persons or molest their property. Should you do so your

Great Father would be very angry with you and cause you to be punished. You have enemies about you but the greatest of them all is whiskey. I learn that some bad white men bring it to you from Taos and sell it to you. Open your ears and listen to me. It is contrary to the wishes of your Great Father that whiskey should be brought here and I advise you whenever you find it in your country, no matter in whose possession, to spill it all on the ground. The ground may drink it without injury but you cannot. I wish you Sioux to remember what I have said to you . . . Your Great Father is the friend of his red children and as long as they behave themselves properly will continue to be so. I have not come among you to bring presents but your Great Father has sent a few things that you may remember what I have said to you.

Kearny Trades with Indians

Following the talk, Kearny gave out a large amount of trade items and then caused the howitzers to be fired. The sight, sound, and action of those cannon astounded the Indians. That night, under a starry sky, Kearny kept a promise he had made the Sioux saying he would send stars to the heavens and the Great Spirit, telling of the meeting that day. What Kearny actually did, of course, was cause a number of skyrockets to be fired into the clear June heavens, saying as he did that he was communicating directly with the Great Spirit.

Skyrockets, howitzers, splendid troops carrying the best firearms and mounted on fine looking horses, together with the powerful speech, impressed the Sioux. The next day Kearny left for South Pass, leaving one company of soldiers behind at the post.

When Kearny returned from South Pass to Fort Laramie, his command traveled due south and passed through Chugwater on their way to Bent's fort on the Arkansas. There they found a supply of grain, rice, salt, and flour that had been stored three years earlier. The act of prematurely storing those provisions surely proved that the Army was looking ahead to the day when a war with Mexico might call for sorely needed supplies.

More Forts Requested

The Mexican War followed shortly after the Dragoons' march to South Pass. The Texas Annexation came in 1845, the resolution of the Oregon boundary in 1846, and at the end of the Mexican War, the Treaty of Guadalupe Hidalgo, in 1848. These dates and events helped the United States expand by more than a million square miles. From now onw, (with time out for the Civil War) the U.S. Army and topographical engineers would spend a large amount of time in what we now call Wyoming.

One noticeable conflict in ideas came from the Fremont-Kearny reports. Fremont believed a string of forts was needed, spaced along the frontier and the Oregon Trail. Not so with Kearny. He advised strongly that a military excursion, a show of might and force, once or twice every couple of years would do the job of keeping the Indians in check and at peace. The government followed Fremont's advice.

Troops Sent Westward

Late in 1848 came discovery of gold at Sutter's Mill in California. With the traffic to the West in 1849 and 1850 reaching into the thousands of hopeful gold miners, the United States government was forced to take a more positive and permanent position along the Oregon Trail.

The entire regiment of Mounted Riflemen (another cavalry unit nearly like the Dragoons— both regiments preceded the actual formation of cavalry regiments so named) was led west by their commanding officer, Colonel W.W. Loring. Loring stopped at a post in Nebraska named after Kearny and left two companies of Mounted Rifles to garrison it.

Fort Laramie Reinforced

Next on the Oregon Trail was Fort Laramie, and here Loring left Major W. F. Sanderson with two companies of riflemen and one company of infantry. They were to garrison the far-flung post, and to construct new buildings, as well as to provide aid, comfort, and security to the endless line of emigrants. Major Sanderson began negotiations to buy Fort Laramie from The American Fur Company and eventually bought it in June 1849 for $4,000. He immediately put his men to work building a bigger and better fort.

Traveling west, Loring stopped at Fort Hall, secured the post, and left two more of his companies of horse soldiers there. Then, with

more than half his regiment scattered from Nebraska to Idaho, the Mounted Rifles colonel marched on to Vancouver (in what is now Washington) where Loring built and garrisoned Fort Vancouver with his remaining soldiers. He had completed his continental journey, erecting governmental posts at strategic places along the Oregon Trail.

Lt. Howard Stansbury of the Corps of Topographical Engineers had been handed orders to survey the Salt Lake area and to determine a new route to Salt Lake from South Pass, if possible. He was also to find an alternate route to the West. Bonneville, the commanding officer at Fort Kearny had much experience in the area Stansbury was entering and was able to give careful advice to the young engineering officer.

Stansbury then marched to Fort Laramie, arriving only three weeks after Major Sanderson bought the post. With him, Stansbury brought his small, compact unit of 18 men, five wagons, 50 mules and horses, and his second in command, 2nd Lt. John W. Gunnison. Stansbury led them west to Salt Lake where he spent the winter and surveyed that great body of salt water. He also **surveyed a new road to Fort Hall in Idaho.** Then in spring of 1850, after hiring Jim Bridger as his guide, he returned on a new route many miles south of the dusty Oregon Trail.

Overland Trail Established

After his expedition, Stansbury reported that a feasible route south of Oregon Trail could be used. It would run east from about where Green River is today, past Rock Springs, through a pass south of Rawlins called Bridger's Pass, named after his guide, and on to Fort Laramie. The route Stansbury suggested could avoid Fort Laramie and head on east to join up with Fort Kearny. This later corresponded roughly to the Overland Trail.

With Stansbury's report, information from Fremont and Kearny, and with the string of posts stretched across the continent, this seemed to be a good time to hold a general council with all the Indians. Before trouble occurred between the Indians and emigrants, it would be best if the rules and regulations were publicly made known so that both red man and white would know how the other felt about the Oregon Trail and the mass of humanity struggling to the West.

Keeping Peace with the Indians

The meeting was called for late summer 1851 and was to be held at Fort Laramie. Thomas "Broken Hand" Fitzpatrick had been appointed agent to the Arapaho, Cheyenne, and Sioux tribes, so, early that summer Fitzpatrick, together with the commandant of Fort Laramie, sent out word in all directions of the meeting to be held.

By mid-August whole villages and tribes of Indians began to arrive at Fort Laramie. Hundreds of Indians rode into the small post each day, until by late August, one scribe said that more than 60,000 Indians, of which 20,000 were warriors, had gathered at the Frontier post.

It was, by any comparison of the past or the future, the largest gathering of Indians at one place in the history of the American nation. The small garrison with hardly more than 200 men struggled to supply the Indians with food, camp space, water, and grass for their horses.

Each warrior brought his favorite horse—maybe two or three—and many more horses were used to transport the tipi lodges and families, so there were at least 20,000 head of horses at Fort Laramie.

Colonel A.B. Chambers, owner of a Saint Louis newspaper, was on hand for the meeting. He brought his editor B. Gratz Brown with him to record the progress of the Treaty of 1851. Both men gave accounts of the long-drawn-out affair, and from them, as well as from stories and diaries written by others who were there, we have a fine record of the event.

The gathering grew so big that the entire assembly had to be moved down the North Platte River to a point 30 miles downstream where Horse Creek joins the bigger body of water, where today, Nebraska and Wyoming join, east of Torrington.

The whole idea of the meeting was to help the government ensure the safety of the emigrants crossing Indian lands. The commissioners tried to win the Indians over to the idea of keeping the peace that the Great Father in Washington wanted. For that, the Great Father would pay the Indians an annuity for the loss of grass, buffalo, and the right to cross Indian lands.

Treaty of 1851 Signed

When the treaty was concluded, the agreement reached was that Indians would receive a $50,000 annuity for the next 50 years, this to be paid out at Fort Laramie. Later, this was amended to extend for only 10 years, but the amount remained the same. Both white and red men would be punished for any raids they took part in. Tribal territories were set and approved. Finally each tribe would be allowed to continue to hunt and fish in its own tribal territories.

On September 20, a wagon train loaded with cast-off Mexican War uniforms and tons of other trade items arrived at the Horse Creek council grounds. Cocked hats, long-tailed uniform frock coats complete with gold tinsel decorated epaulettes, and blue pantaloons were given out to the Indian warriors, chiefs, and headmen. Hangars, or swords, large medals, and various ribbons were also presented to the red soldiers.

As the meeting drew to a close, Colonel Mitchel and Agent Fitzpatrick left with eleven of the more important chiefs for Washington, D.C., where the Indian leaders were to visit President Millard Fillmore in the White House. The Council and Treaty of 1851 were considered by most as having been successful.

VIGNETTE:

"The colorful council of 1851"

B. Gratz Brown, editor of a Saint Louis newspaper, gave the following account of the 1851 council:

It was an interesting cavalcade that moved down the Platte on the well-worn and dusty Oregon Trail. Two companies of troops were in the lead; then followed the white dignitaries riding in carriages prepared for the occasion. Heavy wagons creaking under their loads of supplies followed behind, while all about where Indian villages on the move. Chiefs rode with some decorum, while braves and boys dashed about, displaying their horsemanship and working of surplus energy.

Upon the squaws and girls had fallen the burden of camp moving. After taking down the lodge, they had attached to their horses - travois - prairie buggies - and on these placed their lodge skins, camp equipage, and small children. Some of these buggies were provided with a wicker framework and with skin covering for shelter. Even the dogs were harnessed to small travois which carried light articles.

As each band of village got under way, the horses and dogs assumed a regular order of march. Should some foreigner break into the line ahead of a dog, the aggrieved canine would set up a piteous howl until he was again in his proper line of succession. The cavalcade stretched out for several miles and about it a cloud of dust rose thick and stifling...On Saturday, a large band of Sioux chiefs, braves and men, nearly a thousand in number, well mounted, came down the Platte. They marched in solid column about four abreast, shouting and singing. As they passed over the hill into the plain they presented an imposing and interesting sight. In the center rode their principal chiefs, who carried an American flag, which they say was given them by General Clark in the early days of his superintendency. They marched into camp and formed a circle. Colonel Mitchell gave them some tobacco, and vermillion, and informed them that he would expect them to meet him on Monday morning, at the firing of the cannon.

Later that day, several hundred Cheyennes, also mounted, rode over the hill, in manner similar to the Sioux, came into camp, and were treated with the same presents...(On Monday, following the signal from the cannon, the council got underway)... When the whole body commenced moving to the common center, a sight presented of most thrilling interest. Each nation approached with its own peculiar song or demonstration, and such a combination of rude, wild, fantastic manner and dress never was witnessed. It is not probable that an opportunity will ever again be presented of seeing so many tribes assembled together displaying all the peculiarities of features, dress, equipments, and horses, and everything else, exhibiting their wild notions of elegance and propriety.

They came out this morning, not armed or painted for war, but decked out in all their best regalia, pomp, paint, and display of peace. The chiefs and braves were dressed with punctilious attention to imposing effect. The 'bucks' (young men) were out on horse or afoot, in all the foppery and display of prairie dandies. In their efforts to be elegant, fashionable and exquisite, it must be confessed that the prairie dandy, after his manner, displays quite as much sense and taste as his city prototype, with this advantage. The Indian does not conceal his features with a superabundance of hair. In their bearings and efforts to show pride of dress and tinsel, they are on a par.

The squaws were out in all the richness and embelishments of their toggery. Their displays, according to their stations and wealth of their husbands and fathers, marked their ability to dress and their distingue in genteel Indian society. The belles (that are Indian as well as civilized belles) were out in all they could raise of finery and costume, and the way they flaunted, tittered, talked and made efforts to show off the best advantage before the bucks, justly entitled them to the civilized appellation we have given them. We concluded that coquetry was not of foreign origin. Even more than ordinary care had been bestowed on the dress of the children. They were evidently on their best behavior... some decked out in all the variety of finery that skins of wild animals, beads, porcupine quills, and various colored cloths could suggest. Others were in more simple costume, a string of beads around the neck, and a string around the loins...The ceremony commenced. A large calumet of red pipestone, equipped with a three-foot stem and ornamented with bright colored beads and hair was brought forth. The bowl was filled with tobacco and kinnikinnick. The Sioux interpreter lighted the pipe and passed it to Supt. Mitchell. He took a few puffs and passed it on to Agent Fitzpatrick, from whom it went to the chiefs about the circle. Some, on taking the pipe, extended it to the four points of the compass, then up to the Great Spirit and down to the Bad. A ceremony observed by nearly everyone as solemn protestation of truthfulness was to extend the right hand to the bowl and draw it back along the stem to his throat.

Gathered together for the first time in history were 20,000 Indian warriors from more than eight powerful nations, making up the Red Army of the West.

EPIC:

"Zion"

Not every Mormon following Brigham Young into the valley of the Great Salt Lake liked what he saw, but when the deciding vote was taken, only one dissented.

The Pioneer, or advance party, had done its job. From now on this was to be their home. They had fought hard enough, worked hard enough and certainly prayed hard enough for it—the valley was theirs to settle. One writer has captured on paper, however, some of the bewilderment they evidently felt as they viewed their new home:

> They were easterners, New Englanders and New Yorkers mainly. However well they might bear the hardness of the dry country as a route of passage, they expected something like home at the end, especially if the new place was labeled New Jerusalem. Instead they got gravelly dry ground, bunch grass, cricketts, rattlesnakes, the unfamiliar high horizon of a mountain-rimmed valley, the flame of desert sunsets over a sterile lake. They had to adjust not only to discomfort, but to dislocation from all they knew. In building the Kingdom they had the problem of creating a whole new way of life, learning new arts of tillage, adapting to a new climate and unfamiliar weathers and lights and colors. A child born here would be forever different, responsive to another sort of beauty, to other habits, other customs.

> But it was not totally strange. Foreign as it might be to their personal experience it was close to the biblical echoes to which their faith was tuned. Eighteen miles west of them in this desert that was as bleak as ever Palestine was, lay a Dead Sea of salt as that of the Bible. Into it flowed a stream, the effluent of Utah Lake to the south, that shortly in their consciousness of being the tribe of Joseph they would name the Jordon.

Brigham Young, the Mormon leader, faced a monumental task. He had to settle the valley. He had to ensure that the Book of Mormon would last and always be the main guide to living while he transported thousands of Mormons, Mormon converts, animals, supplies, and equipment across a whole continent to the valley of the Great Salt Lake—their Zion. It would take a true pioneer and, a promoter. Above all else, it would take a dynamic preacher to get the job done. History has proved that Brigham Young was equal to the task, and more.

STORMY WYOMING

By 1850, there were a few missionaries, ministers, and priests who had either come to Wyoming or passed through, enroute to other areas. Most of them were working with Indians. The first white women who crossed South Pass were missionary wives—the wives of Marcus Whitman and Reverend Spalding.

Missionaries in Wyoming

A number of the missionaries and others preaching the Gospel attended the rendezvous on the Green River. Notable among those men of the cloth who observed the mountain men at these summer meetings were Reverend Whitman, Reverend Spalding, Jason Lee, Nathaniel Wyeth, William Gray, and Father Pierre DeSmet. The mountain men especially welcomed them at their summer trade fairs, as all were able to read and write something most mountain men were not able to do. So, any letters to be written home, accounts squared away with fur companies, and Bible readings for mountain men came from theses early day missionaries.

Father De Smet a Favorite

Father DeSmet was a favorite. Nearly all Indian tribes wanted the personable young Belgian priest to come live with them. In fact, it was Father DeSmet who led a large contingent of Crow Indians to the treaty of 1851 at Fort Laramie. There, according to his own accounts, he baptised 955 Arapaho, Cheyenne, and Sioux children in one day!

The Famous Wyoming Missionary Father P.J. De Smet Who Claimed To Have Baptized 955 Arapaho, Cheyenne and Souix Children In One Day.

Brigham Young Leads Mormons

Brigham Young was not to be considered a missionary. While these other men were carrying the Gospel to Indians and mountain men, Brigham Young was not bringing a religion to a people—he was bringing his people to a place where they could follow their religion and their faith in peace without interference or persecution by those who held different beliefs.

The Mormons had been pursued across New York, and finally on the banks of the Missouri River at Florence, Nebraska, they set up their quarters. From there, in 1847, Brigham Young led the Mormons to their "Zion" in the West. Zion, for the Mormons, was the valley of the Great Salt Lake.

In ten years time, Brigham Young had moved nearly 50,000 people into the valley of the dead, salty lake that Jim Bridger and his friends, only twenty-five years earlier, had believed to be an arm of the Pacific Ocean. This mass of people moving to the West had changed the once barren area into a bustling town and an abundant farming area.

In 1849, Brigham Young sent a delegation to Washington, D.C., asking that the area be admitted to the Union as **Deseret State**. (Deseret, according to the Book of Mormon, means Honey Bee.)

The delegation was not successful in getting the State of Deseret admitted to the Union, but a new territory was created, Utah Territory. Young, president of the Mormon Church was named Territorial Governor by President Fillmore. Six territorial officials were also appointed, three of them Mormon and three of them, non-Mormon.

With the Territorial Governor being also the head of the church there were bound to be some problems. First, there simply was no division between church and state. The church would settle any controversial matters first, in their own manner, and only then could the state take action. It was a difficult situation, not to the Mormons, but certainly to the Gentiles, or non-Mormons, and later led to trouble.

New Mail Route from Utah to Missouri

By 1850 a mail route of sorts had been established between Salt Lake City and Missouri. A government contract was in effect, and the mail was to run from Independence, Missouri, to Salt Lake City on a monthly basis. The route was divided into two divisions because the one long run was irregular, due to bad weather. The first division ran from Independence to Fort Laramie where it was supposed to meet the second division mail originating at Salt Lake City. Then, exchanging their packets of mail, each courier returned from Fort Laramie to his starting point.

All the while, thousands upon thousands of gold seekers, Oregonians, and Mormons were cutting wagon ruts deeper and deeper as they made their way westward.

First Indian Battle

The first altercation between red and white men in the area took place June 15, 1853, near Fort Laramie, when some renegade Sioux bucks took control of the ferry boat on the North Platte River. An Army sergeant recaptured the boat, and was fired upon by the Sioux-who claimed later they were just having a good time.

The post commandant, however, ordered 2nd Lieutenant H.B. Fleming to the Sioux encampment where he was to bring back the culprit who fired the shot, breaking the Treaty of 1851. Leading two squads of soldiers and taking an interpreter, Lieutenant Fleming arrived at the large Sioux encampment north of the Army post.

There, Fleming demanded the man who had shot at the sergeant.

Fleming's orders were if the culprit did not give himself up, then Fleming was to find the man himself, place him under close arrest, and bring him back to the guardhouse at the fort.

No Indian volunteered to be arrested. Fleming then took direct action, resulting in a skirmish during which three Sioux were killed and three more wounded. Fleming then captured several warriors, clapped them in irons, and hauled them back to the guardhouse at Fort Laramie.

Almost immediately, the Sioux chief went to Fort Laramie and asked the post commandant to release his men. He did not feel the boat incident warranted any arrests, and certainly not the killing of three of his men, and wounding of three more, or jailing the others.

While the Army post commandant agreed to listen to the chief, he refused to release the jailed Sioux warriors. The Army felt the incident was serious and that its authority had to be maintained over the Indians.

Plains War Develops

The matter stood that way for a full year. Then, on August 18, 1854, a cow was missed from a Mormon wagon train. The theft was reported to Fort Laramie, and this time the commandant of the post was 2nd Lieutenant Fleming. The young commandant ordered Brevet 2nd Lieutenant L. Grattan to go to the Sioux encampment a few miles downriver from the post, where the indians were gathering for their annuities promised by the Treaty of 1851, and bring back the Indian cow thief.

As far as Fleming and Grattan were concerned, the cow incident was no different from the ferry boat incident, and should be dealt with by a firm hand. But there were some different factors involved now: the Indians were still angry over the killing and wounding of their men the previous year. They claimed that the soldiers had shed the first blood, and that the soldiers first broke the provisions of the Treaty of 1851.

Grattan was only a recent graduate of West Point and ignorant of the ways of the Indians. Certainly he had little experience in dealing with matters this serious.

Finally, the French Canadian interpreter whom Grattan took along with his small command to arrest the cow thief, was not well liked by the Sioux. The interpreter, who was drunk at the time, told a number of Sioux that the white soldiers were going to kill them and then devour their hearts!

With all of this against him, Grattan loaded his twenty-nine man detachment into a wagon and pulled two small cannons along to the area where the Indians were camped.

There he had the cannon loaded and made ready for firing while he demanded the man who had stolen the cow be turned over to him to be taken back and jailed at Fort Laramie. Receiving no satisfaction there, and seeing a number of Indians making warlike gestures, Grattan gave the order to his troops to fire. The foot soldiers fired first into a crowd of about fifty Indians, and then the cannon were discharged.

The bulk of the Indians were hidden under a grassy rim, a sort of river terrace just below the ground level. Grattan could not see them, nor could his soldiers. As soon as the soldiers had discharged their rifles and the two cannons, a massed wave of Indians charged, over-running Grattan's position. Within minutes Grattan's entire command was killed. It was reported later that only one Indian died.

The Grattan Massacre angered the U.S. Government, and within weeks the garrison strength at Fort Laramie had been increased by an additional one hundred men, led by a field grade officer, Major William Hoffman, and an additional 100 men. At the same time, headmen among the Sioux tribes who took part in the battle could not control their young bucks and warriors bent upon revenge, and they attacked a number of innocent wagon trains.

Sioux Expedition of 1855

As a result of public pressure upon Congress, the Army was ordered into action. The result was the Sioux Expedition of 1855. Under the command of popular Mexican War hero Colonel William S. Harney, the expedition met and thoroughly defeated a large contingent of Indians at Ash Hollow, Nebraska, in August 1855. Battle casualties listed 86 dead Indians and 4 dead soldiers. Harney then swept into Nebraska and wound up at Fort Pierre where, in March 1856, he concluded the Sioux Expedition with a general treaty in which nine tribes of Sioux participated. However, Harney's campaign and 1856 peace treaties did not stop the trouble, but merely slowed it down.

Mormons Speed to Zion

Wyoming weather also brought death and misery during those years. The Gathering, the term best describing the thousands of Mormon converts who came to Salt Lake City and Utah ran into a series of early blizzards in 1856 which caused great tragedy to those particular groups.

A revolutionary new idea had been promoted to hurry the mass of European converts to Zion that year. Instead of waiting for enough heavy, slow and costly prairie schooners to gather at Winter Quarters to move them all to Salt Lake City they were to push or pull eight handcarts over the 1,400 mile trail from Florence, Nebraska to Salt Lake, Utah. Riding on two high wheels and an even lighter five foot long bed, the whole handcart could easily be pulled by two adults grasping the two shafts enclosed by a crossbar. The father of a family could get inside the shafts, and leaning against the crossbar, pulled the handcart while the mother pushed.

It was an exciting idea and an inexpensive one. But the handcarts were flimsy and fell apart easily. The families could not haul enough supplies to feed themselves on their journey

Photograph of Oregon Trail Ruts

across the continent. Also, the people who pulled and pushed were not the hardy rural stock of America, but converts who came from the city streets, the power looms, the mines and the factories of England and Europe. The first Handcart companies in 1856 made the trip, with only twenty or thirty dying along the way. The last two got away from Florence late and found themselves crossing an ice-slush filled North Platte River at Casper on foot, which froze their clothing, their meager supplies, their shelters, and in many cases, themselves.

The Willie Company, or Handcart Company Number Five was in the lead and were rescued at Saint Mary's Station, near the summit of South Pass. Relief wagons from Salt Lake met them there with supplies and helped them, but many survivors had to have fingers, hands and legs amputated because of extreme frostbite and 70 of the original number died.

Naming of Martin's Cove

Handcart Company Number Six, or the Martin Company, was a week behind Number Five. They fought a tragic and losing battle with the cold from Platte Bridge to Devil's Gate. Finally after a week of this severe struggle they stopped at a cove in the rocky hills just west of Devil's Gate. There the rescue units from Salt Lake finally found them so weak that they nursed them there in camp several days before attempting to move them on to Salt Lake. 156 of the 500 in the company did not live to see Zion and many of the rest suffered amputation because of frostbite. This particular cove on the Sweetwater still bears the name Martin's Cove.

The handcart experiment proved to be a costly one, but it was continued in 1857. But now, instead of no supplies other than those hauled in the handcarts, large wagons followed the companies with extra food and clothing. Certainly no handcart ever started the march so late as the previous year either.

U.S. Declares War On Utah

A new President of the United States had been elected in 1856 and it was customary when a new President, representing a different political party, came into the White House, that he made new Territorial Governor appointments. President Buchanan appointed Alfred Cumming the new Territorial Governor of Utah Territory. Brigham Young refused Cumming the office. That sullen defiance to an act of the President added fuel to the fires of controversy and reports streamed out of Utah which said Young was running the Territory to suit the Mormons, not Gentiles.

Judge W. W. Drummond left Utah in 1857 writing—"The Mormons look to Brigham Young and to him alone for the law by which they are governed---federal officers of the Territory are constantly insulted, harassed and annoyed by the Mormons, and for these insults there is no redress." W.M.F. McGraw, who had been replaced as a mail contractor, also issued a stinging indictment against Brigham Young. Indian agent T.S. Twiss, reported that Utahans were making settlements on Indian lands in violation of the law.

The net result of the defiance, and the culmination of the problems was a declaration of war against the Territory of Utah by the United States. The Mormon, or Utah War has been called "Buchanan's Blunder" after President Buchanan who spent $15,000.00 on the bitter year-long campaign.

The Utah Territory was 1,500 miles from the nearest American city of any size and straddled the trail which led to California. American citizens called Gentiles by the Mormons, were being mistreated and their lives and property was threatened. The defiance to seat the new territorial governor called for governmental action.

The President authorized a military expedition of 2,500 men to leave Fort Leavenworth in June 1857 to march to Utah. It was easier said than done.

An Army of 2,500 men took thousands of pounds of supplies, and the supply lines stretched all the way from Saint Louis to Salt Lake. It was necessary to haul tons of supplies to various points on the Oregon Trail where "supply dumps" were set up. Then, as the army moved West, they were issued rations along the way.

Horses and mules used by the army had to be fed corn every day. The grass had been grazed away from the Oregon Trail for miles in each direction as a result of the thousands of emigrants who clogged the trail every day. In fact, the Army traveled most of the way to Fort Laramie, and from Fort Laramie to the bridge at Platte River (Casper) using the side of the North Platte opposite of the slow moving emigrant trains.

Dispute Settled

All summer long, wagonmasters and their freight outfits and bullwhackers hauled supplies up the Oregon Trail. By September the Army started to move out. They were to face, that fall and winter, the same storms that the Mormon Handcart Companies had faced.

The Army lost hundreds of mules and horses, although only a few men died. Thousands of tons of supplies were lost as Major Lot Smith, leading hard riding Mormon raiders, cut deeply into supply trains and destroyed thousands of pounds of supplies.

The Army made it through the winter intact, weak to be sure, but capable and ready to carry out their orders. By the time the army arrived in Salt Lake City, the war had already been settled. An envoy sent by President Buchanan sailed around the tip of South America and traveled overland to Salt Lake to make peace with President Young, sparing the Army the distasteful task of fighting fellow Americans.

Governor Cumming took his rightful seat as territorial governor, and President Young and his followers were relieved to find the army would not burn the city to the ground as had been rumored.

Settling at Camp Floyd, a new Army post, 40 miles from Salt Lake, the army was more interested in the trouble that was rearing up along the Mason Dixon line east of the Rockies. Keen observers said a war between North and South was only a few years away.

Bull Freight Team

80

Under the command of Lieutenant Colonel Phillip Cooke the 2nd Regiment of Dragoons struggled up the Oregon Trail from Fort Laramie to Utah in October and November, 1857.

An express from South Pass had arrived at Fort Laramie in early October telling of the havoc Major Lot Smith and his mounted Mormon raiders had caused Colonel Alexander, commanding officer of a column of infantry. Alexander sorely needed a cavalry arm in order to keep his supplies intact, and fight off the wily and bold Smith from destroying more supplies. Cooke left Fort Laramie to help Alexander.

Major Lot Smith had caused monumental losses. As one military report said, "This wily leader succeeded in burning 74 wagons laden with supplies and driving off nearly 1,000 cattle. Among the supplies destroyed by Smith were 12,700 pounds of bacon, 167,000 pounds of flour, 1,400 pounds of sugar, 13,333 pounds of soap and 134 bushels of dried peaches."

During his march to South Pass, and beyond, Colonel Cooke kept a daily journal of his impressions of the march. Cooke wrote:

> November 5. We passed Devil's Gate...crossed the little river (The Sweetwater) to within a half mile of a deep grassy valley, extending to the mountain masses of naked granite. On the 6th, we found the ground once more white and the snow falling, but then very moderately. I marched as usual. On a four-mile hill the north wind and drifting snow became severe. The air seemed turned to frozen fog; nothing could be seen. We were struggling in a freezing cloud...(The regiment tried to find shelter in and among the Rattlesnake Mountains) Only a part of the regiment could huddle there in the deep snow, while the long night through the storm continued, and in fearful eddies from above, before, and behind, drove the falling and drifting snow...morning light had nothing cheerful to reveal; the air still filled with driven snow... It is not a time to dwell on the fact that from the mountain desert there was no retreat nor any shelter near, but a time for action. No murmurs, not a complaint, was heard, and certainly none saw in their commander's face a doubt or a cloud...Marching ten

Brigham Young
Leader of the Pioneers

CHAPTER VIII

VIGNETTE:

"The winter war"

miles only...November 8. The mercury that morning marked forty-four degrees below the freezing point! The march commenced before eight o'clock, and soon a high northwest wind arose which, with the drifting, gave great suffering...Ten days later, Cooke arrived at Fort Bridger. November 19. Marched, leading through the mud and snow, as yesterday, fourteen miles, passing the camp of the Tenth Infantry. I encamped several miles above them, on Black Fork, and about three miles below Fort Bridger. From there I reported in person yesterday...I have one hundred and forty-four horses, and have lost one hundred and thirty-four horses. (Major Lot Smith ceased raiding wagon trains when he learned the 2nd Dragoon Regiment had arrived at Fort Bridger. Smith respected Cooke and his hardbitten horse soldiers even if they had fewer horses.) Most of the loss occured on this side of South Pass, in comparatively moderate weather. It has been starvation. The earth has a no more lifeless, treeless, grassless desert; it contains scarcely a wolf to glut itself on the hundreds of dead and frozen animals which for thirty miles nearly block the road with abandoned and shattered property; they mark, perhaps beyond example in history, the steps of an advancing army with the horror of the disasterous retreat.

Of the men who served in the Army in the Utah War many also served in the Civil War. Only a few years later 51 of them would wear stars as generals; some were generals in the South; some were generals in the North; and, all of them, comrade in arms in the Utah War.

"The trail of words"

Of all the trails crossing Wyoming the most unusual was the "trail of words", or the telegraph line. As far as the Indians were concerned, this was a powerful thing, mysterious and full of heat and fire. They called it the "lightning trail" and years later artists depicted the Indian leaning against a lonely telegraph pole listening to the hum of electricity and the wind singing through the wires.

All summer and into the early fall of 1861 telegraph pole crews and survey parties toiled across Wyoming. From the West another line was doing the same as its crews sighted through transits, punched holes in the hard ground, uncoiled heavy wire, fastened insulators to the poles, and raised them in the race towards Salt Lake City.

As they approached each other—one from the East and one from the West—Pony Express riders carried vital messages back and forth, each day their distance being cut down by the telegraph lines marching forward.

When the telegraph line was completed it did not bring about the complete end of the Pony Express. The Pony Express ceased to function along the main telegraph line, but, it did continue to carry messages and urgent mail from the telegraph line to other points which did not receive electronic messages and news.

The two telegraph lines met in Salt Lake City on October 22, 1861. On October 24, the first transcontinental message flashed across the Nation:

Early Surveying Crew

To Abraham Lincoln, President of the United States:

In the temporary absence of the Governor of the State, I am requested to send you the first message which was transmitted over the wires of the telegraph line which connects the Pacific with the Atlantic States. The people of California desire to congratulate you upon the completion of the great work. They believe that it will be the means of strengthening the attachment which binds both the East and West to the Union, and they desire this—the first message across the continent—to express their loyalty to the Union and their determination to stand by its Government on this first day of trial. They regard that Government with affection, and will adhere to it under all fortunes.

(signed) Stephen J. Field,
Chief Justice of California

President Lincoln had been instrumental in getting Congress to appropriate $400,000 to help build the telegraph line, one reason Chief Justice Field had congratulated the president upon the completion of the line. But, even more comforting to President Abe Lincoln were the words saying that the line would help bind the East with the West. The Civil War was in progress, and any news of the West standing firm behind the Union was most comforting to a president who surely did not want to fight a war on two fronts.

The line had been surveyed and close on the heels of the engineers followed crews of men digging holes for the slender telegraph poles. Next came the pole setting crews, and shortly thereafter, the wire crew came with a telegrapher.

As they moved forward—from the East and from the West—Pony Express routes became much shorter in that they picked up news from the end of the wire. In many cases, the Pony Express rider simply raced to the crew coming from the other direction and delivered his news which was then wired to its named destination.

Harrassment from the Indians was not as serious as had been expected. At one place, an Indian stepped in to help a crew holding wire with heavy buckskin gloves during an electrical storm. A lightning bolt struck the wire some distance away, the Indian who was standing on wet ground was shocked with a searing jolt of electricity. Many Indians, as a result regarded the telegraph line as the "lightning trail".

In another case, some marauding young bucks saw in the line an opportunity to knock over some poles, and rip off the wire which they would use for lariats. They did it during a summer electrical storm, and as they rode along in single file, each man holding a section of the strung out wire, lightning struck the wire and almost killed all of them, burning several quite badly. At one place Indians thought the solution in the glass jars which constituted the "battery" or power sources held magical powers. They seized the jars and drank them empty, hoping to have those powers themselves. As most of the elements used during those days were zinc and copper in a solution of sulphate of copper in the glass jar, the results were deadly and the Indians died, in that case, horrible deaths.

Those kinds of situations were rare but the story of them did circulate among the Indians and white men helping hold down incidents along the telegraph trail at first. Within a year, the telegraph line was the only link between East and West as the Civil War raged in the Atlantic States, and the Indian War on the plains prompted raids on the stagelines and Pony Express lines.

CHAPTER IX

CIVIL WAR WYOMING

On April 15, 1861, newly elected President Abraham Lincoln issued a call for 75,000 volunteer troops to put down the rebellion in the South. At the same time, the Overland Telegraph Company was surveying and setting telegraph poles across Wyoming, each day shortening the rides of the Pony Express.

And all the while, emigrants, prospectors, and a few Mormon converts were slowly moving west on the Oregon Trail. Several times each day, the Overland Stage Company sent its dusty Concord stagecoaches rolling and swaying past the canvas covered prairie schooners. Supplies were also a part of this procession, as bullwhackers and teammasters cracked their bull whips over yoked-up oxen hauling the loaded freight wagons westward.

With the Civil War raging, Lincoln knew that the Union Army could not handle another war on the western front. Nor could the Union handle the situation if the westerners were to join the Southern sympathizers. By 1850, Utah was a territory, and California was a State. By 1861, Dakota, Nebraska, Colorado, Nevada, Oregon, Washington, and New Mexico were territories. Idaho came in as a territory in 1863, and Montana in 1864. California, Iowa, Kansas, Minnesota, Nevada, Oregon, and Washington were all organized and admitted to the Union by 1864. President Lincoln knew he needed the support of these new states and territories. The nation could not survive if there was dissension west of the Mississippi and Missouri.

Gold fever continued to rage as gold was found in Montana, Colorado, Idaho, and Nevada. Prospectors, businessmen, a wide array of skillful promoters, and gold camp followers hurried into those areas. The only link the government had with most of these new states and territories was the Oregon Trail with the Pony Express, the stagecoach, and telegraph lines across Wyoming. When the Ute and Shoshone Indians began to carry out daily raids on those lines in 1861 and 1862, impatient demands for military help began to arrive frequently in far away Washington D.C.

Regular troops had been pulled out of the West to strengthen the Union forces at the beginning of the Civil War, and volunteer units began to arrive to fill in the gaps. Many of the volunteers were unhappy with their western assignments because they had enlisted to fight "Johnnie Reb," as they called the Confederate soldiers. Their fear of the sudden attacks of the Indians as well as their fierce fighting, the boredom of the frontier fort and the long stretches between paydays—all these things led to desertions. And when news arrived that a new gold field had been discovered or that there were silver mines for the taking, many soldiers deserted in hopes that they could strike it rich too.

On the whole, however, volunteer troops did a good job. Many volunteers were from the midwest or California and knew about the terrain and the Indians. Few West Point officers ever thoroughly understood their Indian enemies, while most volunteer commanders could call upon previous personal experiences for knowledge in handling a situation. Those volunteers who came from Kansas, Nebraska, Colorado, California, and other western areas were accustomed to the dry climate, dry winds, sudden electrical storms, sloppy thaws, and high rivers in the spring and subzero winter weather.

First Winter Battle

One of the first winter battles ever fought along the continental divide was fought after the Shoshone Indians led by Chief Bear Hunter challenged Colonel Patrick Edward Connor in January 1863. This occurred on the Bear River in Utah Territory a few miles west of Wyoming. Connor was able to defeat the Shoshone, killing 224 Indians. A number of women and children and several hundred horses were captured, and a small white boy being held captive by the Shoshone was rescued. As it was subzero weather, Connor's volunteer California infantry and cavalry outfit had proved themselves as men who could cope with the climate as well as with the Indians!

Cherokee Trail

Until then, Indian battles along the western end of the Oregon Trail near Salt Lake had disrupted all forms of traffic. Connor, who was boosted to brigadier general after the battle, opened the lines of communication and transportation with that decisive battle, using volunteer troops.

On the other end of the Oregon Trail, Ben Holladay had moved his stagecoach lines south and started using what became known as the Overland Trail. This new road ran from Julesburg, Colorado, to Denver, then pointed north, past what is now Fort Collins, and across the Laramie Plains using the Cherokee Trail. In 1849, Cherokee Indians heading for the goldfields in California had used that route; hence the name, Cherokee Trail.

The Overland Trail went to the base of Elk Mountain, and then turned West and crossed the North Platte River and Bridger's Pass, continuing west until it ended in Salt Lake and the Utah Territory. This was nearly the same route that Jim Bridger and Lt. Howard Stansbury had checked out, on Stansbury's mission to find a new route West.

The new trail seemed feasible to Ben Holladay, but it doubled the work of the Army, whose lines were already stretched thin. Having another trail to guard would require more troops.

Chivington Massacre

Meanwhile, another volunteer Army was fighting and was successful in overwhelming the woodland Sioux in Minnesota and eastern Dakota, while Colonel Kit Carson and his volunteers were doing battle with the Apache and Navajo in New Mexico.

In Colorado the governor wanted the Cheyenne and Arapaho to meet with him so that he could, by treaty, clear the way for farmers, settlers, and miners to enter and use their land. The Arapaho and Cheyenne wanted no part of Governor Evans' proposition, but the matter was brought to a head by the ill-famed Chivington Massacre on November 29, 1864. Several hundred Arapaho and Cheyenne, mostly women and children, were badly wounded or killed by the troops under orders of Colorado's famous "Fighting Parson," Methodist Colonel John Mr. Chivington. Chivington was later court-martialed because of this act.

Up to this point, few of the Arapaho and Cheyenne had become involved in the trouble along the Oregon Trail, nor had the western branches of the Sioux been a threat. But when Chivington massacred their people, the Arapaho and Cheyenne sent war arrows calling for help from their allies the Sioux.

When President Lincoln had called for volunteers, an attorney in Hillsboro, Ohio, William O. Collins, paid the expenses of a volunteer cavalry regiment, and the soldiers chose Collins as their colonel. This regiment, the 11th Ohio volunteer Cavalry, arrived at Fort Laramie May 30, 1862. From there it was scattered out in small detachments at the outposts from Fort Laramie west to South Pass. It saw three years duty and fought over twenty official battles and hundreds of small skirmishes, as it sought to police most of central and southern Wyoming.

Fort Collins and Caspar

Colonel Collins gave his name to Fort Collins, Colorado and July 26, 1865, 78 days after Lee's surrender which ended the Civil War, Collins gave his only son: Lieutenant Caspar Collins lost his life in a gallant charge at Platte Bridge Station, the present site of Casper, Wyoming. There was an error in the spelling of young Collins's name in General Orders #49, ordered by Major General Pope naming the small post in his honor; his name was spelled Caspar, rather than Casper. The city Casper proudly bears the name, still misspelled. Orders No. 49 read as follows:

II. The Military Post situated at Platte Bridge, between Deer and Rock Creeks, on the Platte River, will be hereafter known as Fort Casper, in honor of Lt. Caspar Collins, 11th Ohio Cavalry, who lost his life while gallantly attacking a superior force of Indians at that place.

Besides the volunteers from California and Ohio, the states of Iowa, Michigan, Kansas, Missouri, Colorado, and Nebraska also supplied troops. White, black, and red men all fought against the warring Indian nations. 90 Pawnee Indians, hereditary enemies of the Arapaho, Cheyenne, and Sioux, fought beside their white brothers in a company led by Major Frank North. A sister company of Winnebago and Omaha warriors, also blood enemies of the Arapaho, Cheyenne, and Sioux alliance, fought under the command of Captain W.E. Nash. Both Indian units served at various times, not only as "the eyes and ears" of the Army, but as legendary fighters against their red-skinned brothers. Also lending support were the "Galvanized Yanks," Confederate soldiers who preferred to fight the Indian in the West than serve time in a federal prison in the North. As captured Southern soldiers they were given a choice of serving on the frontier or spending time in dark northern prisons. Many came West as U.S. volunteers, officered by Yankee soldiers.

Their strange nickname came from the practice of covering iron dishes and other kitchen utensils

USA Scout Gabe and his friend
Chief Washakie of the Shoshone Indians

with zinc to prevent the iron from rusting. This process was called "Galvanizing." Since the Confederate U.S. Volunteers who came west seemed to have a thin coating of Yankeeism, they were given the name "Galvanized Yankees."

War parties were causing a multitude of problems from Fort Laramie west to South Pass on the Oregon Trail. Usually it was Arapaho, Cheyenne, or Sioux—or a combination of all three—causing the trouble. When they finished a raid, they retreated into the Powder River regions north of the North Platte in order to heal from their wounds, count their coup, divide the stolen horses and mules, and display their prizes before their squaws and old people.

No military commander had yet penetrated the Powder River region, the area where the Tongue, Rosebud, Big Horn, Powder, and Belle Fourche rivers drained into the Yellowstone.

Treaty Signed

Chief Washakie of the Shoshone Indians had signed a treaty at Fort Bridger in 1863 giving his personal guarantee that passage on the Oregon-Overland Trails would not be subjected to any future Shoshone attacks, even though terms of the treaty made it evident that a railroad would soon come west. In exchange for signing this treaty, the Shoshone were to be given $10,000 in annuities for 20 years. Five days later a similar treaty was signed with the Ute Indians.

Even so, small battles took place in the spring of 1864 all along the Oregon Trail from Fort Marshall, a small log structure near present day Douglas, across the South Pass. Three battles took place in February, two in March, two more in April, three in May; and in June, four skirmishes took place.

By now, General G.M. Dodge, commandant of the military district, had placed General Connor over this part of Wyoming, reorganized out of Dodge's military district. Connor was ordered to make retribution against the red marauders, who were hiding in the Powder River regions.

Moonlight Commands Fort Laramie

Colonel Thomas Moonlight, who had the command at Fort Laramie, was impulsive and excitable and showed a regrettable lack of judgment: two Sioux Indians purchased a white woman captive from other Indians, and brought her to Fort Laramie to turn her over to the white commander as an act of friendliness. When the woman told of ill treatment by the Sioux buyers, as well the other Sioux and Cheyenne Indians, Moonlight had the two Sioux stretched by their necks with trace chains and hanged where they were left dead, for public inspection for several months.

It was a grim story. Both the white woman who had been the captive and the post sutler, who had had long experience with the Indians, argued against Moonlight's act of vengeance. But, Moonlight was determined to teach the Indians a lesson.

Next, Moonlight gathered a group of friendly Brule Sioux and commanded them to move East, almost into the tribal territory of the Pawnee Indians, their ancient enemies. An escort of 140 men, consisting of an element of the 7th Iowa Cavalry under the command of Captain W.D. Fouts was ordered by Moonlight to prod the Brule along.

Balking at being moved into the dangerous Pawnee territory, the Brule split into several factions—one warlike and one peaceful—and during the melee Fouts and four soldiers were killed. When Moonlight heard this, he ordered "boots and saddles," the call to arms, and marched off from Fort Laramie, hot on the trail of the rebel Indians. One hundred miles north of the post, Moonlight stopped to let his men and horses rest, and the unfriendly Brule drove off all his horses. Moonlight burned all the saddles and bridles so the Indians could not use them and walked all the way back to Fort Laramie.

Moonlight Relieved

General Connor was infuriated at Moonlight's loss of horses—the campaign Connor was trying desperately to wage against the Indians depended upon those mounts. He insisted to General Dodge that Moonlight be relieved of his command, which Dodge initialed.

Moonlight's loss of command was also prompted when Connor found out that Moonlight had advised a number of Connor's command they could go home since their enlistments had run out. Moonlight was correct in this, but the idea irked Connor: he felt Moonlight had caused a near mutiny when some of the other soldiers and their officers refused to take orders, with their enlistments about to expire. In retaliation Connor had several batteries of artillery loaded and aimed at the sullen troops. The trooops saw Connor was serious, and submitted. Connor told them that their enlistments had not, in fact, ended just because the Civil War was over. They were to serve their full enlistment, and only then could they return to their homes.

Colonel Moonlight, however, was a minor problem as far as General Connor was concerned. The freight bringing necessary supplies to build up strength for the proposed Powder River Campaign was maddeningly slow. Troop enlistments were running out. Horses and mules were in short supply. Besides all these problems, the Indians continued to raid up and down the Oregon Trail, all the way from central Nebraska to South Pass almost without fear of retribution.

On July 26, 1865, Sergeant Amos Custard's wagon train had been nearly wiped out almost within sight of the small post at the bridge crossing the North Platte. Out of 29 men, only three survived.

Connor Swings Into Action

Two days later, Connor shoved his command north into the Powder River country in the classic "pincher" movement. Like giant jaws, two columns would swing wide, and hopefully force the renegade Indians into the jaws of the pincher while two more columns of soldiers would sweep up remnants of stray Indians into the encirclement. All four columns were to rendezvous on the Rosebud River.

The eastern column came out of Nebraska heading toward Bear Lodge (Devil's Tower). Another column would move directly north from Fort Laramie. The western column, which divided

General P.E. Connor Established Fort Connor On The Powder River.

into two columns with one sweeping the foothills of the Big Horns, would forge north into the area near where Kaycee is today and rejoin the other columns before pushing straight up the flanks of the Big Horns to the Rosebud.

With over 2,000 men, horses, artillery, wagons, and scouts at Connor's disposal, his campaign was the most ambitious ever attempted in hostile country where every hill and valley could serve as hiding places for enemy Indians. Connor was fighting the combined tribes of Arapaho, Cheyenne, and Sioux who knew every draw, gully, water hole, and places of concealment in their beloved hunting territory. Even with Major Jim Bridger as his Chief of Scouts, Connor found it nearly impossible to sweep the Indians into his huge pre-planned military net.

Fort Connor Established

Three weeks after taking the field, Connor established Fort Connor on the Powder River. There he left half his own particular command behind to guard supplies and garrison the small cottonwood stockade. The red-headed, Irish-born general then continued north, once his western-most column had rejoined his command.

Connor Engages in Battle of Black Bear

The first fight occurred when Major North's Pawnee Indians killed and scalped every single member of a 27-man war party of Cheyenne Indians. A few days later Bridger reported a large camp of Indians on the Tongue River near where present day Ranchester, Wyoming is located.

At dawn on August 29, 1865 General Connor personally led his men into the large Arapaho village of Black Bear, a well-known and famous war chief of the Arapaho Indians. With 125 cavalrymen and the 90 Pawnee Scouts of Major North's company, Connor slid over the ridge into the camp and completely destroyed it. Forty Arapaho were killed, and at least twice that number were wounded. Connor also captured 500 head of horses, which he sorely needed. Connor's losses were counted at 6 men killed and several wounded.

It was a far superior force which Connor sent his men against, and soon the Arapaho gathered their forces and fought a running battle with Connor's troops all the way back to Fort Connor.

The official report of Connor to Dodge said, "I have the honor to further state that we returned to our encampment at 2:00 AM, on the 30th, having marched one hundred miles, fought the battle, and brought our prisoners and captured stock back to camp in thirty hours. I shall move on again this afternoon to the rendezvous of my columns near the Yellowstone."

As it turned out, the Battle of Black Bear was the one bright spot in his whole campaign. Connor had led the men of the 7th Iowa and 11th Ohio Cavalry Regiments into and out of a battle, victoriously, returned to his base camp with little loss after inflicting serious damage on his foe.

Connor's other columns, however, had run into a whole series of problems. Both had been hit by various Indian groups, and this was a time when they were nearly out of food, the horses were weak from no corn or grain, and early September snow storms had nearly halted the columns. Both columns of soldiers were dismounted since their horses were too weak to carry them, and if it had not been for the howitzers, the Indians would have inflicted even more damage on the two columns.

Connor was relieved of his duty and sent to Utah, and the campaign in the Powder River was called to a halt. A new general named Pope had taken over the military district, and he and the War Department were devising a new method of taking care of Indian problems in the Powder River region.

In 1866, Major General Pope, the War Department and the Indian Commissioner figured that a series of forts could be built and garrisoned on the Bozeman Trail, protecting the gold hungry prospectors heading to Virginia City and Alder Gulch in Montana on the trail. The posts would also serve to provide a base for patrols of soldiers curtailing marauding Arapaho, Cheyenne, and Sioux Indians. These plans did not, however, prove successful.

———————

VIGNETTE:

"Eyes and ears of Connor"

Over the years, the American Army employed the American Indians as special units in time of war. From pre-Revolutionary to present times, American Indians have always served with distinction, proving with their deeds and actions to be fine soldiers.

General Connor used two scouting companies in the Powder River Campaign of 1865. The following account is from Finn Burnett, grandfather of Milward L. Simpson of Cody, a former Governor and U.S. Senator from Wyoming. Burnett was with the sutler on the Powder River Expedition. The sutler provided supplies for soldiers not issued nor carried by the ordinary quartermaster such as writing paper, thread, sweets, combs, etc.

Burnett was impressed by Major North, and his Pawnee Scouts. He also liked Captain Nash and the combined Omaha and Winnebago Scouts. This account explains why.

Two or three days later a Pawnee scout was running into camp yelling, Sioux! Sioux! He reported that he had seen a war party come to the river (Powder) from the east, ten or fifteen miles down the river, north of the fort (Connor). Captain North thinks this war party was the same Indians who killed Caspar Collins a few days before at Platte Bridge as many scalps found in their possession was mute evidence that they had successfully attacked and killed a number of soldiers and that the age of the scalps would tend to verify the times as being the date of the Lieutenant's death. General Connor ordered North to go after them, in fact his scouts were going without orders as fast as they could catch their horses. A.C. Leighton (the

sutler) who as an intimate friend of Major North received permission for himself and I to accompany them... (once locating the Sioux after hard riding) finally the scouts came in and reported that they had located the Sioux camped in the timber a few miles ahead of us. Major North ordered the Pawnees to surround them, and wait until early dawn before attacking them. They were surprised and fought manfully until the last one was killed. There were forty-two of them, and two of them were women; none of them escaped. They had evidently been raiding along the Overland Trail as they had a number of whitemen's scalps, among them which we took to be a light curly haired girl; they also had a lot of clothing, both women's and men's. They also had a number of Ben Holladay's horses, they were fine lot, all branded B.H......

All through the Powder River Campaign, the Pawnee Scouts looked for their blood enemies—the Arapaho, Cheyenne, and Sioux. Burnett reports an ingenious way they trapped them.

...The Pawnees had a white horse which they used as a decoy. They would take this horse out at night a short distance from the camp and secret themselves around it. All Indians pride themselves as being expert horse thieves. This characteristic and this white horse caused a number of gallant horse thieves to lose their top-knots during this expedition. The Pawnees never took prisoners, but manifested great pride in exhibiting scalps, horses, guns, bows, arrows, clothing, or anything captured from an enemy.

EPIC:

"The Fetterman fight"

Chief Red Cloud and his Red Army of the West made the work of building Fort Phil Kearny a miserable and frightening task during the summer and fall of 1866. Hardly a day went by without the wood choppers sustaining an attack from Red Cloud's hard riding warriors.

Usually the Indians went back to their hunting territories with the coming of fall, to prepare for and go on a big fall buffalo hunt. But the fall of 1866 was different: Red Cloud kept his army fighting, and few went on the hunt for buffalo. There was bigger game. It wore a blue uniform and was called "Walk-a-Heap" if it was infantry and "Yellowleg" if it was cavalry.

On the cold and clear morning of December 21, a messenger hurried back to Fort Phil Kearny with the word that the wood detail was being hit by Indians again. They needed help fast. Colonel Henry B. Carrington, post commandant, sent Captain William J. Fetterman to the rescue. In sending Captain Fetterman out to help the wood detail, Colonel Carrington made it plain that only a rescue was needed, and that once the rescue was

achieved the rescue unit and the wood detail were to return to the post. Fetterman was ordered not to go beyond Lodge Trail Ridge. Beyond that ridge help might not be coming, since Carrington believed Red Cloud's forces were superior in number. Besides, it would be foolhardy to fight the Indians on their own terms in their home terrain.

With many women and children on the post, Carrington did not dare risk losing his men in a skirmish. His forces were already cut down due to the summer campaigns and many of them being sent to garrison Camp Connor and Fort C.F. Smith. Major Jim Bridger, Carrington's personal advisor and scout, agreed with Carrington's observations.

Fetterman Disobeys Orders

Captain Fetterman, who had won glory during the Civil War was not as cautious as Colonel Carrington. On more than one occasion he let it be known at Fort Phil Kearny he felt Colonel

Carrington was too conservative for his tastes. In fact, Fetterman boasted that if he had command of 80 men, he could ride through the entire Sioux Nation!

Colonel Carrington put Fetterman in command of various elements of Companies A, C, E, and H of the Second Battalion of the 18th Infantry Regiment and part of Company C of the 2nd Cavalry Regiment the morning of December 21. With those men, supporting officers, Captain Brown, Lieutenant Grummond and two civilians, Fetterman sallied forth. In less than an hour, all 81 men had been slaughtered by Red Cloud.

Fetterman did rescue the wood detail in quick order. Then, seeing the Indians slipping up and over Lodge Trail Ridge, Fetterman gave chase. Once over the other side of the pine covered ridge, Fetterman's command was swamped as hidden red soldiers poured in from all directions. Like a

huge tidal wave, the Indians smashed Fetterman's force in what became one of the worst military defeats ever suffered by the Army.

Although many have called this a Massacre, the name is not really applicable since resistance with arms was offered by Fetterman's command. It was, a military defeat suffered in battle. Worse, it left Carrington in a very poor military position since no information was arriving or leaving the post as couriers were cut off by the Indians.

''Fetterman's folly'' was laid on the doorstep of Colonel Carrington, who as commanding officer, took the blame. The blame probably should have been placed on the desk of a War Department official in Washington, D.C., the Indian Commissioner in Washington, D.C., and the military district commander in Omaha, all of whom were actually uninformed as to the Indian affairs on the Bozeman Trail.

Gold Discovered in Montana

Gold was discovered in Montana just before the Civil War ended. Earlier, there had been a succession of gold rushes during the Civil War to Nevada, Idaho, and Colorado, and the Rocky Mountain area was full of gold miners and prospectors.

So, when the discovery of gold was announced in Montana, the rush was on and hundreds of people swarmed into the southwestern tip of the territory, where the gold discoveries were centered—in the area of Virginia City and Alder Gulch.

The only problem was, it was difficult to get there. A prospective gold miner would have to follow the Missouri River to the Great Falls area, and then follow a trail slanting southwest to the gold area. Or, he could go to Salt Lake, and head north up the rugged edges of the Wind River mountains and the Tetons. But both of these routes were long and tedious.

John Bozeman Blazes Trail

An easier route planned by John Bozeman and John Jacobs had been blazed north from the Oregon Trail near Douglas, Wyoming. Pointing northwest from present-day Douglas, the trail turned and followed the eastern flanks of the Big Horn Mountains once it struck Crazy Woman Creek. After fording the Big Horn River, the trail followed west up the Yellowstone River until the gold camps were reached.

It was a fine trail, not having too many big hills to pull up or slide down. Heavy mining equipment could be hauled in with bull teams, and since there was plenty of grass and water and game to be found all along the trail, even a tenderfoot could make the trip in good shape.

There was only one drawback: the trail cut through the heart of the hunting territory of the Arapaho, Cheyenne, and Sioux Indians, and they did not want any white men there at all. But, to people hoping to strike it rich, a few pesky Indians were no bother—they plowed right on and by 1864 were moving up the trial named after John Bozeman.

That same year Jim Bridger set out to locate a new trail leading from Fort Caspar into the Big Horn Basin, north to the Yellowstone, and then west to the gold fields. Washakie, Chief of the Shoshones of that area, was a friend of Bridger's and gave him permission to go ahead, promising

---

CHAPTER X

THE BOZEMAN TRAIL

to give no trouble to emigrants and gold miners on their way through to Montana. But the trail was tough, the first 100 miles, crossing desertlike terrain. And following was the hard pull, up over the southern end of the Big Horn mountains and down the other side. After fording the Big Horn River, the road was passable, but not as good as Bozeman's road.

Red Cloud Fights Back

Permission from the friendly Shoshones, however, was not enough to give the white man safe passage: The Sioux Red Cloud and his allies had seen what had happened along the ''Big Medicine Trail,'' or Oregon Trail. Disease had resulted and debris, bad whiskey, Indians turned into beggars, scarce game, and scarce grass for miles on either side of the dusty road. Red Cloud did not want this to happen to the Powder River country. Promises from prospectors, emigrants, and soldiers that the hoards of people were just passing through was not good enough. Even if they *were* only going through the region, he knew bad results would follow. So, Red Cloud's Indians fought back. They were not going to let the lush hunting grounds in the Powder River area be subjected to the ruin seen along the Oregon Trail.

Armies Dispatched

On the eastern side of the Mississippi the Civil War came to an end, and thousands of Americans, weary of war and hearing of gold and land for the taking, headed west. People from the East and the South were looking for a chance to get ahead, the Southerners leaving the ashes of defeat behind. To them the Indian problem was just one more obstacle to overcome, on the road to where they were going.

The volunteer regiments of the army were steadily using up their enlistment time and heading home. Newly recruited regular soldiers were put into old regiments and sent West. Some of these soldiers were newcomers to America. The bulk of the regiments coming west were American by birth, but they were quickly followed by Irish, German, English and Canadians, who enlisted in the United States Army to gain American citizenship. Others enlisted because soldiering was the only trade they knew.

Leaders in Congress and those representing the Army and the War Department wanted to end the Indian raids, especially along the Bozeman Trail. One idea was to send an Army out West to finish off any Indians on the warpath. The Indian Commissioner and his Bureau had an entirely different idea of what to do, desiring to set up treaties, talk with the Indians, and organize permanent reservations for them to live on. However, a few bad men had succeeded in getting jobs with the Indian Bureau and by cheating both the Indians and the government on supplies and money they made a muddle of everything.

There was not enough agreement among those in government to form a common plan, and the people who were hurt were the emigrants seeking a home in the West, the soldiers trying to carry out orders to protect them, and the Indians trying to protect his hunting, his home, and his family.

Treaty Denied

An example of this dilemma took place at Fort Laramie in 1866. The Indian Bureau set up a Council with the Sioux tribes to get them to agree to allow emigrants to pass along the Bozeman Trail. They were still sitting in council when Colonel Henry B. Carrington, at the head of an army of 2,000 men, marched into the fort led by a 36-piece band on their way to build forts along the Bozeman Trail. Not yet having come to an agreement, the Indians could not miss the supply wagons with equipment to build blacksmith shops, a saw mill, mowing machines to make hay and the many troops.

One chief told the Peace Commissioners, ''Great Father sends us presents and wants new road, but white chief goes with soldiers to steal road before Indians say yes or no.''

Consequently not all of the Sioux headmen at that 1866 Council signed the treaty. Certainly Red Cloud did not, as he withdrew his Oglala warriors and other Sioux leaders and prepared to redouble his efforts to cause trouble on the Bozeman Trail.

Colonel Carrington's orders were plain and simple: He was to take his men, build posts at the southern and northern ends of the Bozeman Trail, and re-build Fort Connor, as well as protect the American citizens using the Bozeman Trail

By the fall of 1866, 160 American lives had been lost and at least that many wounded. A number had been taken captive. The number of horses, mules, and oxen kept at the forts were seriously reduced. Supplies were on short ration basis. And it was doubtful if fresh troops were on their way to help out Forts Reno (formerly Fort Connor), Phil Kearny, or C.F. Smith.

Captain W. J. Fetterman Killed By Sioux Indians
Near Fort Phil Kearny December 21, 1866.

Carrington Reports Fetterman Disaster

Worst of all, Carrington (headquartered at Fort Phil Kearny) had no real idea of the strength of Red Cloud. He did feel that the Indian leader could overwhelm the post if he chose to do so. As the wagons hauled in the 81 dead following the Fetterman disaster, Carrington was making up his mind to allow John "Portugee" Phillips, a native of the Portuguese possession of the Azores, to ride to Fort Laramie calling for relief and reporting the tragedy. Phillips had been back and forth from Fort Laramie a number of times on his job as a freight contractor and knew the trail.

The colonel allowed the use of his own Kentucky-bred horse on the 240 mile ride, and Phillips slipped through the water gap of the stockade the night of December 21. The message was to be dispatched from Horseshoe Station, the first telegraph station he would reach enroute to Fort Laramie. In the message Carrington described the action costing the lives of 81 men and the plight of the post, and asked for immediate relief.

A Wyoming blizzard blew in soon after Phillips left. The temperature dropped to 30 below. Soldiers could only stand guard 15 minutes at a time because of the cold.

Phillips rode under cover at night, and on during the day as much as possible, in spite of the weather, and arrived after three days at Horseshoe Station. He sent wires to Omaha and Fort Laramie and then, not completely trusting the telegraph, rode on arriving at Fort Laramie in the midst of the Christmas night dance. He was able to give his report in person, fortunately, as his wire had not been received. Colonel Carrington's gallant horse died soon after their arrival at the Fort.

Back at Fort Phil Kearny, the men had finished digging a common grave for the enlisted men, burying officers in individual coffins lined with tin cans pounded flat. Nothing was heard from Phillips for three weeks. No one dared venture out of the post, and the sentries on the walls reported Indians along the skyline of Lodge Trail Ridge time and time again.

Then, wading through deep snow, the relief showed up. It had taken four companies of infantry and one company of cavalry over three weeks to reach the isolated and frozen post. Many men of the relief were so badly frostbitten on the trail that they were left at Fort Reno.

Carrington Relieved

A week later, Colonel Carrington was relieved of his command. He was first sent to Fort Caspar, and arrived with his escort, the same regimental band that had hailed his arrival at Fort Laramie the previous June.

Under a new post commander now, Fort Phil Kearny steadied down to a long and cold winter. In the meantime, nothing had been heard from Fort C. F. Smith, a hundred miles north near the Big Horn River. From November 1866 until March 1867 that post had been isolated. Then, two sergeants volunteered to snowshoe to Fort C. F. Smith to see how the command was faring. They made the trip in February, spent a day there gathering mail and telling what had happened at Fort Phil Kearny, then turned around and plowed back to their starting place. They took an Indian interpreter with them on the return trip. At one point, all three men were separated from each other in a running battle with some Sioux Indians, but all three arrived safe and sound, although at separate times, back at Fort Phil Kearny. They

W.H.J. 1930

lost the mail from Fort C. F. Smith but escaped with their lives.

Fort C. F. Smith was doing well, but at Fort Phil Kearny the situation grew increasingly more critical. Each day more men were sent to the infirmary with scurvy—diseased gums, loss of teeth, pains in legs and arms—as the long winter progressed. Finally, in late May the snow had melted enough so that the "scurvy crew" from the post infirmary were able to go out to eat the green grass just beginning to poke up from the wet ground near the post. They pulled the grass, dug for roots, savored the wildflowers—anything that would help them regain their health.

Breech-Loading Rifle Introduced

The arrival of green grass also saw supply trains arriving from Fort Laramie. Several wagons were loaded with the new Springfield .50 caliber breech-loading rifle. Seven hundred of these guns were sent to replace the antiquated muzzle-loading Springfields the troops had been issued. The drawback to the earlier Springfields was that after firing a round from the muzzle-loading rifle, it took time to ram the charge and then fire again. During that lull, the Indians often tommahawked the soldier in the act of trying to fire a second round. Now, with the rolling block at the breech, it was a simple matter to fire, reload, and fire in a few seconds.

The coming of spring also released many of the Indians who had spent their time in winter quarters. As the grass became greener, it was easier for Indians on the prowl to range farther away from their villages. So, Indian raids increased and through the summer months as in the previous summer were frequent and ferocious. When wagons moved along the trail, they moved as large units and with military guards whenever possible. The civilians did not like it, but many of their wagons were halted at Fort Phil Kearny until the military felt it safe enough for them to proceed to Fort C. F. Smith. To those who were dreaming of gold, such delays seemed intolerable.

New Type Fortification

At the northern post, Lt. Sigismund Sternberg had designed a temporary log and willow corral around the haying crew tents, two miles from the fort, where the men were putting up hay from a large natural meadow. At six-foot intervals upright logs were set in the ground, with one log laced to the poles on the ground and another higher up on the upright log pole. This type of fortification was screened off with willows, and the whole structure built into a rectangle of about 100 feet by 200 feet.

A corral fortification was in use at Fort Phil Kearny, also, to protect the wood choppers and sawyers, should the Indians attack. The fort consisted of sixteen wagon boxes tipped over on their sides and formed into an oval, or corral. Two were left out of the oval and set in strategic places, where they could hinder any horsemen attempting to ride down the wagon box corral. Each man—civilian and soldier—had been given instructions as to where he was to fight from, in case of an attack, and 7,000 rounds of ammunition were stored at the corral of wagon boxes.

The positions of Fort Smith and Fort Phil Kearny had been chosen because they were entirely defensible. Any attacking forces would have to travel in the open and expose themselves to a well-directed stream of gunfire. Further, they were situated in places where it was nearly impossible for an opposing force to fire down into the camp or rake the positions with long-range rifle fire.

Red Cloud Gathers Army

All spring and early summer, Red Cloud had been busy too. He was getting an army together with Minniconzou Sioux for one big battle, meaning to destroy Fort Phil Kearny, the hated little post on the banks of Piney Creek. Red Cloud had trouble convincing the Minniconzou to strike Kearny, as they wanted to attack Smith instead. Finally, the Indian army split into two forces, and each one set out to strike both posts at about the same time.

The American soldiers were ready to fight. In fact, they were anxious to come to grips with Red Cloud; they were still smarting from the statements about the Fetterman disaster made by the Commissioner of Indian Affairs in his report to Congress in January, 1867:

> Now, I understand this was the fact: These Indians being absolutely in want of guns and ammunition to make their winter hunt, were on a friendly visit to the fort, desiring to communicate with the commanding officer, to get the order refusing them guns and ammunition rescinded, so that they might be able to procure their winter supply of buffalo. It has been reported that some three thousand to five thousand Indians assembled to infest the fort. The number of Indians is not there. The whole is an exaggeration, and although I regret the unfortunate death of so many brave soldiers, yet, there can be no doubt that it was owning to the foolish and rash mismanagement of the officer in command of the post.

The men and officers serving at Reno, Phil Kearny, and C.F. Smith did not learn about that statement until the winter and spring had lifted enough so that lines of supply and communication could be re-established. By that time Colonel Carringtion had been relieved at Fort Phil Kearny, sent to Fort Caspar, and then sent on farther to Fort McPherson in Nebraska.

Carrington had no defender in sour old General Phillip St. George Cooke. Cooke had changed from the hard-bitten and abled commander into a sour old man vainly trying to hide his deep disgust and disappointment at not being given a battle command during the Civil War. No one really trusted him since he was a Viginian—a Southerner by birth, even though he remained loyal to the U.S. government and his own son-in-law was the dashing Southern cavalryman, General J.E.B. Stuart. Cooke had failed to send supplies to Carrington, the new breech-loading rifles, or an adequate supply of ammunition. And it was Cooke too, that remained silent as the Indian Commissioner heaped abuse upon the shoulders of the Colonel Carrington.

Thus, the Indian Commissioner's remarks went unchallenged. The officers and men were bitter about that report and were anxious to prove the Commissioner wrong.

The "Hayfield Battle"

That was the situation on the morning of August 1, 1867, when the northern force of Red Cloud's army paused at the hay field corral enroute to Fort C.F. Smith to do battle. They just wanted to whet their appetite, so to speak, on the sixteen men that they found, half of them soldiers, half of them civilians.

As it turned out, those eight civilians and eight soldiers fought a day-long action which has since been nearly forgotten. They won an overwhelming victory even though the post commander, Colonel Luther P. Bradley, did not attempt to send help to them. Captain Edward S. Hartz had seen the battle start, but when he reported it to Colonel Bradley, the colonel ordered the gates closed on the seven company strength post. Late that afternoon he sent a company of soldiers with a howitzer, but by then the Indians had retreated and were mournfully dragging their dead and wounded away.

Fortunately, that keen and able writer of action along the Bozeman Trail, Finn Burnett, was there and left an account of the battle, the "Hayfield Fight." From it we learn that Lieutenant

Sternberg, who had designed the log and willow corral and positioned the men inside, was killed among the first shots fired, so the command fell upon Al Cotton, a civilian and former Civil War Captain who had served under Union General Buell. Al's brother Zeke was at the Hayfield fight, too, and fought heroically beside his brohter. Not more than two years earlier, Zeke was a Confederate captain serving the cause of the South. This was the first time the two brothers could fight together in a common cause against a common enemy.

When Lieutenant Sternberg died, Burnett said, "The savages had seen the officer fall and, heartened at the thought that the defenders would be leaderless, they charged down again from all sides. Straight from the hills they hurled themselves recklessly at the corral, to be met by a flashing stream of lead that swept them back again.

"Time and again they reached the enclosure, and their hands and moccasins flashed on the rails as they attempted to climb over to mix hand-to-hand conflict, but in every instance they were blown back to add their bodies to the heaps outside...an injured sergeant who had a gaping wound in his shoulder was carried to a tent...but a loaded revolver was kept ready for him, and throughout the day, at every attack, he stumbled out, to fight besides the others. Then, when another lull would occur, he would be helped back into the tent, exhausted..."

Suddenly, the battle was over. Only one mule survived out of thirty mules that the men had inside their corral. It was estimated 300 Indians were killed, and at least 300 wounded. Only two soldiers were killed and one civilian. Four more defenders were wounded, three soldiers and one civilian.

The Hayfield Fight, or Battle, is not well known. One reason it was not given much publicity is that the Army was not proud of the fact that more than 400 soldiers sat safely inside a walled fort as 16 men held off the huge Indian force in a battle that raged all day. Only when the battle was over had the post commandant offered help. The post and battle field are actually over the Wyoming state border now, inside Montana. The Bozeman Trail forts, however, knew no political subdivisions then and are to be considered as one part of the Bozeman Trail saga in the history of Wyoming.

Red Cloud Musters Forces

A hundred miles south, Red Cloud was bringing his huge force of warriors for quick work in demolishing and destroying Fort Phil Kearny, not knowing that the northern wing of his army had been thoroughly defeated by 16 men. Red Cloud let his men stop off to fight the 32 defenders of the oval of wagon boxes, and then, once his men had tasted the thrill of battle, he would direct them against the hated fort.

Major James Powell commanded the company of infantry, a part of the 7th Infantry Regiment, in the Wagon Box Fight. Half of his men escaped from the pinery, the actual place in the timber where sawyers and choppers were felling trees, and returned safely to the fort. Some of them, including four civilians, retreated to the wagon box fortification when the first Indians began to drift out onto the small plain where the temporary fort was located.

Major Powell was a veteran remaining calm and cool all through the battle after informing his men that they would have the fight of their lives that day, and to be sure to make every shot count. His total battle casualties were counted as three killed with the men killed at the wagon boxes. Two men were wounded. His immediate command was 32 men, and the odds against this tiny unit had been as high as 70 to 1.

Swarming like angry bees, the Indians first ran off all the mules and horses, cutting off any planned escape. Meanwhile, Powell's men reported to the ammunition dump where 7,000 rounds were stored and then took their positions according to the pre-arranged battle plan.

A thousand yards away the Indians were still milling around, shrieking, yelling, and assembling for their first charge. It was about 9 A.M. on August 2, 1867, the day after the Hayfield Battle.

Powell's command, now in place, watched the Indians racing up and down their lines, defiantly shaking war lances and shields, brandishing rifles and tomahawks, and yelling at the yellowhides who lay behind their fragile barricade watching and waiting.

Eyewitness Account

Private Sam Gibson said later that he was only 18 years old at the time, and that the expression on the faces of his companions as they faced the overwhelmingly superior forces that morning would haunt him forever. He said it was not so much the look of fear, but a look of resolution. Gibson said most of the soldiers took their shoes off and untied the laces, tying one end of the lace to the trigger of their rifle, and the other to their big toe. That way, when a man stood he could pull the trigger on the extra long rifle and kill himself, rather than being taken alive. Gibson prepared to do the same, as the Indian cavalry began to ride in circles closer and closer to the oval corral.

Gibson, who was to serve many years in the Army, said, "I have served in the Army forty-eight years, taking active part in the Sioux Campaign of 1876 and also in the Wounded Knee Campaign of 1890-91 at Pine Ridge Agency, but never before or since have my nerves been put to the test sustained on that terrible second of August, 1867, when we fought Red Cloud's warriors in the wagon box corral."

Arrows tipped with pine tar and set afire began to fall into the small fort, igniting the straw and hay scattered there for the mules and horses. The defenders had no time to put out the small fires, and the smoke drifted upward into the azure August sky, while the defenders grimly waited for the horsemen to make their charge.

Suddenly, the whole force of mounted men wheeled and charged straight at the men inside the wagon boxes, hanging low over the outstretched necks of their horses, carrying lances, rifles tomahawks, or war clubs at the ready. They knew the yellowhides would have to re-load their clumsy rifles, and during that period they would break through the flimsy fortifications and, as at Fetterman last winter, they would kill everyone within minutes.

Thus, the Indians were prepared for the first sheet of fire and flame erupting from the 32 rifles as they made their charge. They kept right on coming, dead certain they could arrive at the Fort before another death broadside could decimate their ranks.

With their new Springfields the soldiers re-loaded in a split second and fired a second volley, then a third; and at the sound of the fourth well-directed volume of fire, the attack broke off to either side as the Indians rode for safety. Behind them they left over a hundred dead and wounded.

Undaunted by the turn of events in what should have been an easy victory, the Indians formed up again and once more charged at the smoke-shrouded fort, after showering it with long-range rifle fire and more of the fire arrows. Once again the defenders sent well-aimed bullets cutting through the Indian ranks, costing them more dead and wounded.

During the lull that followed, the soldiers watched in admiration as two enemy horsemen, riding side-by-side, would swoop down on a wounded Indian, grabbing a leg or arm, and then wheel and drag him to safety. Out of respect for their courage, the soldiers withheld their fire and let the brave riders carry their wounded off the battlefield.

By noon, Lieutenant John C. Jenness, Private Henry Haggerty, and Private Tommy Doyle had been killed. Several others were wounded. The battle was three hours old, and what little water the soldiers had was in a wood barrel which had been pierced, several times over, with bullets and the water was seeping out. Private Gibson and Private John Grady made a run for the cook tent where several large kettles still held water and scampered back to the safety of the wagon boxes. Gibson said his kettle took a bullet, but he did not receive a scratch, nor did Grady, and they brought back enough water to slake the terrible thirst the men had developed from the battle, with the hot sun burning down upon them and the slow burning fires heating up the air all around them.

For three more hours Red Cloud sent the cream of this red army, horseback and on foot, against the tiny wagon box fort. He seemed to be single-minded about wiping it out to the man. But long-range, quick loading rifles, the well-directed and orderly aiming and shooting, and the almost limitless supply of ammunition all took their toll of Indians, over and over with each charge.

One last full-fledged frontal attack took place, when the Indians gathered together into a sort of flying wedge and ran on foot directly at the center of the oval fort. Major Powell coolly directed the volley upon volley of rifle fire at the charging Indians, who were dropping in heaps beyond the fort. At last, the charging Indians got so close that Gibson said he could see the whites of their eyes and, as each Indian was vividly painted for battle, he clearly saw the vivid white, yellow, green, and red-painted figures.

Gibson said he had never hated the Indians. "It was their lives or ours. We had not forgotten Massacre Hill [The Fetterman Fight]. We were not fiends, gloating over the suffering of their wounded, but that bloody day of December 21 [When Fetterman's command perished to the man] was fresh in our minds, and we were filled with grim determination to kill, just as we had seen our comrades killed. There was no thought of wavering. We knew from their countless numbers that if they overwhelmed us they could easily capture the fort [Fort Phil Kearny], but six miles distant, where there were helpless women and children. We were fighting for their lives as well as our own. It was not revenge but retribution."

Last Charge Fails

Fortunately the last charge of Indians faltered and failed. At nearly the same time, the supply of

John Portugee With Major James Powell

ammunition had dwindled down so that each man had only a few rounds left. They had fired nearly 7,000 rounds.

At nearly the same moment, howitzer fire was heard in the distance: a relief column was on its way to help the small command. But the battle was over when the utterly tired defenders wearily stood and accepted the congratulations of the relief column.

Red Cloud's forces had taken two terrific defeats at Fort Smith and at Fort Kearny in two days' time; but Red Cloud continued his attacks on the Bozeman Trail.

Two New Forts Erected

Two new forts appeared in Wyoming that summer. Fort Fetterman was erected on the banks of the North Platte near present-day Douglas, and Fort D.A. Russell was built at the new railroad town of Cheyenne. Feelers for a peace treaty were sent out by the government, and all summer long, in 1868, Indians came into Fort Laramie to sign it. Finally, Red Cloud came to Fort Laramie in November, and he too signed the treaty.

By then, however, Fort C.F. Smith and Fort Phil Kearny had been abandoned and dismantled by the Army. A composite fort built from their remains was erected on the North Platte River, a few miles east of where Rawlins is today, and it was named Fort Fred Steele.

Red Cloud may have lost the Hayfield and the Wagon Box battles, but he had not relinquished his position on the Bozeman Trail.

David A. Russell

CHAPTER X

VIGNETTE:

"The life of Riley"

The soldier's life at the western post was not all hardship and danger or monotony. Much of their off-duty time was spent in hunting and fishing. This was the kind of recreation the post commander encouraged, knowing antelope, deer, elk, buffalo, or trout as well as grouse or sage chicken would allow the cooks to provide a break in the beef and pork diets.

Riding horseback after wolves and coyotes was approved. It kept the men in shape, and the horse gained stamina running over the rugged terrain. Baseball, foot races, horse races, rifle matches, boxing, and wrestling were encouraged. These were often arranged in elaborate tournaments which ended in a great championship bout on the Fourth of July.

Privates received about 50 cents a day in wages or about $16 per month. On the second year of a four year enlistment, an extra dollar was added to the base pay. Two more dollars the third year and at the end of the fourth year, he was still receiving only $19 per month. For this reason many deserted in hopes of striking it rich in the gold fields.

Justice was harsh. Henry Morton Stanley describing military justice on a western post in 1867 reported that men were often tied to a wheel and lashed until the blood ran down their backs. Punishment often consisted of digging a hole or trench and then filling it up. More often it was an extra assignment of ordinary work on the post such as cleaning stables, white-washing buildings, cutting wood or ice, or doing extra guard duty. A military post was usually built by the same men sent to garrison it. So, a soldier learned how to mix concrete or cement, make adobe bricks, roof buildings, handle a shingle, saw in a lumber mill, plant and irrigate gardens, and build walls.

There was so much work on a post that sometimes the soldier actually looked forward to the field campaign where he only had to walk twenty to thirty miles a day, carry his rifle and ammunition, and fight. It almost seemed easier than working! Besides, barriers between officers and men on the post were soon eliminated in the field, as they strove together toward the common goal of survival.

Disease had to be constantly guarded against on the frontier. Usually the post had a doctor who was primarily a surgeon. His surgeon role was used in extracting bullets, binding wounds, and removing an arm or leg. His other duties sometimes included being veterinarian and gardener.

At Fort Laramie the surgeon and chaplain had a 2-1/2 acre garden. In 1868 they put out 6,000 strawberry plants, 250 raspberry, 250 blackberry, 100 currant, 600 asparagus, and 50 rhubarb plants. All of these would provide vitamin C to combat scurvy, the dreaded disease of the army.

The posts were usually located near pure water and where there was good grazing nearby, whenever possible. A natural hay meadow near the post where hay could be cut and stored was highly desirable. Ideally there was a plentiful supply of timber for building-lumber and for fuel to heat and cook with. Also, a post ought to be located so melting snow or surplus rainwater would readily drain off.

Most of the western army posts were built around an open parade ground with the buildings forming the perimeter, with enlisted men's barracks on one side, officer's quarters on another and the warehouses, stables, guard house, shops and all the rest forming the other parts of the quadrangle.

Not many western Army posts had stockades built around them. Forts on the Bozeman Trail like Reno, Kearny, and Smith were exceptions to the rule. Most of them like Fort Laramie had broad open parade grounds, with barracks for enlisted men a part of the quadrangle and officer's quarters, and other buildings for military affairs completing the other sides of the open area. There was usually a guardhouse, a quartermaster supply depot and warehouse, stables for the animals, main administration buildings, carpenters' shops, the blacksmith, and "Suds Row." The last was an area where some of the wives of the enlisted men took in washing, earning extra money. The sutler's store was like an old time mercantile store with canned goods, tobacco, candy, shelves of yard goods, plus a card and pool room. Off to one side and separate from those two rooms was a place where a man could buy a beverage to quench his "big dry," or thirst.

In the sutler's store at Fort Laramie it would not be uncommon to see the famous chief of a tribe buying his wife a bolt or two of gaily colored calico while he sucked on a peppermint candy stick. In the same room might be a field grade officer with his wife buying the same material as the officer considered some new twisted tobacco stocks. Both men could possibly be facing each other over iron rifle sights the next week, but in the sutler's store an armistice clearly existed.

In 1867 Fort Laramie had the following buildings: An adjacent office with 3 rooms and 10 desks: 6 officers quarters with 30 rooms, a Provost marshall's office (millitary police) with one room and 2 desks; 2 officers stables for 20 horses; 1 arsenal magazine where the powder was stored with 2 rooms; 1 building for company shops with 8 benches to work on; 2 bakeries that could turn out 1,200 rations of bread per day; 3 kitchens for enlisted men; 5 barracks, 3 for one company each, and 2 for 2 companies each; 1 farrier's quarters where horses and mules were cared for; 2 mess houses in which 400 men could be fed at once; 1 guard house big enough for 40 men; 1 band room where 10 men could practice together; 1 ice house which could handle 40 tons of ice which was sawed, cut and put up during the winter from the river; 1 musicians quarters with 2 rooms; 3 laundresses quarters for 8 laundresses (suds row); 1 saddle shop with 10 benches; 1 blacksmiths's shop with 6 fires; 3 storehouses for the commissary and quartermaster which held 250,000 rations; 1 quartermaster storehouse with a single storeroom that held 200 tons of food; 1 commissary office and storeroom which could hold 250,000 extra rations; 1 carpenter's shop with 14 benches; 1 post office with 2 rooms; 1 hospital with 24 beds; and 3 cavalry stables for 200 horses.

Fort Laramie was set up for a permanent garrison of at least 7 companies. A company in those days consisted of about 60 men, as Fort Laramie probably had around 500 permanent garrison troops stationed there at that time.

As the years went by, towns grew up in the vicinity of the Army post and depended upon the Army payroll to support their economy.

"The anvil chorus"

To a nation still licking its wounds from the Civil War, the building of the Union Pacific and Central Pacific Railroads was an exciting event. An army of newspaper correspondents and photographers followed the progress of the railroad and reported the good things to the public leaving the financial storms to the boards of directors of the two railroad companies. In 1867 there was hardly a dissenting voice being raised about government subsidy, troops pulled out to aid the railroad construction crews, or other incidents connected with the mighty engineering feat taking place. All America was cheering and watching the two lines as they raced toward each other. It was almost considered unpatriotic to say, write or print anything bad about the great project.

One writer, W.A. Bell, told in a few well chosen words how the Nation felt. "We, pundits of the far East, stood upon that embankment, only about a thousand miles this side of sunset, and backed westward before the hurrying corps of sturdy operators with a mingled feeling of amusement, curiosity and profound respect. On they came. A light car, drawn by a single horse, gallops up to the front with its load or rails. Two men seize the end of a rail and start forward, the rest of the gang taking hold by the twos, until it is clear of the car. They come forward at a run. At the word of command the rail is dropped in its place, right side up with care, while the same process goes on at the other side of the car. Less than thirty seconds to a rail for each gang, and so four rails go down to the minute. Quick work, you say, but the fellows on the Union Pacific are tremendously in earnest. The moment the car is empty it is tipped over on the side of the tracks to let the next loaded car pass it, and then it is tipped back again, and it is a sight to see to go flying back for another load, propelled by a horse at full gallop at the end of sixty or eighty feet of rope, ridden by a young

Jehu, who drives furiously. Close behind the first gang comes the gaugers, spikers and bolters and a lively time they make of it. It is a grand 'Anvil Chorus' that those sturdy sledges are playing across the plains. There are ten spikes to a rail, four-hundred rails to a mile, eighteen hundred miles to San Francisco—twenty-one million times are those sledges to be swung—twenty-one million times are they to come down with their sharp punctuation, before the great work of modern America is complete.''

Burly, hamfisted Irishmen working for the Union Pacific, led the contingent of tracklayers who came from all over the world. From the West, the Central Pacific employed the smaller, but just as tough and just as hardworking, Chinese.

They were destined to meet at Promontory, Utah Territory on May 10, 1869. At 10:30 a.m. that day the golden spike, uniting the two lines would be driven.

RAILROAD WYOMING

In Cheyenne spectators watched the track-laying crews of the Union Pacific Railroad work furiously as they sought to stabilize enough of a roadbed, railroad ties, and rails to support a steam driven locomotive into the new Wyoming city.

The date was November 13, 1867 and by mid-afternoon amid celebrating citizens the locomotive did arrive, tooting its whistle and announcing the end of one era and the beginning of another.

Only three months before, the Wagon Box Fight had taken place near Fort Phil Kearny. Only two months before peace commissioners, trying to maintain friendly relations with various elements of the Sioux, Cheyenne, and Arapaho had given them a large supply of ammunition hoping to implant by this gesture the message in the redmen's minds that they wanted peace. Only one month before, peace commissioners had sent word to Red Cloud that they wanted him to come to Fort Laramie and sign a peace treaty.

Everyone except Red Cloud wanted to wind down the war on the plains, and even Red Cloud would do it if the Army would abandon Forts Reno, Phil Kearny and C.F. Smith on the hated Bozeman Trail.

Earlier that year, just after fresh troops and more supplies including 100,000 rounds of ammunition and 700 new breech-loading Springfield rifles were on their way to Fort Phil Kearny, Major General Grenville M. Dodge was on the prowl in Wyoming. Now, however, he was not the soldier in charge of the military district, but the chief engineer in charge of the construction of the "start and stop" Union Pacific Railroad.

The "start and stop" phrase means that the promoters of the transcontinental line had seen nothing but trouble from 1862 through 1865, starting and stopping the progress a number of times. Few people would consider such an engineering feat possible. Then, with the Civil War involving the entire nation, supplies, men and money were hard to come by.

But now, the war was over and the cry "Manifest Destiny" and all its proponents were still lingering, and the people cried out for more and more westward expansion. There were a million men who had been under arms during the Civil War who were now free to fill up the West. In addition, over 300,000 people had moved into the western states and territories, and in the wheat and corn growing states of Illinois, Wisconsin,

Kansas, Iowa and Nebraska nearly a million immigrants from Europe had broken the sod, built their cabins and sod houses and were farming.

Homestead Act of 1862

The Homestead Act of 1862 helped by giving 160 acres to a man if he could prove he had not fought against the United States, was the head of a family, or was twenty-one and was a citizen, or at least had filed first papers to become a citizen. That act and its provisions included nearly everyone and so on and on came the homesteaders to the West. They were joining the crowds of miners and prospectors heading anywhere in the West where gold or silver could be found.

The railroad was looking forward to immigrants from Europe filling up the empty plains, and the miners and the others filling the remainder of the land. The railroads had to have passengers and it had to have freight so they were happy to see the throngs going west.

Remember that General Dodge was looking for a good route going west with a party consisting of General U.S. Grant's chief of staff. Major General John A. Rawlins, a geologist, a surveyor, two companies of cavalry and two companies of infantry.

City of Cheyenne Located

At the Black Hills (actually the Medicine Bow range) Dodge met with Major General C.C. Augur. As commander of this military district, Augur had orders to locate a military post at a place designated by Dodge. That meant that when Dodge chose a division point for the railroad, Augur would also set up a military post there. That is how Cheyenne was born. Dodge picked a place on Crow Creek and named it Cheyenne after the Tribe of Indians and the mountain pass just to the West. Augur promptly picked the site for Fort D.A. Russell at a point just a bit north.

On the Fourth of July, 1867, General Rawlins gave a patriotic speech at Cheyenne. Since then this has become an annual event throughout Cheyenne's time as territorial and later state capital.

Dodge noted in his book, *How We Built The Union Pacific Railway*, that a couple of days after Rawlins gave his talk, a party of Indians made an attack on a Mormon grading crew that was plowing and leveling the land ahead of the track-laying crews, and killed two men. "We buried the men and started the graveyard of the future city," Dodge observed.

Cheyenne, WY 1867

Dodge had been a railroad engineer before the Civil War. During the war he had served under General Sherman repairing damaged railroads throughout the South, and serving Sherman's fast moving army with supplies. Dodge had also been departmental military commander in the Wyoming area. Thus, the Union Pacific Railroad people had found in Dodge, the perfect engineer having good connections in Washington, D.C. and a man who not only knew the land the railroad was to travel through, but also something of the nature of the Indian problem.

Following their adventures in Cheyenne, Dodge and Rawlins continued West and crossed the North Platte River to the future site of Fort Fred Steele. A little further along the way West they stopped to look for water, as Rawlins suffered from an asthma condition and needed lots of water, especially while on the arid plains of Wyoming.

City of Rawlins Site

Dodge said, "The country from the Platte to Bitter Creek is very dry, no running water in it, and before we reached camp, General Rawlins became very thirsty, and we started out in an endeavor to find running water, and I discovered a spring in a draw...When General Rawlins reached this spring he said it was the most gracious and acceptable of anything he had had on the march, and also said that if anything was ever named for him, he wanted it to be a spring of water, and I said to him, 'We will name this Rawlins Springs.' It took the name. The end of one of our divisions happened to be close to this spring, and I named the station Rawlins, which has grown into quite a town and a division point for the Union Pacific road."

Historic Ames Monument Stands In Memory Of
Oakes And Oliver Ames.

Two other men who were driving forces in the construction of the Union Pacific were General Jack Casement, the man in charge of grading and track-laying, and Thomas C. Durant, vice president of the railroad company.

Ames Monument

The Ames Monument, high on top of Sherman Hill stands today, a huge granite pyramid to the memory of Oakes and Oliver Ames. The sixty feet high native granite tower was completed in 1882, and either side are likenesses of the Ames brothers who placed their personal fortunes behind efforts to build the railroad.

A few years after the multi-ton monument was in place, an Irish justice of the peace in Laramie by the name of Murphy made a trip to Cheyenne to check up on the land patent where the monument was erected. Murphy got to wondering if the monument was on Union Pacific land, or public land and found that it was indeed on public land. So, Murphy filed on the land and then wrote Omaha to the Union Pacific headquarters telling them he would be pleased if the railroad would come move the monument off his farm!

At first, railroad attorneys thought it was funny even if the land was now safely in Murphy's hands. But, when they found out that Murphy wanted a considerable sum for his homestead, it ceased to be a laughing matter. After a conference with a shrewd railroad attorney, and with some pressure from the local law, Murphy was persuaded to exhange his homestead for two railroad lots in Laramie!

Private funds were not enough to provide adequate funds for the building of the railroad. The national government helped by providing incentives in the form of subsidies. The subsidies amounted to a strip of land twenty miles wide on each side of the center of the track which was given to the railroad. The land was to be owned in a checkerboard fashion by the Union Pacific while alternating sections of land were to remain public land. Also, a government loan to the railroad of $16,000 for every mile built on level ground was made. The loan increased to $32,000 a mile on semi-level ground and went to $48,000 per mile in mountainous areas. Interest on the loan was 6 percent and loans were to be paid back in thirty years. In this manner for the first six miles of track west of Cheyenne, the railroad collected $16,000 per mile. The next 150 miles was worth $48,000 per mile since it was through the mountains and more difficult to build. The rest of the way to Promontory Point was worth $32,000 a mile. A grand total of $27,000,000 was loaned to the railroad company and was paid back on time.

Race to Promontory Point

Dodge was an organizer who put together a group of men who could do the advance work on the railroad vital to building the line. Survey parties included a chief, who nearly always was an engineer, plus several engineering assistants, rodmen, flagmen and men who pulled the chain. The chain was the measuring device that stretched from one surveyed point to another often reversing itself from one end to the other until the point of destination was reached.

The rodmen held upright rods at each surveyed point as the surveyor peered through his transit, a sort of telescope. Using a reference point, of which there were several marked off on the rods, the surveyor was able to keep an accurate record of the ups and downs—the profile—of the hills, valley, plains, and level ground measured for the railroad.

Once all this information was passed on to the engineers in charge of drawing up the plans for laying out the actual track they could let General Casement know what his crews could expect in terms of filling a draw, adding more soil to a section, or building a bridge or trestle over a creek or canyon.

Coming east, the Central Pacific Railroad had the tremendous job of plunging directly into the Sierra Nevada mountains. Beset by huge snowfalls, heavy spring run offs of melting snow, solid granite walls to tunnel through and treacherous grades perched on the sides of tall mountains, the Central Pacific moved ahead slowly but surely. It was an engineering feat of the first magnitude!

Appearance of Railroad Towns

There were some difficult spots on the Union Pacific also. One of these was the crossing of Dale Creek. Located between Cheyenne and Laramie there was no way to detour around the deep, wide chasm. A trestle 136 feet high and 650 feet long would have to be built to span the canyon. Good planning, optimism and clever men put it together. It was built of logs which had been cut in Michigan and marked as to exactly where they were to be placed. They were then shipped out and matched into their right places. When the big bridge was finished it was steadied by many guy

wires stretching from the bridge to granite walls of Dale Creek Canyon. The first train chugged across the engineering marvel in June 1868.

During that construction, Dale City was born. Like many towns along the railroad right away, Dale City grew almost overnight and had three hotels, half a hundred log cabins and walled tents for the men to live in. Another settlement a few miles away grew with Dale City. It was the tent city found always at the head of the railroad. Inevitably the tent city was a lawless, gathering place for gamblers, dance hall girls and gunslingers.

When the bridge was finished, both towns gradually disappeared. Just as Benton rose and fell, so did many other tent cities rise and fall. Benton was located a few miles east of where Rawlins is today. For a brief period of time its dusty street embraced a population of several thousand or more.

A young photographer, working his way up and down the railroad with his traveling darkroom, took a number of photographs of Benton. The professional cameraman was Arundell C. Hull, a twenty-two year old native of Minnesota. He said of Benton, "At one time the population reached five thousand, with rough characters and outlaws making up the majority."

> All the daylight hours the streets thronged with people...a motley crew of peddlers, miners, gamblers, Indians, Mexicans, Chinamen, railroad workers, bullwhackers, muleskinners, capitalists, cappers, ministers, and prospectors. The fine alkali dust was six inches deep in the streets and the wind was unceasing. An eastern dandy, who stepped off the train in a black broadcloth suit, soon looked as if he had crawled out of a flour barrel. There was not a blade of grass or a growing thing in sight, but there were twenty-three saloons and five dance halls. The greatest institution of them all was a frame structure forty by one hundred feet, covered with canvas and floored for dancing, but serving as well for gambling. It was called 'The Big Tent' and it had stood by in turn at Julesburg, Cheyenne, and Laramie.

Hull had tried to enlist in the Army for the Civil War. But, he was too young, too tall, and too thin. However, he knew photography, and so he went

West, taking pictures as he went. He arrived out in the West a full year ahead of famed William Henry Jackson, the dean of American photographers, and worked with Jackson during 1869 taking pictures up and down the Union Pacific right of way.

Water had to be hauled to Benton in great wooden barrels from the North Platte River. There it sold at 10 cents a bucket and $1.00 a barrel. Many thought whiskey was cheaper and it lasted longer. The whiskey, however, added to the fact that Benton experienced one or two violent deaths every day.

In August, 1868 Buffalo Bill Cody was the master of ceremonies at a political rally at Benton. The occasion was the campaign of General Ulysses S. Grant for president. Grant was there and made a speech. Afterwards Cody, who was known as a Pony Express Rider, buffalo hunter, and Army scout, auctioned off an old gold watch owned by Grant to help defray campaign expenses.

Casement Brothers Build Railroads

Dodge expressed best the vital work Jack Casement and his brother, Dan Casement produced when he noted that the two brothers did all the track laying and a large part of the grading of the railroad.

General Jack Casement and Dan Casement built the entire track and most of the grading...Their force consisted of 100 teams and 1,000 men, living at the end of the track in boarding cars and tents, and moved forward with it every few days. It was the best organized, best equipped, and best disciplined track force I have ever seen. I think every chief of the different units had been an officer of the army, and entered on his work from the moment they were mustered out. They could lay from one to three miles of track per day, as they had material, and one day laid eight and a half miles. Their rapidity in track laying, as far as I know, has never been excelled. I used it several times as a fighting force, and it took no longer to put it into fighting line than it did to form it for its daily work. They had not only to lay and surface the

track, but had to bring forward to the front from each base all the material and supplies for the track and for all workmen in advance of the track. Bases were organized for the delivery of material generally from one hundred to two hundred miles apart, according to the facilities for operation.

Railroads Blazed the West

Those places were Fremont, Fort Kearny, North Platte, Julesburg, Sidney, Cheyenne, Laramie, Benton, Green River, Evanston, Ogden, and Promontory. Thus, the railroad started city life in Wyoming.

Along with city development, local real estate booms rose and fell as the track-laying crews marched forward each day. Along with the growth of towns came town government, and suddenly people woke up to the fact they belonged to Dakota Territory, which meant they were ruled from far away Yankton, the territorial capitol. They felt it was too far away and that something would have to be done about it.

Track-laying had been slow at first—only forty miles laid down in 1865. By 1866, two hundred and sixty miles reached West. In 1867 with more mountains and valleys to cross only two hundred and forty-six miles were laid. In 1868, the railroad company was so thoroughly organized, five hundred and fifty-five miles of tract were laid! One hundred eighty-six miles were added as sidings and the grand total for the Union Pacific was nearly 1,300 miles of rail gleaming in the Western sun.

Promontory Point

The Irish, under the Casement brothers, laid the next to last rail, and the Chinese workers slammed their sledges against the very last spikes in the last tie. The time had finally arrived, and crowds arrived at Promontory Point for the grand finale to the epoch-making event of driving the last spike.

The 21st Infantry band was on its way West with several companies of regiment, and so amid the martial strains of stirring music, "Jupiter," the Central Pacific engine chugged up to the appointed place. From the East, the Union Pacific "No. 119" inched forward until men standing on the cow-catchers of the locomotives could nearly reach out and touch each other.

Then, arguing about which company would drive the golden spike because the Central Pacific

Union Pacific Railway Commission, 1867

had provided the real gold spike and had begun construction first, while the Union Pacific had built longer, and faster, it was finally decided not to strike a gold spike at all. It would, instead, be inserted into a specially drilled hole while a polished steel spike would be hit by both Leland Stanford, president of the Central Pacific, and Thomas C. Durant, ranking Union pacific official present at the ceremony. Attached to the spike was a telegraph wire, and the exact moment the sledge hammer descended, it would electrically, notify the nation on a coast-to-coast telegraph hookup that East and West coasts were finally and officially united by rail.

It still took diplomacy to keep the peace between the two railroad officials. The silver maul, used to drive the steel spike was handed to a lady whose name, unfortunately, is lost to history. She took the first few swings at the spike, although one observer said she wasn't much of a "spiker," the title of the sledge hammerman.

Once the unknown woman had completed her task, the maul was handed to the official who completed the work—the last work on the trackage. Then, the two engines drew close enough so the men could lean forward and hand

bottles of champagne back and forth, toasting each other as the band played and the locomotive whistles tooted!

Actually, several ceremonial spikes arrived at Promontory. One from Arizona was made up from iron, silver, and gold. One from California was all gold. The one from Nevada, appropriately enough, was silver. All of them were tapped into place in a piece of laurel wood from California representing part of a tie, and a silver engraved plated attached describing the momentous occasion. Even the spike with the telegraph wire still attached was driven into the highly polished California wood and placed in a museum.

While the driving of the steel spike announced loudly and clearly and electrically to the world the end of one era and the beginning of another, the exit from Wyoming the year before by Jim Bridger was significant too. Bridger had come to Wyoming as a teenager and had grown into one of the most renowned mountain men, as highly regarded by his peers as by those who read or heard about him. When the men in blue began to fight the Red Army of the West or survey the Country, it was Bridger to whom many of them turned for advice or sought him as their guide.

113

Jim Bridger Retires

Now he felt his work was done. He left Cheyenne in 1868 on July 21 where the Army had paid him off and discharged him on that date. He was nearly 65 years old, his neck with a large goiter bothered him, his bones ached with rheumatism, and his eyesight was failing. He was going back to his farm near Westport, Missouri to "think on it."

Dramatically enough, Jim Bridger, whose names and titles ran the gamut from Young Jim, to Old Gabe, to Blanket Chief, and the military titles handed him but never officially recorded of Captain, Major, and Colonel, rode the Union Pacific out of Cheyenne that day in July, 1868. He had come to what was *to become* Wyoming, wearing moccasins and riding a horse in 1823. Now, he was leaving what *was* Wyoming on a steam train, still wearing moccasins.

Jim Bridger's work was done, and Wyoming was straining against its harness yearning for more people, more gold and more government.

James Chisholm drifted into Cheyenne in late March 1868. He was a native Scotsman, who had come to Chicago in 1864 and landed a job as a newspaper reporter with the *Chicago Tribune.*

Stopping off in Cheyenne, he was on his way to the "Green River Mines" to report the latest gold rush which was then in progress near South Pass. Caught in one of Wyoming's late winter blizzards, Chisholm lost his way and nearly froze to death crossing from one side of a Cheyenne street to another. He safely reached a clothing store where he spent the rest of the day and night resting up on a pile of buffalo robes.

His report on Cheyenne was generally favorable. He said, "Cheyenne is scarcely eight months old...it is already a compact, well-bulit city full of good hotels, and spacious stores well stocked with wares of every kind, and with a daily living tide flowing through its streets as one could find in a city ten times the size and age."

The violence there alarmed him, however, a vigilante committee had just finished lynching several local toughs. Chisholm said, "A little westward of the city, near Crow Creek, was a companion picture (of a man dangling from a telegraph pole) and rumor has it that three more were hanging somewhere in the vicinity. The two bodies were cut down by the order of the authorities and deposited in City Hall. From thence they were soon conveyed in a wagon—the rope still around their necks—to the Coroner's office, where an inquest was held, the jury having no difficulty in arriving unanimously at the conclusion that they both had come to their death by strangulation."

On leaving Cheyenne, Chisholm promised he would come back. Then, where he went for the next few months is a mystery. He casually mentions in a journal he wrote, which was recovered years later, that he had so much "of camp life lately that it gives me a kind of seasickness to resume it." He wrote those words as he was entering South Pass City, and a good guess is that the errant Scot had been at the head

CHAPTER XI

VIGNETTE:

"Wyoming goldrush"

of the railroad with Jack Casement and his Irish crew before returning to his reporterial duties for the Chicago newspaper.

He was finally compelled to write the truth of a mining rush, not for the newspaper, but for his logged journal. Chisholm wrote;

> In 999 cases out of a thousand, the men who pursue the varied avocations of western life, do not even acquire a decent competence. They would have been better and they know it, to remain where they came from, practising a wise economy with the modest earnings of their trade or profession. The populations in the States are on the average better off than the floating populations out in the mountains. One hears a very general regret unconsciously expressed, as in the case of sailors, that they ever adopted this kind of life. And yet they hang on to it, partly from habit, partly because they are reluctant to return to their friends in a state of poverty, and partly because there is always the hope that they will make a 'big strike' some day. One man in a thousand makes the big strike, and the 999 linger on, upheld by the expectation of doing the like.

That was Chisholm's way of saying the gold rush to South Pass City, Atlantic City, and Hamilton City had not turned out to be the bonanza finds as first reported. In fact, Dr. T.A. Larson in his fine HISTORY OF WYOMING emphasizes that point, noting that most of the better books written about gold rushes actually ignore the South Pass area. Larson points out that the late Dr. S.H. Knight, who headed the University of Wyoming's fine Geology Department had documented the fact that between 1867 and 1873 only $2,000,000 in gold came out of the area.

Still, gold was there and it did draw people, among whom was the lady who has been recognized by many as the mother of woman suffrage in Wyoming—Esther Hobart Morris.

With track laid all the way across Wyoming and law and order at a very low point, the Union Pacific officials saw a distinct need for organized law in the area. They were joined in this idea by other men who had come to the western part of Dakota Territory intending to settle. These men were those who remained in the boom towns of Cheyenne, Laramie City, Green River and Evanston after the "boom" had settled to normal proportions and the tent cities were gone.

Real estate booms were deflated now and the shacks that had been built to last while the track-layers were in town were collapsing under the weight of the winter snow. No one lived in them just as no one now lived in Benton, Bear River City, Dale City and others.

The biggest payroll in Wyoming was that of the railroad which was now starting to mine coal near Rock Springs. It had plans for a set of railroad repair shops in Cheyenne, a rolling mill in Laramie city and more coal mining at Evanston. Those towns were "hanging on" and one of them, Cheyenne, was rapidly becoming an "army" town

with Fort D.A. Russell on its outskirts but more importantly Camp Carlin also nearby was providing a centralized supply depot for the Army of the West.

In 1867 most of the present day Wyoming was Laramie County, Dakota Territory with its county seat at Fort Sanders about three miles from Laramie City. It was a long way from Yankton, the territorial capitol. Most of Dakota Territory recognized the problem and had sent a memorial to the 40th Congress recommending that the western part be made a territory on its own.

At nearly the same time General Jack Casement appeared in Washington, D.C. acting as a delegate to Congress. His election had no legal background as no legislature had met to elect him. Casement, nevertheless, went to Congress starting the movement for a new territory to be created from the western part of Dakota Territory. One of the men who worked hard for Wyoming Territory was Dr. Hiram Latham, a former Union Pacific surgeon who had settled in Cheyenne. His quiet manner, good taste, and background went a long

CHAPTER XII

EPIC:

"Selling Wyoming to Congress"

Wyoming State Capitol Building, Cheyenne, WY.

way in creating friends for Wyoming in the national capital.

Latham created a circular, and had it sent to each member of Congress.

"WYOMING"

To the Honorable Members of the Senate and the House of Representatives:

The people of Western Dakota have commissioned the undersigned to express to the Members of both Houses of Congress their earnest desire for a separate territorial government. The following are some of the facts and reasons that render the measure both desirable and necessary:

There are now 35,000 American citizens within the limits of the district called Wyoming. That district embraces 110,000 square miles, and is nearly twice the size of any state East of the Mississippi. Its eastern boundary is about 300 miles from Yankton, the capital of Dakota, and nearly one half of the people reside more than 1,200 miles from that capital. The Union Pacific Railroad is now finished for a distance of 250 miles within the limits of Wyoming, and by November next the cars will be running on the road across the Territory from east to west, a distance of nearly 500 miles. The facilities afforded by the Union Pacific Railroad

for reaching Wyoming, the exhaustless mines of gold, silver, and copper with which the territory abounds, its mountains of iron and thousands of square miles of coal lands, its millions of acreas of unequaled pasturage, and the salubrity of the climate, are now attracting to that district of the country a vast throng of enterprising people.

It is confidentially believed that in one year from this time Wyoming will have a population of 60,000 white people, nearly all American citizens. Cheyenne, the principal town in the Territory, has now a population of more than 5,000 souls, and it is not yet a year old.

The people of Wyoming are practically without government and without law. Vigilance committees usurp the functions of the courts, and the only restraint upon the evil disposed is the fear of violence at the hands of those self constituted tribunals. While the public lands remain unsurveyed, permanent improvement will not and cannot be made. For the people and for the Union Pacific Railroad there is a great and constantly increasing necessity for an early survey of the lands along the line of said road.

The people of Wyoming earnestly desire and respectfully ask that the Senate bill establishing a Territorial government for them become a law in this session of congress.

H. Latham

Agent For The People Of Wyoming

On July 25, 1868, President Andrew Johnson signed the Organic Act which created the Territory of Wyoming by Act of Congress, thanks in part, to the devoted efforts of Latham and Casement.

The editor of the *Cheyenne Leader* was more eloquent in his statement calling for the territory. Nathan A. Baker editoralized Saying "Dakota is a slow coach; we (in Wyoming) travel by steam."

While Dakota was still using stagecoaches, Wyoming was moving ahead, and traveling by steam.

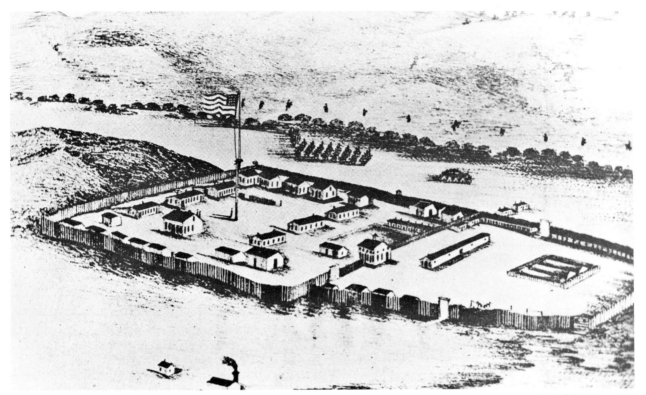

Fort Phil Kearny—1867

CHAPTER XII

TERRITORIAL WYOMING

A month after President Andrew Johnson signed the Organic Act creating Wyoming a territory on July 25, 1868, the Stars and Stripes were hauled down at Fort Phil Kearny and Fort C.F. Smith. Red Cloud had won his war, or at least it looked that way to him. To the Army, it meant complying with the provisions of the Treaty of 1868, which gave a huge tract of land to the Indians as a reservation. Named the Great Sioux Reservation, it included a vast area north of the North Platte taking in all of the Powder River Country and western Dakota.

Forts Dismantled

The hated forts inside that area had to be removed. Once they were dismantled and the sections that could be saved were hauled away, Red Cloud's warriors set torches to them and watched in glee as they burned to the ground. Only when they had been completely destroyed did Red Cloud come to Fort Laramie to put his signature to the treaty.

In the meantime, Jim Bridger helped haul what was left of them to erect Fort Fred Steele, a few miles East of where Rawlins is today. That post now joined the southern tier of posts in the new territory which included Fort D. A. Russell at Cheyenne, Fort Sanders at Laramie City, Fort Bridger near Evanston. All of them helped guard the Union Pacific across the territory to Salt Lake City.

Forts Fetterman and Laramie were situated on the southside of the North Platte, and so were not actually in violation of the Treaty of 1868. Both of those posts were to be out posts and centers of supply for the Army. Any future Indian trouble meant that Fetterman and Laramie would instantly become strategic jumping off points for Army columns.

Over at Jim Bridger's old fort a council of peace commissioners had met with Chief Washakie, and out of the meeting 2,774,700 acres were set aside and called the Wind River Indian Reservation. Washakie's Shoshone people liked it, but the Bannocks returned to Idaho leaving the Sho-

119

shone Indians the sole owners of the land. Situated between the Popo Agie and the Wind River, the reservation reached West to the crest of the continental divide beyond the towns of present day Riverton and Lander, and is today the only Indian reservation within the boundaries of Wyoming.

Up to this point, the huge tract of land now called Wyoming Territory had been claimed by a number of foreign nations, and had been a part of various territories. England had claimed the land first, then Spain, followed by France. The Louisiana Purchase made most of the land American although, a small section of southwestern Wyoming had been ceded by Spain to Mexico in 1821.

In 1835 Texas seceded from Mexico and that small portion of Wyoming formerly belonging to Spain, then Mexico, was now a part of the Republic of Texas. That lasted until 1845 when the United States annexed the Republic of Texas.

Russians had moved from the Alaskan area south along the Pacific coastline and, along with England, France and Spain, claimed a section of the Oregon Country which drained the Snake-Columbia River system. The United States laid claim to that area, partly because Spain had ceded her rights to the United States in the Treaty of 1819.

In 1824, Russian claims to the Oregon Country were given up to the United States and twenty-two years later in 1846, England relinquished her claims south of the boundary line of 49 degrees north latitude from the towering continental divide west to the Pacific Ocean to the United States. A small part of Wyoming in the West had been a part of the Oregon Country for a long time, and it was now officially a part of the United States.

So, Wyoming as a territory had been actually a part of England, Spain, France, Mexico, Russia and Texas. Six foreign nations had the right in the past to hoist and fly their national flag over parts of Wyoming.

Naming of Wyoming

As the United States began its westward expansion in pursuit of ''Manifest Destiny,'' Wyoming, as we know it, was once part of a number of territories including Louisiana, Missouri, Nebraska, Dakota, Idaho, Oregon, Washington, Utah and Indian, or Unexplored Lands.

When the creation of the new territory was under discussion, a number of names were proposed for it. Indian tribes that had lived, hunted, or fought in the area were given close consideration including the Arapahoe, Cheyenne, Crow, Pawnee and Sioux. Dr. Larson pointed out in his book, *HISTORY OF WYOMING*, that the United States Senate spent more than a little time trying to figure out a name and included the names of rivers such as Big Horn, Platte, Sweetwater and Yellowstone. Lincoln was a favorite of many, but finally they named the area Wyoming. It was already being called that, the name having been proposed by Congressman James M. Ashley, who in 1865, had come from Pennsylvania where there was a Wyoming Valley. Wyoming is a Delaware Indian word, and it means ''at the end of the plains'' or ''on the plains.'' It was even suggested the Senate liked the new name because it was easy to spell, and it was easy to pronounce.

Counties Established

Before Wyoming became a territory, the first county had been created by the Sixth Dakota Legislaive Assembly. It embraced all of the western half of Dakota from the present state line to the eastern edges of Utah and Idaho territories. This huge county had for its county seat, Fort Sanders. The date for creation of Laramie County, as it was named, was January 9, 1867.

The Seventh Dakota Legislative Assembly created Carter County, and named South Pass City the county seat by splitting Laramie County in half and this was the western half. That was on December 27, 1867. In 1869, Carter County became Sweetwater County. The same Seventh Dakota legislature also changed the Laramie County seat from Fort Sanders to Cheyenne.

On December 18, 1868 the Eighth Dakota Legislative Assembly created Albany and Carbon counties naming Laramie City as the county seat for Albany, and Rawlins Springs, the county seat for Carbon County.

By the time Wyoming became a territory and finished its internal organization, it had four counties. What little portions of both Utah and Idaho Territories were within the boundaries of Wyoming were unorganized from July 25, 1868 until December 1, 1869 when the first Wyoming Territorial Legislative Assembly created Uinta County which included the Utah and Idaho areas. The county seat was Merril. Merril lost by one vote to Evanston the next year, and the County seat was changed to Evanston.

Census taken in 1869 in the four counties revealed only 8,014 people contrary to Dr.

Latham's enthusiastic report and circular given to the members of Congress. Albany County had 2,027, Carbon County had 400, Carter County 2,862, and Laramie County had 2,665.

Officials Appointed

The people in the new territory looked forward with a great deal of interest to the list of officers appointed by the President. President Andrew Johnson was having a battle with Congress. Also, 1868 was an election year and General Grant was the President-elect. Anyone President Johnson appointed had to be confirmed by the U.S. Senate, and this meant that no one was appointed and confirmed until after the inauguration of Grant which did not take place until March 1869. Even then, it was not until May 1869 that the new governor and his staff arrived in Cheyenne to take office.

In the meantime, law and order was a loose, free-wheeling affair. The same problems, as a result of being too far from Yankton carried on during the long period of 10 months before the new governor arrived to take office. Law breakers operated pretty much as they wanted. Titles to land were still unsettled. In fact, both civil and criminal law was at a standstill until May 1869. Of course, vigilante committees did their work—outside the law—while the appointments to territorial offices were being made.

Besides the post of territorial governor, a territorial secretary, three judges to the supreme court, who would also act as district judges, a surveyor general, land officer receivers and registers, a United States Marshall, a United States District Attorney, and a long list of postmasters were also posts that needed filling.

Territorial appointments had been considered "political plums." A man who had worked tirelessly for the presidential election could hope for a good job in a territory. And, in some cases, the farther West the appointment, meant the lower the scale of being vital to the election of the new President. Wyoming, at that time would have been measured as a territory close to the bottom of the political pay-off scale.

Since President Grant had turned to his Civil War officer friends for help in his campaign, a great many of his appointments came from the officer class left without work following the long and bitter war.

First Territorial Governor

Wyoming got a former brigadier general as its new territorial governor. He was John Allen Campbell, an Ohio native who had served on the staff of General Schofield during the Civil War. Campbell had later on become the assistant Secretary to War. He took his oath of office April 3, 1869 and arrived in Wyoming a month later

John Allen Campbell—First Territorial Governor

amid the strains of the Fort Russell military band and the cheering citizens of Cheyenne. The new Territorial Governor also carried the title of Superintendent of the Wind River Indian Reservation (a title which was changed two years later).

The Territorial Secretary was Edward Merwin Lee from Connecticut. He had been captured during the Civil War. After his release, he won the silver star of a brigadier general. He founded, while in Wyoming, the *Wyoming Tribune*, a Cheyenne newspaper.

Governor Campbell appointed Benjamin **Gallagher from Iowa, Territorial Auditor. The post** also carried with it, at that time, the position of Superintendent of Public Instruction, an exofficio job, meaning he got the work by virtue of his office. It also carried an additional $500 a year as a salary. Gallagher had been a post trader, or sutler in the West for a number of years.

Cheyenne banker, and a former native of County Clare, Ireland, John W. Donnellan was appointed Territorial Treasurer. He had been a colonel in the Civil War, and then came to Cheyenne in 1867 where he went into the mercantile business and in 1868 opened a bank.

President Grant appointed John H.Howe from Illinois Chief Justice of the Territorial Supreme Court. Howe had been a brigadier general in the Civil War. John W. Kingham from New Hampshire and William T. Jones of Indiana were appointed Associate Justices of the high court. Both men were high ranking Union officers in the Civil War. All three men served as district court judges too.

The United States Attorney was a young Delaware native, Joseph M. Carey, who had earned a law degree from Pennsylvania University. He had been too young to be in the Civil War, but was old enough to have worked long and hard for Grant in Delaware. The rest of his life, political and personal, would be tied closely to Wyoming as he would serve in the future as a city mayor, Territorial Delegate to Congress, U.S. Senator, and Governor of Wyoming.

While the judges were busy holding long overdue terms of court, and the marshalls were trying to establish law and order, the new Governor went about his task of organizing the territory into a House of Representatives and a Council (like the State Senate). Using the census taken earlier, and based upon population, 13 members of the House of Representatives were assigned to the vast area. Laramie County received 4, Albany County 3, Carbon County 1, **Carter** County 3, and the unorganized part of Utah and Idaho got 1, and the "At large faction" got 1 more seat.

The Council was represented by 9 members. Three came from Laramie County and three from Carter and the Utah-Idaho combination.

The Republicans and Democrats then held conventions and chose their candidates for the territorial legislature. One other office was to be voted upon — Delegate to Congress from Wyoming Territory.

In the meantime, Indian trouble around the South Pass area had brought bad news to Governor Campbell. Several people have been killed and wounded, warranting a plea for assistance to General Augur. Troops were dispatched, and rifles and ammunition were issued to the civilians to defend themselves.

By the time the trouble settled down, the party conventions had picked their nominees for office. Election day was September third.

The elected Congressional delegate was **Stephan F. Nickolls, a Virginian, a Democrat and a Cheyenne merchant. In fact, Democrats won all the seats in the First Territorial Legislature.**

Woman Suffrage Bill

The Territorial legislature went into session on October 12, 1869 and met for 50 days. William H. Bright, of South Pass City, was chosen President of the Council and S. M. Curran, of Carbon County was Speaker of the House. J.M. Freeman, representative of the unorganized territory never came to the session. Although Governor Campbell and Secretary Lee were Republican, the two branches worked together well.

Bills for mining regulations were passed, Cheyenne was named the territorial capitol, the penitentiary was to be located at Laramie City, property taxes were set, game laws were established which forbade the wholesale slaughter of one of Wyoming's great natural resources, its wild animals.

What would have been an ordinary legislature, turned into an historic session where President Bright introduced the woman suffrage bill. He introduced only the one bill during the entire session in which time 104 bills were introduced. The bill simply said that women should have the right to vote and hold office if they were twenty-one years of age and resided in the territory. It is clear that it was one of the most famous, if not the most famous piece of legislation ever to come out of a Territorial or State Legislative Assembly in Wyoming history.

In the House, the woman suffrage bill took a week to over come any objections. It passed the House 7 to 4. In the Council, the bill passed 6 to 3.

Looking back now, there are several reasons why the woman suffrage bill was introduced and passed. First, the thin population of Wyoming needed more citizens. By giving women the right to vote and hold office, it was hoped a landslide of women would move to Wyoming. Also, Democrats were looking ahead to the next election thinking since they had given women the right to vote and hold office, they might possibly count more voters coming their way from grateful women voters. The action, it was felt, might also embarrass Republicans who were seeking to gain suffrage for black voters following the Civil War.

None of these three factors came to pass. Wyoming only counted 1,104 more people in the Census of 1870. The Territory was off to a slow population start, and that fact would plague Wyoming politicians for years to come. Only in recent years has there been a few candidates satisfied with keeping Wyoming a land of "low multitude and high altitude."

"Women suffrage in Wyoming"

Mrs. Esther Morris—The Mother Of Woman Suffrage

124

Publicity, articles, and speeches about woman suffrage and the crying need for it may have swept the headlines in Eastern America, but it was Wyoming, and then Utah and other Western territories and states, that first gave women the right to vote and hold office.

Right after Wyoming and Utah Territories enfranchised women, Colorado and Idaho followed so that by 1914 ten out of eleven Western states had granted women suffrage. Only New Mexico held out.

This led to the proposal of the 19th Amendment to the United States Constitution on June 4, 1919 and ratification of that Amendment on August 26, 1920.

First came the Wyoming Territorial Act which read:

"AN ACT TO GRANT TO THE

WOMEN OF WYOMING THE RIGHT

OF SUFFRAGE AND TO HOLD

OFFICE

"Be it enacted by the Council and House of Representative of the Territory of Wyoming:

Sec. 1. That every woman of the age of twenty-one years, residing in this territory, may at every election to be holden under the laws hereof, cast her vote. And her rights to the elective franchise and to hold office shall be the same under the election laws of the territory, as those of electors.

Sec. 2. This act shall take effect and be in force from and after its passage.

The 19th Amendment, the culmination of all those efforts is as follows:

ARTICLE XIX

(Proposed 4 June 1919; Declared Ratified 26 August, 1920)
The right of citizens of the United States to vote shall not be denied or abridged by the United States or by any State on account of sex.

The Congress shall have power, by appropriate legislation, to enforce the provisions of this article.

So, what was initiated offically into law in Wyoming Territory on December 10, 1869 finally became the law of the land as the 19th Amendment fifty years later. Both acts were brief and pointed. No one had ever had any doubts as to what they meant, certainly not women who had stood in the wings of government waiting their chance to take their rightful place alongside men to vote and hold office.

It took Governor Campbell four days to think about the suffrage bill before he finally signed it. Dr. Larson said among those who urged Governor Campbell to sign the bill were several women, two of the three Supreme Court Justices, and Territorial Secretary Lee, who may have had more to do with the bill than is generally supposed. Owing to his military career during the Civil War where he attained the rank of brigadier general, Lee was called "General" by all those who knew him personally. He even carried the title with him as he was elected to serve a term in the Connecticut State Legislature. During his term in the Connecticut Legislature, and long before he came to Wyoming, General Lee had introduced legislation for a women suffrage amendment which lost by the narrow margin of 93 to 111. When he came to Wyoming as the new territorial secretary, one of his first acts had been to purchase the *Wyoming Tribune* which openly advocated women suffrage **before** the act became a reality.

It has been suggested that General Lee had much to do with helping William H. Bright produce the only piece of legislation he offered during the entire territorial legislative assembly. Bright came from South Pass City, a town whose population stood at about 460 persons in 1869 and was the home of miner-saloon-keeper, John Morris. According to a number of persons then living there, Mrs. John Morris entertained the two candidates for Council at their home before the election. While serving tea, she asked them to support a woman suffrage bill. Both men, H.G. Nickerson, who lost, and W. H. Bright, who won, promised to carry out her wishes if elected.

Mrs. Morris, a New York native, had moved to South Pass City in 1869 from Illinois to join her husband and sons in the little mining community. In 1870 it was General Lee, while Acting Territorial Governor, who appointed Mrs. Morris as justice of the peace. She held this post for eight and a half months. In 1871 she had moved to Laramie, and in 1876 moved on to Cheyenne where she died in 1902.

Because of her efforts with Bright, and her work as justice of the peace, she was acclaimed in 1913 by Wyoming University professor Grace Raymond Hebard as "The Mother of Woman Suffrage." Today, Wyoming is represented in Statuary Hall in the national capitol in Washington, D.C. by a statue of Mrs. Morris, placed in 1960.

Thus, a little over 100 years later, the first woman suffrage act in the United States was recognized with the placement of the statue of Esther Hobart Morris in Washington, D.C. The work of art had come a long way, and many had helped put it there, not the least of whom was General Lee, and W.H. Bright. Mrs. Morris had won her right to acclaim as she lobbyed with Bright and Nickerson, and diligently handled more than 70 cases as the first woman to hold public office.

More than any of these facts, it must be remembered that Wyoming women, few as they were, worked side-by-side with their husbands, no matter whether they were merchants, professional men, soldiers or ranchers.

They earned their right to vote, and Wyoming justly earned the right to the title of "The Equality State" following the passage of the woman suffrage act.

William H. Jackson

CHAPTER XIII

EPIC:

Dr. Ferdinand Vandeveer Hayden, well known as the father of the United States Geological Survey, hired a young photographer to accompany his 1870 geological survey crew across the southern half of Wyoming. The photographer was William H. Jackson, a young Civil War veteran who had just completed a full year working at the new art by taking pictures recording the building of the Union Pacific Railroad. His photographs of that construction are, even today, considered masterpieces of the camera art, and were instrumental in Hayden's decision to employ the young photographer.

Young Jackson's Civil War service had been as a Green Mountain soldier with his home state's Vermont Infantry. After the war, Jackson went West. Reaching Nebraska City, Nebraska he hired out to drive a wagon to Virginia city, far up in the newly discovered gold fields of Montana. He wrote his father that his boss, Mike Rayan, was going to whack a bull train up the Bozeman Trail "if the redskins weren't still on the warpath."

As it turned out, Ryan's bull train had to go to Salt Lake City because 1866 was not considered a safe year for travel on the Bozeman Trail. Thus the train traveled the Oregon and Mormon Trail. At Salt Lake City it had a choice of detouring north via the western trail route to Virginia City, or traveling on to California, via the California Trail. Jackson chose the latter.

Jackson was not taking pictures as he left

"Potato John and the photographer"

Nebraska City, because he was driving a wagon, but, he did sketch various scenes. He had learned to draw early in his life, and once during the Civil War he had worked as a draftsman for his commanding officer. Later, the drawings he made of the Oregon Trail would come to life as fine water colors and line drawings, still considered among the finest examples of art work recording Oregon Trail scenes.

Among these scenes are drawings of the Platte River Bridge near Casper and the Deer Creek area at Glenrock. He recorded buildings at Deer Creek which were in flames from an Indian raid. Soldiers were pursuing the Indians when he made his sketches.

By the time he crossed the continental divide at South Pass, the twenty-three year old bull whacker had grown stringy, lean, and tough. After making the choice to go to California, he proceeded to Los Angeles where he spent the winter of 1866-1867. He worked at several stage stations that winter, and when spring came, hired on to help drive a herd of half broken horses east to Julesburg, Colorado. The horses where to be used to help build the Union Pacific Railroad.

Jackson's trip East was as interesting as his trip to California. After a great many adventures, he arrived at Julesburg in August 1867 and was paid the magnificent sum of twenty dollars for his long, hard trip. This sum helped him to find his new occupation.

Having studied and worked as a photographer in Vermont, he knew enough of the business to hire out as a helper to an established Omaha photographer. Within a few months, his brother Edward had joined him. The two brothers opened two Nebraska photographic galleries in 1868.

Leaving brother Edward at Omaha, in 1868, Jackson joined young Arundel C. Hull, another photographer, and the two worked their way west along the Union Pacific taking and developing photographs. They took pictures of anything and anyone, staying up half the night to develop them.

Jackson and Hull spent six days in Cheyenne. Jackson has written of the Cheyenne period:

They were busy days. Every available moment was spent in making negatives, taking pictures, and printing them. Albumen paper was silvered by floating it in a bath of silver nitrate, and fumed with ammonia when dry; this work we did at night. The printed paper was then put through several washings, tonings, and fixing operations, and dried, trimmed, and mounted. Naturally we were elated, after all this work, when fine pictures resulted, and were correspondingly depressed when the finished product turned out poorly. Photography in those pioneer times was still largely in the experimental stage.

127

It was as a result of this pioneering work that Hayden hired Jackson to make the survey trip across southern Wyoming in the summer and fall of 1870. On this expedition Jackson produced superb pictures. Among them are photographic studies of Chief Washakie and his tribe of Shoshone Indians near South Pass; studies of the Flaming Gorge area; studies of Independence Rock; clean, clear pictures of Red Buttes near present day Casper; and many other photographs, forming important photographic records of early Wyoming.

Jackson's employer, Dr. Hayden was no stranger to the West. He had earned the title of "The-man-who-runs-after-rocks" from the Sioux in 1860. The ardent geologist had been looking for fossil specimens when several Sioux caught him, made him turn inside out a sack he was carrying, and finding the sack full of rocks, left him unharmed, thinking him insane. Since Indians regarded crazy people with deep respect, that is probably all that saved Hayden's life. His work at that time was as a geologist with the Raynolds-Maynadier Expedition of 1859-1860. During those years he had listened to the famed guide, Jim Bridger, and desired to come back to Wyoming and explore the regions Bridger had described.

First Hayden had to arrange the 1870 geological survey to Salt Lake. One of the men, John Raymond, the cook on the survey trip had been dubbed "Potato John." Raymond was the cook for the expedition, not by profession, but because it was the only remaining berth on the crew. He was better, most of the crew said, as a guide and packer than a cook. He proved that theory when he tried to boil potatoes at 12,000 feet above sea level in the Uinta Mountains. After trying for two days to bring the spuds to a boil, he was informed by the amused scientists, with the survey, that cooking at that altitude was tough! The higher the altitude, the lower the temperature at which water boils. So, named "Potato John" by now, he gave up boiling the potatoes, and resorted to his frying pan. The cook-guide-packer, "Potato John" was a particular friend of Jackson's and often took time to help the photographer load his bulky equipment on top of "Hypo," Jackson's balky white mule.

In the winter of 1871, Dr. Hayden listened to Nathaniel Lanford give a talk in Washington, D.C. regarding an exploratory trip Lanford had taken to Yellowstone. Lieutenant Gustavus Doane, Henry Washburn, and Cornelius Hedges had been on the same 1870 trip with Langford, but small attention was given to the trip. In fact, most people had listened skeptically, if at all.

But, to Hayden, those stories reminded him of those of Yellowstone he had heard ten years earlier from Jim Bridger. So, Hayden formed an 1871 expedition to explore and survey the Yellowstone regions. Thomas Moran was added as the official artist. Moran, who had a reputation as a fine landscape artist, could work together with Jackson exchanging views as they traveled to record the sights of the mysterious and fabled Yellowstone area.

Assembling at Ogden, Utah Territory, in June 1871, were 35 men and their pack animals. They had been outfitted at Cheyenne's Camp Carlin a few weeks before, and then rode flat cars to their Utah jumping off point. Fifteen of the men, including "Potato John" were cooks, teamsters, guides, and packers. Twenty were artists, photographers, geologists, entomologists, engineers, and topographers.

Jackson and "Potato John" loaded two cameras on "Hypo." One camera was 6-1/2" by 8-1/2" that he had used the previous year. In addition, he had a new camera with a fine 8 by 10 inch lens which could produce bigger and, Jackson hoped, clearer negatives. Each camera was carried in a set of specially built packs made from heavy leather, designed to be as dust proof as possible. The previous year Jackson had carried a small keg of water for washing his photographic plates in areas where there might be no water. The keg had been hard to handle. This time he carried the water in a rubber container which fit the pack saddles easier and was not so bulky. In the leather pack saddles, Jackson had supervised the construction of special compartments that held his dark box, his "black tent" (where he developed his work), glass plates, bath holder, and chemicals.

William H. Jackson In Wyoming 1870

Jupiter Terrace, Yellowstone National Park

Thus, Jackson rode on one mule, and pulled "Hypo" along behind as they joined the long column headed north into Idaho, Wyoming and Montana. "Potato John" was not far behind and the whole column of men and animals labored north.

Jackson wrote many years later that the expedition entered the Yellowstone region almost breathlessly. The wonders of what they saw were to be captured forever by the young photographer with the help of "Potato John" as they intermittently coaxed, and then cursed "Hypo" up and down mountains and valleys. Hayden had allowed two other photographers to come on the trip, but both men ran into trouble. One had lost his camera when a sudden gust of wind toppled it into the yawning reaches of the Grand Canyon of the Yellowstone. The other photographer lost his plates of the expedition in the great Chicago fire a year later.

It was the photographs of Jackson, then, that survived and were used to give proof that the stories Colter, Bridger, and Langford told were true. Their tales of the wonderous geysers, the fabulous paint pots, the roaring falls dropping hundreds of feet into the mighty Grand Canyon, the mystical high altitude Yellowstone Lake, the vast herds of buffalo, the huge flocks of birds and abundance of speckled Native trout were proved to be real by Jackson's photographs.

As the bill was prepared requesting Yellowstone be set aside for a national park, various specimens of minerals, rocks, flowers, and other items provided reasons why the land should be set aside. But, the real proof came when Jackson's photographs (blown up and bound into a fine leather folio by Hayden) were presented to each member of Congress.

This led to the birth of America's first national park. The bill was passed asking that 3,578 square miles be set aside for all Americans to enjoy forever. Much of the idea to reserve the land had come from the Washburn-Langford Expedition, but the real clincher for the Senators and Representatives, sitting a long way from Wyoming came when they opened up their personal folio of Jackson's pictures.

President Grant signed the bill into law, March 1, 1872.

Well—what happened to "Potato John" Ray-

129

mond? And, "Hypo"? They continued to travel with Jackson, who the next year photographed the Teton range of mountains in what was to become the Grand Teton National Park. Thomas Moran was also along and Mount Moran was named in honor of that great American landscape artist.

Jackson continued his trips and his great photographic work in the Colorado Rockies, recording the Garden of the Gods, Estes Park, San Juan Park, Mesa Verde, and the Cliff Dwellings. In 1877 Jackson climbed Fremont Peak in the Wind River Mountains and photographed the wide Wyoming vista seen from that high rocky point, and then took more photos of Atlantic and Pacific Creeks, the Shoshone Indians. He also made another trip into the Yellowstone region.

His son wrote years later, "To my fellow photographers who look at his (meaning his father's) pictures, but have had limited personal experience with pioneer photography, it may be not amiss to point out that practically all of them were made with cumbersome and erratic equipment of years ago. Heavy cameras, packs of plates and chemicals, dark tents and all the rest had often to be lugged up mountainsides where mules would not go—and they were lugged on the back of the photographer.

"The process of preparing a wet-plate and developing it called for great skill and art. I recall, as a small boy, seeing my father coat an 18 x 22 inch plate. He balanced it carefully on the thumb and fingers of his left-hand, poured a pool of collodion in the far, left-hand corner of the plate, and then slowly worked the thick fluid about the edges and all over the plate until it reached the near, right-hand corner. So sure and careful was his hand that never a drop was spilled, nor was there any fluid left to be returned to the collodion bottle. This was hard enough to do in a building, let alone on top of a mountain in driving gales, after packing camera, plates and plate holders up over ledges slippery with ice and across treacherous fields of snow."

While Jackson and Moran were recording their impressions of the Yellowstone-Grand Teton regions, a jury of women was being impaneled in Laramie; stockmen were organizing an association in Cheyenne; and, Walter D. Pease in Johnson County was recording the first homestead entry in Wyoming.

It was a busy time for Wyoming, as the territory was marched toward civilization.

———————

CATTLE WYOMING

Sublette Brings First Cattle

The first cattle that came to Wyoming were 12 animals of English origin, brought by Captain William L. Sublette. Sublette had left Saint Louis heading for the rendezvous which was held at the junction of the Wind River and the Popo Agie July 16, 1830. Enroute, Sublette gave a Fourth of July talk at the base of a large grey monolithic rock near the Sweetwater River, and in toasting the Nation's birthday named the rock, appropriately enough, "Independence Rock."

With the growth of traffic along the Oregon Trail a few years later, thousands of oxen were yoked up and pulled lumbering wagons as they plodded across Wyoming. These animals were often traded at Fort Laramie or Fort Bridger for fresh stock. A pool of oxen in good condition were on hand at both posts, and the emigrant or bull whacker needing to replace a used up animal could make the trade at 2 for 1, or 3 for 1, allowing the wagon or freight outfit to move on to the West. The weak animals were turned out to graze and fatten up, and when they had regained their strength, they were traded off to some other emigrant in need of help.

So, on the Western end of the Oregon Trail, herds of cattle and horses and mules soon built up. Eventually, better breeds of cattle were brought in, some of which seemed particularly adapted to the climate, the grazing, and the

higher altitude. It was from the Oregon Trail, and its sister trails, the Mormon and California, that the cattle industry in Wyoming began. A great many cattle were driven from Oregon into Wyoming, reversing the usual direction of travel.

A long way south of Wyoming, it was reckoned in Texas by 1860 that 4,500,000 head of cattle were scattered over the Lone Star state's 262,398 square miles. That meant about 2-1/2 cattle per square mile. When the Civil War was over, the railroads began to push West. Cattlemen in Texas drove their herds to railheads like Dodge City, Abilene, and Wichita. At those points, buyers took over and shipped the cattle to Kansas City, Saint Louis, and Chicago for further feeding. Then, they were re-sold to packing plants. It was a short jump then to restaurants, stores, butcher shops, or canning factories and eventually to the final consumer.

Cattle Drives a Part of Wyoming History

The Texas cowman, once having made his sale, turned around and went back to Texas to the job of rounding up another herd and preparing for another cattle drive to the railroad.

Those cattle drives took place across Indian country and past great herds of buffalo. Soon the buffalo hunters thinned out these herds and sent the meat to railroad crews and Army posts. The hides went East. But, with the reduction of the buffalo herds, the demand for beef soared.

The cattle trails went even further north when the Union Pacific Railroad sliced across Nebraska, Wyoming, and Utah. The Chisholm Trail started out at San Antonio and led to Abilene and Wichita. The Shawnee Trail also took off from San Antonio, but headed to Kansas City, and Ogallala. A part of that trail came into Wyoming near Pine Bluffs. Crossing Wyoming, the trail passed near present day Lingle, Lusk and up into the Powder River region before splitting off to the Dakotas in the East, Milk River and Montana in the North, and Gillette, Buffalo and Sheridan on the West.

Cattle Survive Wyoming Winters

Seth Ward, one of the sutlers at Fort Laramie, had started to winter cattle in Wyoming in 1852, not expecting to see them when spring came. That spring, however, Ward found the cattle alive and in fine shape.

Alexander Majors, of the great freighting firm of Russell, Majors & Waddell, had the same experience. Majors learned that cattle could survive Wyoming winters when his firm was supplying the Army in the war against the Mormons in the winter of 1857-1858. A great number of cattle wintered on the Sybille Creek near present day Wheatland. Because of the excellent condition of the stock when spring came, Majors continued to leave cattle in that area for many winters.

The next year, Elias Whitcomb of Virginia wintered 1,200 cattle for a freighting firm in the Chugwater area. Once again, the cattle wintered well.

At Fort Bridger, Jim Bridger got into the cattle business as he swapped rested cattle for weak ones with the westward bound emigrants.

The Army purchased Fort Bridger, and then installed Judge William Carter as the post sutler during the Mormon War. The judge was at various times, local judge, postmaster and goldminer, trader, merchant, and cowman. When the Union Pacific line was built through Wyoming, Carter went East and brought back a carload of purebred Shorthorn bulls, upgrading his sizeable herds. By 1877, Carter was advertising that he had entered into an agreement with the Union Pacific to build shipping yards. They were complete with corrals, pens, scales and what he called "commodious lots and extensive enclosures" capable of handling large numbers of cattle. He said he would ship East for the cattlemen at a reduced rate. Judge Carter did a good business, and was well liked and respected for his honesty.

The cattle industry in Wyoming was slowly but surely taking hold. There were, of course, drawbacks to Wyoming even if the range was good. One was the Indian problem. An Indian saw little difference between a good cow buffalo and a good beef cow. They tasted about the same, and with the buffalo herds declining, beef cattle looked increasingly good to the Indian.

Another problem was that all the land north of the North Platte River had been reserved for Indian use by Treaty of 1868. It was however, ideal for the range cattle industry—having acres and acres of abundant grass and plenty of good water.

Cattle Industry Blossoms

The Indian Treaty did not stop Nelson Story, a Ohio gold miner who had made a sizeable strike in the Alder Bulch area of Montana. He took his gold to New York where he converted it into greenbacks, made a profit, then headed for Texas in 1866 and bought a thousand head of longhorns, mostly cows with calves, and headed north. He did not stop at Abilene, or Dodge City, or Cheyenne, but kept on until he arrived at Fort Phil Kearny where he was stopped by the Army who

told him he could not go north. There were too many Indians, they said, who would kill him and his trail crew and run off the cattle.

But Nelson Story would not listen. In the dark of night, he shoved his herd north and before dawn was out of sight of Fort Kearny, not even stopping at Montana's Fort Smith. Story kept moving until he was back where he started in Montana. He had successfully brought the first herd of cattle up the Texas Trail.

Luck continued to ride with Nelson Story. And, by 1886, he was the biggest cattleman in Montana.

Story was the first man to drive cattle across Wyoming. There would be many more in the future.

John Iliff brought cattle to Cheyenne, from Texas and then sold them to local butchers. One of the young cowboys with that herd was John B. Kendrick, who would come back to build a cattle empire of his own near Sheridan, get into politics and serve as a Governor and U.S. Senator from Wyoming. Wyoming's first year-round permanent herd was established by W. G. Bullock and B. B. Mills in 1868. They built their herd near Fort Laramie from cattle driven in from Kansas, Iowa and Missouri.

Part of the expanding beef market were the financially secure government contracts to supply beef to Army posts. Wyoming Army posts needed a large, reliable supply of beef and in the 1870's many cattle came from Texas and were delivered to Forts Russell, Sanders, Steele, Fetterman, and Laramie. Also, even if the Treaty of 1868 did not allow cattlemen on the vast Powder River range, the treaty did provide that beef be supplied to various tribes of Indians. Contracts were awarded and herds of Texas cattle pushed into the reservation.

By 1870, the first herd of Wyoming bred cattle was being shipped out of the territory, the first time a home grown herd was sold to outside interests and shipped on the Union Pacific line to another area.

The seller was H.B. Kelley of Chugwater. He sold only 750 cattle, but they went to French buyers who needed beef to feed their soldiers then engaged in the Franco-Prussian War.

From that time forward, cattle shipments from Wyoming railroads mounted steadily. The following table will serve to indicate the rate of progression in the mid-1870s:

1873.....186 cars of cattle
1874.....738 cars of cattle

In those days about 20 head of stock were able to find space enough in a cattle car to make the trip from Wyoming to Chicago. The Union Pacific was charging about $140 a car—at least from the eastern side of Wyoming from where Kelley shipped his 1870 herd. That meant the cowman had to deduct approximately $7.00 a head for shipping costs, plus figure on shrinkage that the cattle would suffer on the trip from lack of feed and water. In order to reduce this factor, many cattlemen drove their cattle east of the Ogallala to ship them, thus cutting down on freight and shrinkage losses.

Up to now most of the cattlemen in Wyoming were Wyoming pioneers. They were men who had settled the area before it was known as Wyoming Territory. By 1871 their herds of cattle were stocked on the range between the North Platte River, and on the Laramie Plains east of Fort Laramie and Pine Bluffs. Inside that triangular section of land the herds jumped from a few thousand head of cattle in 1869 to around 100,000 head in 1871.

The best water, land, and grazing was being selected for the future by these early pioneer cattlemen. Most of them had only recently

become cattlemen. What they needed now, in addition to more cattle, were the cowboys who knew the range business as well as raising cattle. They also needed horses to carry cowboys in their work.

Horses and Cowboys Needed

Texas cowboys came, bringing their own horses, and fulfilling the need for experienced horses. In fact, one writer said that 35,000 Texas cowboys came up the various trails north into Kansas, Colorado, Nebraska, Wyoming, and Montana. Between 1869 and 1885 those same 35,000 men supplied an amazing 1,000,000 head of horses to those states.

Stock Association Formed

The next thing the territory also needed was a cattlemen's association. Many cowmen had already joined the Colorado association, and some had joined the newly organized in 1871, Wyoming

Stock Grazier's Association which embraced both cattlemen and sheepmen.

After visits to Colorado, and many meetings in Cheyenne, ten pioneer cattlemen met in Cheyenne on November 29, 1873 and formed the Laramie County Stock Growers Association. They named Cheyenne as their headquarters. Nearly six years later on, March 29, 1879, the name was changed to the Wyoming Stock Growers Association. This organization was to have a big role in the future development of Wyoming, and nearly 100 years later remains a potent political force in the State.

By that time it was recognized by those who understood politics that there were now two dominant political forces in Wyoming—the Union Pacific Railroad and the Wyoming Stock Growers Association. For years these two groups would provide political, economic, and social leadership in Wyoming.

VIGNETTE:

"The cowboy in Wyoming"

Wyoming has seen a succession of "Types" who visited, stopped or traveled through the state. From prehistoric man through the various tribes of Indians, the blue skies over Wyoming have been the roof for these ancient and less ancient North Americans.

White man came looking for a way West, first as an explorer then as a beaver trapper, and then in a combination of military-survey teams. Following these came the military units taking positions of strength along the various trails helping to protect emigrants moving across the state.

Then came the hoardes of emigrants—religion emigrants, gold loving emigrants, land seeking emigrants and mixed with all of them, some emigrants leaving a shadowy or sorrowful past. Many travelers used Wyoming only as a bridge to get where they wanted to go.

The railroad crews and engineers and track-layers and "Hell on Wheels" people followed. As they came, roots went down drawing bankers, merchants, businessmen, lawyers, and a wide assortment of men and women—good and bad.

All these groups brought with them their own styles of language and their own styles of living and dress. Among them were the Irish, Canadian, English, French, Mexican, Spanish, Basque, and later, Central Europeans as well as emigrants from every state in the Union.

The cowboy played a key role in caring for the far flung herds owned by the cattle kings. The term cowboy originated in the southern Appalachian mountains in the early 1800's. The cattle industry at that time was very different from that which developed in the West. Most of the industry then was confined to fenced pastures. With the

Mr. John B. Kendrick

development of the open-range industry in Texas the life of the cowboy as depicted in western novels and movies began to develop. The long drives northward brought the cowboy to the fore.

Life on the long-drive was not easy. Long hours on horseback were followed by sleeping under the stars. Some men stood guard every night to protect the herd. One of the key dangers was that of a stampede. Cattle were easily frightened into a stampede. Reestablishing the herd and calming it was difficult and dangerous. Many cowboys lost their lives trying to control a stampede.

As is often depicted in literature and movies the cowboys worked hard and played hard. His pay of thirty to sixty dollars a month was often spent on a wild night in one of the trail towns.

Most cowboys were young, usually under thirty years of age. Few had much education. Many were on the move because they were fleeing trouble. Many came West after mustering out of one of the armies at the end of the War between the States. While it is true that some set themselves up in the ranching business by stealing from their employers, most were extra-ordinarily loyal.

Although some cowboys had a deep interest in the fancy clothing so often depicted in Western movies, most dressed in clothing appropriate to the life they led. The broad-rimmed hat helped protect him from sun and weather. His necker-chief was often drawn across his face to protect him from dust. His chaps protected his legs while riding through brush.

The cowboy said he spoke a ''lingo'' all his own, and he was right. He never walked a hundred yards if he could ride them on his cow pony. But, above all else, the cowboy was characterized as a strong silent type who might be hard riding and hard fighting, but always a champion of the underdog and the fairer sex.

One of Wyoming's great cowboys was John B. Kendrick. He was a cowboy all through, and came to the territory from his native Texas with a herd of longhorn cattle. At the age of twenty-two, he arrived in Wyoming Territory in 1879. It was a five month trip up the cattle trail to Wyoming from Matagorda Bay, Texas where young Kendrick started from that year.

Kendrick said years later;

> The scenery was ever-changing. As we traveled northward, we had almost perpetual spring. The trip was indeed beautiful, the wide level stretches of country covered with a splendid

growth of grass and ornamented with all kinds of fragrant flowers. The element of danger, that was part of every day's experience, did not detract from the fascination of the trip.

The Texas Trail resembled a great river with many branches and tributaries. Side trails led in and out in all directions. Cattle included all ages and kinds except calves which were either given away or destroyed to avoid delaying the herd...As a rule, the size of the herd was about 3,000 head; 3,500 was known as a large herd.

The ordinary outfit with a herd consisted of a foreman, cook, horse wrangler and from seven to eight cowboys; a mess wagon drawn by four horses or mules, and a band of about fifty saddle horses. The owner furnished the horses but the saddles and bedding were supplied by the cowboys...We started by branding. At that time we roped and threw the cattle almost entirely on foot (in order to spare our horses for work on the trail.) The roping was very hard on horses, and extremely dangerous because of the viciousness of the cattle. It was less difficult for a man to dodge and escape fighting cattle (on foot) than for a horse. Employers thought best to use men and hire extra help, than risk the horses. Men were cheaper than horses. Our best help were Negroes and Mexicans, who were the most proficient ropers on foot that I have ever know. The cattle were thrown by roping them by the front feet.

When our herd was complete, we started our travels...We averaged about fifteen miles a day. The men were divided into two reliefs in the daytime, and four reliefs of night guards. The last guard called the cook, and turned the cattle from the bed ground to graze. When breakfast was finished, the foreman would go ahead, followed by the cook wagon, and locate water for the noon site. After the discipline of a few days on the trail,

the cattle would march like soldiers following their natural leaders. If possible, they were not allowed to take one step except in the direction of their destination. In this way they would often cover two or three miles while grazing in the morning and again in the evening...

The vicissitudes of the trip were many, including long drives across barren country with a shortage of grass and water. Whole herds of cattle were known to go blind after suffering intense thirst for several days... During the frequent electrical storms at night, instead of being 'off and on' relief, were 'on and on' to hold the frightened herd together and prevent stampeding. The only thing visible was electricity on the points of our horses' ears, and lightning crawling along the ground. More than once I have seen cattle killed within thirty feet of me. When the cattle did stampede and break away, we would gallop with them in the darkness and try to turn them to mill in a circle. I do not recall a single instance when, without rest for twenty-four hours, we did not start on the trail the next day intent on making our usual twenty miles...

The next time Kendrick came up the trail, he remained in Wyoming. He served as Governor of the State, and in the U.S. Senate, Kendrick served from March 4, 1917 until the day he died in Sheridan in Powder River country on November 3, 1933.

The Powder River, in the future would become the backdrop for the Johnson County War, and the cry of ''Powder River, let'er buck!'' would become the slogan of Wyoming men.

Led by a one-armed veteran of the Civil War, the river-born Powell Expedition penetrated the mysterious blank on the map of the West called the Grand Canyon of the Colorado in 1869.

Beginning at Green River, Wyoming Territory on May 25, 1869, the ten man party pushed off on a voyage that was to last nearly 100 days down an uncharted river whose twisting and winding course extended nearly 1,500 miles, and whose elevation would drop from a high at Green River of 6,075 feet above sea level to a low of 700 feet above sea level at Rio Virgin, Arizona.

No one man could describe the haunting beauty of the perpendicular canyon walls nor could they say for certain what this intrepid party would encounter in terms of friendly, or unfriendly Indian tribes. No man could foretell the rapids, falls, cataracts, and smooth water which the exploring group would have to navigate. Certainly none knew if the boats they had could survive the buffeting they knew was ahead.

General Ashley had taken a trip down the Green River in 1825 and stopped about where the Unita River joins the Colorado. For some curious reason, Major John Wesley Powell, the commander of this expedition, had never heard of Ashley's trip. Thus, when he saw " ASHLEY 1825" printed high on the walls of a canyon, he was astounded.

The expedition consisted of O.G. Howland, Seneca Howland, Frank Goodman, Jack Sumner, Bill Dunn, George Bardley, Andy Hall, Billy Hawkins, and Walter Powell, the Major's brother. Powell had four boats built in Detroit for the trip. One, called "No-Name" was sixteen feet long with a four foot beam. It was light and, Powell hoped, durable. The other three were double ribbed and twenty-one feet in length with four foot beams. One was called "Emma Dean" after Powell's wife. The second was called "Kitty Clyde's Sister," and the fourth boat was called "Maid-of-the-Canyon."

Why not join Powell as he tells the real story in

CHAPTER XIV

EPIC:

"Down the green"

John Wesley Powell 1834-1902

his journal? The date was June 8, only two weeks after leaving Green River.

The 'No-Name' was stove in and sinking slowly. Howland apparently decided to run her as long as possible and try to reach a sand bar in midstream, a couple of hundred yards below. The current carried the boat into another rock-filled riffle. The boat was taking a terrific thumping and was starting to break up. At the instant Goodman was washed overboard Howland leaped free. Howland reached the sand bar and saw his brother (Seneca) safe on the bar about a hundred feet farther downstream. Fifty feet above, Frank Goodman was hanging on for dear life to a boulder as big as a barrel, begging weakly for assistance. He had taken in so much water he was in danger of drowning. The Howland brothers managed to get a piece of driftwood to him, and he clung to it until his companions reached him.

During this time the men on shore were rushing down to help the crew of the 'No-Name' but by that wild ride they had been carried out of sight. The marooned trio build a small fire after drying their matches, but their plight was precarious. The river was rising rapidly. Meanwhile the rest on shore were lifting down the 'Dean'. When the instruments were dumped out, Sumner, at great risk, took the 'Dean' across the channel and brought back O.G. Howland, Seneca Howland, and Frank Goodman. We were glad to shake hands with them as if they had been on a voyage round the world and wrecked on a distant coast. They were unhurt except for some bruises.

They had lost everything except shirts and drawers—the uniform they wore in passing all bad spots. Their clothing, bedding and other personal belongings were gone. So were two thousand pounds of provisions. One-third of their larder had vanished, half of the mess kit, and three of the barometers. The men sat glumly by the campfire at the head of a rapid more than a mile long, gazing at the test which awaited them in the morning. They called the spot 'Disaster Falls.'

But after a hot breakfast and with their spirits lifted, they sailed on down the twisting river, their hearts in their mouths, their blood pounding throughout their bodies as they sank deeper and deeper into the unknown. Eighty-five days later they would pull up at Rio Virgin, near Callville, Arizona, their trip over.

Goodman left them at the Uinta River junction July 2, and on August 28, only three days short of the end of the trip but with a terrible rapids facing them, the Howland brothers and Bill Dunn decided to strike out on foot. Their rations were nearly all gone, they were exhausted, and their spirits were at their lowest ebb. They climbed a cliff and disappeared from sight.

The 'No-Name' was sunk. So, the remaining members of the Powell Expedition beached the "Emma Dean" and climbed into the "Kitty" and "Maid" and bet their lives they would survive the rugged stretches of tumbling water ahead. Three days later they were safe. While Goodman lived, the other three were all killed by Indians. The remaining members lived to see their homes in the East.

When Powell returned to the East, he was proclaimed a national hero. So were the members of the expedition. Later on, Powell made another trip into the vast reaches of the Colorado River and Green River System.

Later On, Powell would become the head of the United States Geological Survey, and at the same time, the Director of the Bureau of Ethnology.

Powell, Wyoming was named after Major Powell. A reclamation camp set up as headquarters for the Shoshone Reclamation Project had been named Camp Colter. It was re-named for Powell in honor of his contribution in courage and exploration of the West.

First Camp of Powell Expedition Down Green River

GUNS AND GOLD

After the Union Pacific Railroad was built, the vast army of workers left. The small towns of Cheyenne, Laramie City, Rawlins Springs, Green River and Evanston which had mushroomed into existence, suffered badly as the payrolls diminished and they felt the deep bite of depression settle upon them.

In fact, the whole nation was desperately trying to dig its way out from under a depression. Even as the nation prepared for the celebration of its 100th birthday, great banking houses like Jay Cook and Company closed their doors. Beef prices were down, and people all over America were cast out of work as railroad construction nearly stopped, and industrial plants shut down. Bread lines appeared in Philadelphia where the Centennial Celebration was to be held.

Merchants and businessmen in Cheyenne knew there had to be a way to save their town, their territory, and their own personal fortunes. They yearned for a first class gold rush like those in Colorado and Montana. The only gold found in Wyoming, at South Pass, was not the hoped for bonanza, and because it was so far from Cheyenne, little of the glitter of gold and the business of outfitting miners attracted entrepreneurs.

Still, rumors of gold in the Big Horn mountains had been the subject of more than one conversation over the years. "The Lost Cabin" gold mine, or the story of it, sounded good to the Cheyenne businessmen. Over the years an occasional Indian would fish out a gold nugget found in the Black Hills to pay for trade items purchased at Fort Laramie.

The only trouble was that the Hills, as everyone called the Black Hills in those days, were inside the reservation set aside by the provisions of the Treaty of 1868. Also, part of the Big Horn region was controlled by Chief Washakie of the Shoshone Indians.

The merchants decided to do something about it, going to Chicago publicizing the fact that both the Big Horns and Black Hills were brimming over with gold and silver. They intended to form an association to hunt for the riches, and anyone wishing to join could come to Cheyenne in the spring of 1870 and be outfitted for the venture.

Only 127 men outfitted themselves in Cheyenne and took off towards the Big Horn country early that spring. When General Augur learned about it he argued with expedition leaders that the men should stay west of the Big Horn mountains and stay out of the Wind River Indian Reservation.

Gold Miners and Prospectors
Violate Indian Treaty

The Big Horn and Black Hills Mining Association got as far as Meeteetse in violation of the Indian Reservation when they were caught by the Army. They were fortunately kept from certain death as messages winking from one mountain to another by Indians proved the redmen knew they were there. The group returned to Cheyenne, torn by dissention and disgust, and with nothing to show for efforts except lots of publicity and an angry General Augur.

Shortly after this attempt by Cheyenneites, a group of Sioux City businessmen in Dakota Territory tried the same thing. They formed the Black Hills Mining and Exploring Association of Sioux City and like the Wyoming group, it was made up of many prominent businessmen. Once more the Army stepped in and halted any attempts to cross reservation and treaty lines.

Still, these attempts by men of substance and the newspaper stories about them, and the gold they figured was hidden in the Hills and the Big Horns, was heralded in the depression-ridden East. Also, gold miners with experience now looking for new bonanzas heard about the rumored gold in the Hills and began to trickle into Sioux City and Cheyenne.

Troops Called In

In 1872, a whole detachment of soldiers from Fort Randall in Dakota Territory had deserted to form another gold-seeking expedition in the Hills. The 1873 Dakota Territorial Legislative Assembly urged Congress to open up a part of the reservation for gold mining and white settlement.

President Grant and nearly all of his advisors did not view protection of Indian reservations as a proper military duty. So, when General Sheridan asked that rumors of gold in the Hills be settled once and for all a full-fledged military expedition into the region, complete with experienced geologists to check out the areas which might produce gold, the idea was quickly approved.

Expedition Dispatched

Lieutenant Colonel George Armstrong Custer and the entire Seventh Cavalry Regiment, a thousand man expedition, entered the Black Hills July 1, 1874. Two respected men with mining experience accompanied Custer. They were Horatio Nelson Ross and William T. McKay.

Entering the Hills from the North, the expedition scout Charlie Reynolds was dispatched

Lieutenant Colonel George Armstrong Custer

to Fort Laramie with a cautious message from Custer to General Sheridan that carried little hope for gold miners. Custer said in the report, "I have on my table forty or fifty small particles of gold in size averaging a small pin head," proving that not much gold had been found in over thirty days of prospecting. Even the official geologist for the expedition, Horace Newton Winchell, was not promoting the Hills; he added that he had not seen one particle of gold!

At the end of 1874, the Commissioner of Indian Affairs made his annual report to Congress. Based upon the fact that not one Indian skirmish took place while Custer's army traveled through the Hills, the Commissioner said, "The feeding process which has now continued for six years with the Sioux, has so far taken the fight out of them."

The Indian Affairs Commissioner went on to say that non-treaty Indians had not been able to get those Sioux on the Reservation to go to war, as he said, "...to risk the loss of their coffee, sugar, and beef in exchange for the hardships and perils of a campaign against soldiers."

Then, the Commissioner proudly said, "To have tamed this great and warlike nation down to this degree of submission by the issue of rations is in itself a demonstration of what has often been urged."

Brigadier General George Crook 1876— "Grey Fox In His Uniform Of The Big Horn"

Public clamor and public pressure mounted as newspapers carried more stories about gold that could be found in the Hills. With the Sioux quite docile, why not try to dig the gold and not distrub the Indians?

But, General Sheridan did not believe the Commissioner of Indian Affairs. He remembered, as did many soldiers, what the Commissioner had said following the Fetterman fight scarcely ten years earlier. The Commissioner had said in 1867 that scarcely 3,000 Indians lived in the whole Powder River-Black Hills region who were able to fight.

Indian Fighters Imported

So, Sheridan began to import and transfer good Indian fighters to the region. Men like Brigadier General George Crook, lately chasing Apache Indians in the southwest arrived at Fort Laramie. More troops came in and they were stationed at Forts D.A. Russell, Laramie, and Fetterman. Sheridan meant to be ready—just in case his suspicions about the Indian Affairs report came to pass.

Miners Rounded Up

Sheridan sent Crook into the Hills to round up miners now crossing into the region. Crook met with the miners who liked the wily and eccentric mule-riding general. They decided to follow Crook out of the Hills, and let the Army try once more to establish if gold could be found in quantities or let the government bargain with the Indians for mining rights.

A second expedition under Lieutenant Colonel R.I. Dodge slipped into the Hills in May 1875. W.P. Jenny and Henry Newton, two outstanding New York geologists went with the Dodge Expedition. Dodge even had a woman on the trip, masquerading as a soldier. She was Calamity Jane, otherwise known as Martha Jane Canary, a lady of dubious character who seemed more at home in a saloon than costumed in the uniform of a soldier. Dodge had her sent back to the guard house at Fort Laramie when he found her in uniform!

The New York geologists and Dodge agreed that farming would be a better occupation in the Hills than gold mining. Scout "California Joe" (Moses Milner) also agreed. He said, "There's gold from the grass roots down, but there's more gold from the grass roots up."

Newspapermen seized upon this statement and forgetting the last half, announced to the world that there was a fact, "Gold from the grass roots down!" And, the stampede for gold in the Black Hills was on.

Cheyenne began to feel the thrust of prospectors, miners, and soldiers arriving almost daily and business staged a revival. The only opposition to Cheyenne came from Sidney, Nebraska. East of Cheyenne, the Nebraska town vied for the oncoming mining business. Since Sidney was reached first by those traveling on the Union Pacific from the East where the main traffic came, there was no question in Cheyenne business circles that Sidney was a very serious business rival.

If Cheyenne wanted to be the place to outfit miners, then there would have to be a first class stageline leaving Cheyenne daily for the Hills. That would take the edge off the race between Cheyenne and Sidney for the bulk of the mining business. With the building of an iron bridge across the North Platte at Fort Laramie, part of the problem was solved.

Wyoming Territory had been asking for the bridge for several years, and the Army agreed, saying the bridge was necessary as many emigrants and others had lost their lives trying to ford the deep and swift-moving river over the years. More than once, Army troops had been thwarted in their efforts to take up the chase against Indians due to high water or quicksand. When the bridge was completed and ready for use in January 1876, organizers financing a stageline from Cheyenne to the Black Hills, were ready to move too.

Jack Gilmer, Monroe Salisbury, and M.H. Patrick started the Cheyenne and Black Hills Stage and Express line, and soon hired Luke Vorhees as their superintendent. In turn, Vorhees hired Walter Scott "Quick Shot" Davis to captain the shotgun guards needed to ride the top of the coaches acting as armed guards on gold shipments.

Then, Vorhees turned his efforts to hiring division agents, drivers, stock tenders, blacksmiths, and bringing in good teams of horses, new Concord coaches, as he set up stage stations along the proposed route from Cheyenne north to the Hills.

Indians Called To Washington

The government finally recognized that there was gold in the Hills, and that the Indians had to be called in for a council. But first they took Chief Spotted Trail and a delegation of other chiefs to Washington, D.C. in 1875 to meet with President Grant and Interior Secretary Columbus Delano. Both officials discussed their ideas for a new treaty, but, nothing concrete came from the trip. A second meeting was called in September at the Red Cloud Agency.

A government commission told the Indians gathered at the Red Cloud Agency that the Indians ought to bend to the needs of the government which was feeding them and that the Army just could not keep the miners out of the Hills. The Commissioners also told the Indians that the mineral wealth would be useless to the Indians, but once it was extracted, the Hills would be handed back to the Indians.

The Indian leaders knew the Army was trying hard to keep the miners out of their beloved Hills. They respected the Army for what it was trying to do, but they were angered at the idea that they were dependent upon white man for their food. They also wanted to know why the gold was considered useless to them.

No Agreement Reached

The commisssioners offered the Indians $400,000 a year until a top price of $6,000,000 was reached, all of which was to be paid in goods, beef and other trade items. The Indians countered this offer and asked for $70,000,000, breaking up the meeting. The commissioners went back to Washington to make their report, and the Indians went away angry.

Immediately after the meeting, hostile Indians began to raid lonely ranches and solitary mining operations. As the raids increased, President Grant ordered troops out of the Hills. The gate was now wide open, and the miners poured in with picks and shovels by their sides. They came on horseback, by shank's mare, in wagons, and riding on the coaches of the newly formed stage lines. Stage lines were coming now out of Sidney, Cheyenne, Yankton, and Pierre.

Indians Ordered to Reservation

Ten thousand people stormed into the Black Hills the winter of 1875-1876. At the same time the Commissioner of Indian Affairs, safe in Washington, D.C. was making another annual report to Congress. The report was again the product of a point of a view emanating from the East and was uniformed, singleminded and coated with superiority. The Commissioner said that a general Indian War could never occur in the United States again. He also demanded that any Indians off the reservation should return by January 31, 1876, or the Army, as he said it, "Would come and get them."

Indian War of 1876

The Indians did not go back to their reservations, and the Indian War of 1876 exploded contrary to all the pompus predictions and promises made by the Commissioner of Indian Affairs. Furthermore, unlawful trade with the Indians took place that winter during which hundreds of rifles and thousands of rounds of ammunition, much of which was superior to any the Army was issued, came into the hands of the Indians.

In March General Sheridan ordered General Crook to mount an expedition and move north into the Powder River country from Fort Fetterman. Riding his favorite grey mule, Crook led his thousand man column against Chief Crazy Horse and the Sioux, and various groups of Northern

145

Arapahoe and Northern Cheyenne on the Powder River. (Chakadee Wakoa). On March 17, just across the border into Montana, Colonel J.J. Reynolds hit a big encampment of Indians. Outnumbered, Reynolds was luckily saved from annihilation by the quick support thrown behind his cavalry attack by infantry units of Crook's command. With the weather ranging from zero to 26 degrees below zero, with a number of wounded men, and with his supply lines stretched to a breaking point, Crook wisely withdrew leaving Chief Crazy Horse the victor.

That was the opening gesture of the year-long war. General Sheridan drew extensive plans, with the focal point being the Wyoming-Montana border country where the Tongue, Little Big Horn, Rosebud, and Powder Rivers joined the Yellowstone River, the region the Indians seemed to like best because of good game, lots of grass and water, and abundant cover.

Following this war, Sheridan sent General John Gibbon southeast from Fort Ellis in Montana, while General A. H. Terry was to drive West from Fort Abraham Lincoln in the Dakotas, and then these two columns would meet General Crook marching north from Fort Fetterman. They were to rendezvous at the junction of the Powder and Yellowstone Rivers.

Crook engaged the enemy first on June 17 on the Rosebud River. Discovering the Indians in very large numbers, Crook's command came under attack by a superior force. Crook took his thousand man unit off the field of battle by withdrawing after inflicting a large number of losses upon the enemy. Crook lost nine men killed and over twenty wounded.

Crook knew his contact with the enemy was enough, if he were to complete the sweep that Sheridan had contemplated. Thus, secure with the knowledge that the enemy was in front, and not too far away, Crook withdrew to his temporary base located on Goose Creek at the present site of Sheridan, Wyoming.

Col. Custer Proceeds With 7th Cavalry

While Crook was fighting, Terry detached Lieutenant Colonel George Armstrong Custer with the entire 7th Cavalry Regiment and ordered him to proceed up the Rosebud River. Custer was to try to locate a large trail left behind a big movement of Indians which scouts had seen. While keeping south far enough so he and Crook, Gibbon and Terry could encircle the wily enemy and draw them into the pincer-like trap.

146

Parting on June 21, each commanding officer was intent on carrying out his share of the encirclement and ultimate trap. Custer moved fast since he was not encumbered by infantry. Within a few days his scouts reported a large movement of Indians, and without waiting to determine Gibbon, Terry, or Crook's position Custer struck the enemy.

First, Custer divided his forces and gave Major Marcus Reno command of Troops A, G, and M. Troop B was under the command of Captain McDougall and they guarded the supply train. Captain Frederick Benteen was commanding Troops H, D, and K. Custer, himself, took direct command of Troops C, E, F, I, and L.

Custer then moved north up the right side of the Little Big Horn. Reno was on Custer's left, and Benteen, even further to the left.

Reno made direct contact with the enemy the afternoon of June 25. He fought a desperate battle losing 18 men killed and accumulating 46 wounded men before he effected a river crossing to establish a defensive position on a hill overlooking the Little Big Horn. All the time, hordes of the enemy kept his command under constant attack.

Benteen and McDougall soon joined Reno building Reno's command strength to nearly 400 men. At nine p.m. that night, when the attacks lifted, Reno had his men dig rifle pits and build interior lines of communication while he sent water details down the hill to the nearby river. As the men worked at their rifle pits they could hear the defiant yelling and shrieking from a scalp dance being held by Indians not too far in the distance, but out of sight. At 2 a.m. more Indians delivered rifle fire upon Reno's command.

Benteen Under Attack

At 9 a.m. June 26 the enemy charged the hill on foot, and Benteen took command of the lines under the heaviest attack. Benteen not only helped beat off the attack, but personally led a charge that turned the tide.

Reno led a charge on the other side of the encircled command, running off Indians trying to kill or steal the horses of Troops D and K.

The last flurry and attack ended around noon on June 26. The Indians departed by twos and threes, slowly riding their horses away from the battlefield. Hope was high at this point that Custer was coming, and that was the reason why the Indians broke off their attack. In fact, all through the battle, the questions foremost in the

Buffalo Bill And Chief Sitting Bull

147

minds of the embattled soldiers was, where is Custer? Why hadn't he come to their aid?

The fact is, Custer was dead as was his entire command. The sole survivor was the personal mount of Captain Miles Keogh. "Commanche," as the fine horse was called, had been severly wounded, but was nursed back to health and lived until 1891 when he finally died at the age of 28 years.

All totaled, including Custer, Reno, and Benteen's men, the battle cost the Army 226 dead and 54 wounded. General Terry's men counted 197 dead on the field where Custer's command perished. It was by all counts, the most decisive loss the Army had absorbed during the Indian Wars on the Plains.

In his official report, General Sheridan said, "Precisely what was done by Custer's immediate command, subsequent to the moment when the rest of the regiment last saw him alive, has remained partly a matter of conjecture, no soldier or officer who rode with him into the valley of Little Big Horn having lived to tell the tale."

One thing the Custer defeat did was harden American attitudes about Indians. Nothing the Bureau of Indian Affairs, or the Commissioner of Indian Affairs could say for a long, long time would sway Americans. Nearly everyone in America was bent now upon crushing Indian resistance.

Crook Regroups Army

Crook finished out the rest of the summer and early fall of 1876 on the Big Horn and Yellowstone Expedition. He left Fort Laramie in July. Marching every day, constantly hounding his foe, Crook finally cornered enough Indians at one place to fight the Battle of Slim Buttes, north of the Black Hills on September 9. He marched 800 miles in ten weeks, and scattered the Indians out over a wide area. His command nearly perished at the end. Desperate from the lack of food and water, they shot and ate their horses and mules before stumbling into white settlements on the northern edges of the Black Hills near Belle Fourche on September 12, 1876.

A month later, the seemingly tireless Crook re-organized his command at Fort Fetterman in October. Then, with 11 companies of cavalry, 4 companies of artillery, and 11 companies of infantry Crook led his men north into the Powder River country once more on a winter campaign.

He gave command of the infantry and artillery to Colonel R.I. Dodge. The cavalry command was given to Colonel Ranald Mackenzie. Crook held over-all command.

After meeting with General Sheridan, Crook was ordered out to fight the winter battle. They both felt he could win a big battle by striking hard

at hostile Indians when they were in their winter quarters.

Using Arapahoe and Shoshone as scouts, Crook's column marched north from Fort Fetterman on November 14 across the snow covered frozen wastes into the Powder River country. A fierce blizzard halted the command for several days near the site of old Fort Connor, now called Cantonment Reno. With the temperature hovering around the freezing point all day each day, it slid below the freezing point each night. But, Crook crunched through the icy weather and snow, intent upon his task.

While at Cantonment Reno allowing his men to rest up and to build up a supply dump, Crook gave a talk to all the Indians scouting for his command. He said, "...all these vast plains, all these mountains and valleys would soon be filled with a pushing hard-working population, the game would be exterminated, domestic cattle would take its place, and the Indians must make up his mind, and make it up now, to live like the white man and at peace with him, or be wiped off the face of the earth. Peace, the white man wanted. War he was prepared for."

Mackenzie Battles Chief Dull Knife

On November 20, a scouting party reported a large village of Indians ahead. Camping on a fork of Crazy Woman Creek near the present site of Kaycee, Crook issued Colonel Mackenzie's cavalry with enough food and ammunition for 10 days, and sent him ahead. Mackenzie's cavalry effective fighting force was 1,100 men. A third of that was made up of Indian scouts including Major Frank North and his famed Pawnee Scouts.

All night long, dismounted, the cavalrymen slipped and slid over icy hills and draws as they stealthily approached the Indian camp. At dawn on November 25, they charged into the camp. As the morning mist lifted, they found themselves fighting a very large contingent of Northern Cheyenne Indians led by Chief Dull Knife.

Fighting in the red-walled canyon most of the day, Mackenzie finally won the battle while losing seven men dead and twenty-six men wounded. At least 50 Indians were killed and easily twice that number were wounded. One of the soldiers killed was Lieutenant John A. McKinney. A post was to be named in his memory in Wyoming in 1877.

The real victory was not in the battle's dead and wounded, but in the destruction of the village of 200 or more lodges and the confiscation of huge stacks of rifles and ammunition stored in the village. Tons of buffalo meat went up in flames and most of the enemy horses were killed or captured, leaving the Indians destitute in midwinter!

Mute evidence indicating that members of the village had fought Custer came to light as horses branded with 7C for the 7th Cavalry, saddles, canteens, uniform blouses, caps, and other paraphernalia bearing 7th Cavalry markings were found by the victorious soldiers. Letters were also found. They were from members of the 7th Cavalry. They were still sealed and ready for the first mail home to loved ones.

Crook's men and those of Mackenzie too, whatever their feelings about attacking a village, felt more than justified in their work that day as they dug through the camp and found more and more evidence that Dull Knife's warriors had helped administer the coup de grace to Custer and his command on the Little Big Horn.

The Dull Knife Battle was the end of an era. From now on, the nation would be solidly behind the Army and soon the soldier-Indian battles of any consequence would end on the Plains.

Luke Vorhees

"Trail to gold"

"Arose before six o'clock this morning, in order to breakfast and be ready for the stagecoach sharp at seven. One advantage of this early hour in April of 1877 in Cheyenne, Wyoming Territory, is the fact that the wind was not blowing: so the dust was not flying through the street in front of the Inter-Ocean Hotel, as it certainly *would* be, later in the day.

"I had been warned to limit my luggage, so I had by valise of work clothes, a gold pin and a shovel that had been highly recommended to me by the local hardware man the day before; and I chose to wear my new boots and heavy coat over my one suit of clothes.

"Promptly at 7:00 am, Luke Vorhees pulled up in front of the hotel with a flourish. He already had two passengers in the Concord coach, and there were three of us there ready to board—all bound for Deadwood and the fabulous Homestake gold mining strike. The coaches were colorful vehicles with their yellow bodies and red trim. They accommodated nine passengers on the inside with two seats facing forward and one against the back of the driver's perch facing to the rear. The driver was usually accompanied by an armed guard who sat beside him up front. Luke Vorhees, who was part owner of the Cheyenne and Black Hills Stage, Mail and Express, used three teams on the coach; so speed was kept at a maximum and the run was completed in less than five days. There was a luggage rack on the top and "boots," or holders, fore and aft so that there was room for many

things beside the luggage of the passengers. The stage driver brought many items for the station keepers along the trail, as well as the express and mail which was carried by contract.

Leaving the town of Cheyenne quickly behind and heading north we found that signs of settlement were soon very few and far between. The wind began to blow across the breaks, and in places the going was rough, with several small streams to be forded.

"The first night's stop was made at Horse Creek Ranch where supper was simple but generous, and accommodations were crowded.

"The next day, we settled into the routine and monotony of the ride. In this area there was no danger of bandits, Indians—friendly or marauding—were seldom seen, and the passengers had exchanged all necessary pleasantries by this time. Toward evening we approached Fort. Laramie, which was the most important station on the route. Everyone perked up to observe the new iron bridge across the North Platte which had just been built in 1875 and was quite the engineering feat of the territory.

"The night was spent at the Rustic Hotel just south of the military reserve, where we were able to purchase a fine meal for $.50. I spent some time in the sutler's store, which seemed well stocked for a frontier post. It, like most of the buildings of the Fort, was built of adobe, painted, and kept in good repair.

"The next day was a long, hard run to Hat

Creek and from there into Jenny's Stockade. We were now in the area of the holdups and bandits. The many canyons and broken terrain lent itself to the robber's advantage—however, they seldom bothered the stages going north because about all the loot they could hope for was the money and jewelry of the passengers—which was usually not a great deal. Frequently the run from Deadwood to Jenny's Stockade was made at night, but going the other way that week we set out during a beautiful sunny day in late April, and it was an inspiring trip. The very last of the snow was melting, in many places, the earliest spring flowers were beginning to bloom, everything was greening up, the air was fragrant, and the meadowlarks were singing.

"When we pulled into Deadwood after dark that night, it was as though we had entered into another world. The single street was crowded with man and mules. Music poured from the open doors of many saloons, along with loud voices, much laughter, and occasional cursing. Our progress through the stage stop was slow as men clustered around, but finally we were able to alight and claim our baggage. What next, I wondered, as I turned and looked down the crowded street of Deadwood? The end of the trail to gold!''

The above might well have been the account of the last lap of a young easterner's journey to Deadwood to join the last mad gold rush of the western frontier. This could have been any time during the period of 1875 to 1886, as the Deadwood-Black Hills Stage Lines operated these eleven years in spite of weather, bandits, and other competition to get the gold from the mines to the railroad to be carried to the outside world.

"Beef bonanza"

EPIC:

The only thing that had held cattlemen out of the vast Powder River regions was the Army attempting to enforce the Fort Laramie negotiated Treaty of 1868. Custer's famous defeat caused all signs of Indian appeasement to disappear. The voters of the nation were angry and the politicians in Congress reacted. The result was the passage of the Sioux Bill on February 28, 1877.

By this Act, Congress would no longer treat the Indians as foreign nations. Thus, ratification of any treaty with Indians by the U.S. Senate was no longer required. The Sioux Bill ordered the Sioux back to their reservations. If they refused to go, no food would be available to them and they would starve. In any event, the bill required the Army to round them up and drive them back to the reservations.

In effect, the public, the Congress, the Bureau of Indian Affairs, and the Army were tired of war in the summer and peace in the winter.

Sioux Chief Crazy Horse brought his Sioux warriors to their reservation in May 1877. The Northern Arapaho were awarded (at least temporarily) a portion of the Shoshoni Wind River Reservation the same year. Chief Joseph fought a losing battle across Idaho, Wyoming, and Montana in the famed attempt to move his Nez Pierce to friendlier Canada, but was finally forced to surrender in October 1877, short of his goal. The Northern Cheyenne fought their way north from the Indian Territory across Kansas in 1877 before finally agreeing to take refuge at Camp Robinson, Nebraska. Even then, they made another desperate stab at freedom and their desire for a reservation in the north before calling off their war in 1879.

Along the White River in Colorado, the Indian Agent had been trying to make farmers out of the Utes. He wanted them to live in cabins. But, the

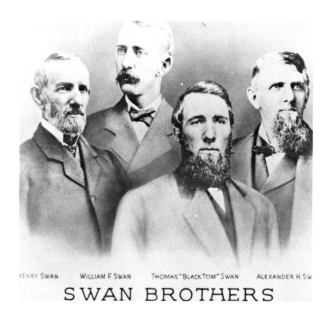

HENRY SWAN   WILLIAM F. SWAN   THOMAS "BLACK TOM" SWAN   ALEXANDER H. SW

SWAN BROTHERS

experiment was not successful and resulted in the Ute Indians fighting the only battle in their history against the Army. They lost the fight, but not before killing the Agent and over twenty of his helpers and soldiers. Many others were wounded. That action accounted for several thousand troops being rushed from Fort D.A. Russell at Cheyenne to Rawlins, then south into the Ute country in Colorado.

Swan Cattle Company Formed

For the most part, the Indian Wars were over by 1880 and the miles and miles of grasslands in northern Wyoming were wide open for cattlemen. Within weeks following the signing of the Sioux Bill, cattlemen drove their herds to the water and grass of the Powder River region. Then began the process establishing rights to this huge new tract of public domain. The vast opportunities led, now to a new twist in the cattle business.

Up to now, early settlers and Texas cowboys had been building the cattle business in the new territory of Wyoming. Now they were joined by the Lords and Lordlings. Lords were the foreign-born men of nobility or rich landowner classes from England, Ireland, Scotland and other nations in Europe who formed large companies, invested in cattle, and ran huge cattle-ranch combines. Lordlings were capitalists from the eastern United States who either joined the Lords or came West on their own and built their own cattle holdings. Generally speaking, all Lords and Lordlings were heirs to large fortunes or had access to large family fortunes. Further, as the possibility of profit became apparent, combined with availability of vast sums for capital collected

from Civil War profits in both the British Isles and the Eastern U.S. money began to pour into the territory. Absentee ownership of Wyoming ranches in the Cody country, the Platte Valley and the Powder River Valley. Scotch money established the vast Talland Cattle Company and the huge Swan Land and Cattle Company whose Chugwater based operations had probably the greatest impact on the whole American cattle business. The Swan company, or individuals connected with it, established the Omaha Stockyards and supported the vast meat packing industry there—an establishment which became the world's largest and the major market for Wyoming beef. It was Swan interest who established the Wyoming Hereford Ranch, near Cheyenne, sometimes called the center of the developemnt of the Hereford breed; and Swan interests were well-represented at Cheyenne's famous Cheyenne Club where Wyoming Stockgrowers gathered to literally direct the fate of the industry and the territory. It was on Swan properties that the first Wyoming rodeo was held and a Western tradition begun. The purpose of this event was to entertain 150 visiting Swan investors in order to acquaint them with the skills needed to acquaint them with the skills needed to manage huge herds of cattle.

Out of the array of titles and vast wealth from both sides of the Atlantic Ocean being invested in Wyoming and elsewhere in the Western America cow country grew the so-called cattle kingdom.

Books like *The Beef Bonanza, or, How To Get Rich On the Plain*, by General James S. Brisbin, U.S. Army, published in 1881 captured speculator's minds and pocketbooks.

Cattle Industry Thrives

Many other books were written regaling the enormous profits to be gained and the cattle business in Wyoming skyrocketed. The cattle boon was on and hundreds of thousands of dollars and English pounds fed the fires of the boom as the Lords and Lordlings invested in cattle in Wyoming.

The land was free, the demand for beef was never better, the economy of the nation was on the upswing and all one had to do, it was said, was turn a herd loose on the open range and let them reproduce.

The demand for beef was apparent. The European and English markets had been hard hit with disease and those beef-producing herds had been nearly decimated by anthrax. Besides, the U.S. Army had bought 12,000,000 pounds of beef in 1870 to feed reservation Indians. By 1880, the figure reached 40,000,000 pounds.

"Squatters"

Taking up land using the Homestead Act, the cowboy simply squatted on the land until it came up for sale. Then, he was the first man to have the right to buy the land. He could also resort to the Desert Land Act of 1877, under which all he had to do was pay 25 cents an acre for 640 acres of land that could not be cultivated without irrigation and occupy that land for three years. At the end of that period, he paid $1.00 per acre and it was his. He had to appear to get irrigation to the land, which was often accomplished in more than one case by simply plowing up a couple of furrows, calling them irrigation ditches, thus answering all inquiries from a "not-too-curious" government official.

Some cowboys appeared to comply with government acts, only to simply turn over the land to his bosses for a fee. Sometimes the cowboy filed on acreage that rested alongside each other by using different land acts, meaning he could take up more land with good water rights and good grazing.

It was easy to do in those days; and many cowboys took their fees and spent it all on a wild time in town on a Saturday night while the Lords and Lordlings nailed down title to land vital to their operation. The remainder of the land remained open range free to the use of all.

The cattle boom also enriched the pioneer stockmen and the Texas cowboy-turned-Wyoming rancher. Fighting for their very existence only a few years earlier, they now found willing partners or corporations asking them to throw in with them; and in due time they sat at the same corporate board meetings with the Lords and Lordlings.

Old cattlemen who had kept the calf tally on a shingle, whose only book had been a checkbook, and who knew the state of their affairs only by the balance or overdraft at the bank, found themselves sitting at directors' meetings where eastern capitalists deferred to their business experience and judgment. It was all so simple. The United States furnished the grass; the East, the capital; and the western stockman, the experience.

It was exhilarating exciting business!

Growth of Stockgrower's Association

The Wyoming Stock Growers' Association (WSGA) which had been organized by ten Laramie County Stockmen in 1873 now became a major social, political, and economic factor in the entire new territory. Instead of the 10 man organization of 1873, it now embraced business in a half dozen states, over 400 members, and 2,000,000 head of cattle.

The WSGA used their vast power in meeting their stated objectives: planning and regulating roundups, inspecting brands, and lobbying in the territorial legislature and the halls of Congress. Soon they had obtained the necessary legislation to virtually control the industry.

WSGA said a "maverick," or cattle without a mother and carrying no brand regardless of age, was to be branded by the roundup foreman with a WSGA brand, and then sold at an auction to the highest bidder. The money from the sale, after 10 per cent had been deducted for the foreman's work, was placed in the Association vaults to be used for operating expenses.

Brand Inspection

Other WSGA sponsored legislation gave the Association the right to inspect brands and outlawed the use of "running irons." Running irons were used to alter brands, thus making it possible to claim other people's cattle. Association inspectors were highly trained to indentify altered brands. They could recognize every legal brand and were present at every stockyard and cattle shipping point. Any animals not properly branded were seized and slaughtered. When the rightful owner could be identified he was reimbursed. The seller was usually arrested. A seller handling cattle with a brand other than his own had to prove ownership by presenting a bill of sale.

Another law protected Wyoming cattle from disease. Most significantly the Territorial government gave the Association legal power to enforce its own regulations. This contributed to much of the tension which soon swept the Cattle Kingdom.

In 1881, nearly 300,000 north-bound cattle crossed Wyoming. Upon inspection by WSGA officials, about 2,000 "mavericks" were cut out of these herds, branded with the WSGA brand, auctioned off, and a neat $76,000 went into WSGA coffers.

Detectives and Gunslingers

Rustling was a direct challenge to the kingdom and the WSGA could see it was getting worse. Even newspapermen wrote about it. Bill Nye, a Laramie writer, said in one of his columns that a man came up from Texas leading a one-eyed steer with one hand and carrying a branding iron in the other. Within a short time, Nye said, he had a herd of three hundred, "the ostensible progeny" of the old steer!

Surely Nye's wit drew a laugh, but rustling nevertheless, was a real problem. In defense of its interest, the WSGA put out hard-eyed, two-gun range detectives. Others were privately hired by individual stockgrowers. One of these was Tom Horn.

End of the Beef Bonanza

Rubbing elbows with the Lords and Lordlings in the Cheyenne Club a swank social palace set up by rich Cheyenne cattlemen gave pioneer Wyoming stock social standing. Until then, a man was as good as his word and his actions. Now, money not only helped his reputation, but gained him a foothold in the social standings generated by the Lords and Lordlings as Wyoming got its first real taste of class distinction.

All of this irked the small cowman and the cowboy. Both were bound by the regulations set by the WSGA. Regulations provided, for example, that one black ball cast against a man by WSGA officials and members meant no work for that man. Further, that man could not join the WSGA. He had no control over holding a roundup, he could not brand a maverick even if he found it, and was tied down to regulations he had not control over, and had not helped form. He particularly resented the fact that special legislation gave the WSGA regulations legal force.

The old time days of the camaraderie between boss and cowboy were fast disappearing. Always the Wyoming weather waited in the wings as the beef bonanza boomed. The day of reckoning was coming and a combination of poor prices, bad weather and rustling would result in that day of reckoning people now call the Johnson County War and the end of "the beef bonanza."

Johnson County Invasion Group—1892

155

LET US HAVE STATEHOOD

Construction Of The Capitol Building Cheyenne, Wy 1886

It took Wyoming Territory twenty-one years, eleven months, and two weeks to build enough political muscle to become the forty-fourth State in the Union. During that two-decade period the buffalo disappeared from the plains of Wyoming, three more railroads built their twin bands of iron in Wyoming, the Indian Wars came to an end, and the forces that were to shape the destiny of the raw state were forming—railroading, stockgrowing and mining.

From a population of only 8,014 in 1869, the population rose to 62,555 in 1890.

The territory survived the Panic of 1873 by buying into the Black Hills gold rush and becoming the main artery of supply, communication and transportation to the Black Hills as Cheyenne became the headquarters of the famed Cheyenne-Deadwood Stage Road. With the miners and prospectors pouring into Wyoming and then on to the Black Hills, it would not be long before minerals of one type or another would be discovered in Wyoming even if it was not gold. Coal was already being mined in the Rock Springs-Green River area, and iron, copper and other minerals made their appearance during the next few years.

So, while the rest of the nation was miserable, wallowing in the throes of a depression, gold was gushing south from Deadwood to Cheyenne on its way to the U.S. Mint. Some of it stayed in Cheyenne and in Wyoming where it joined the Army and Union Pacific payrolls helping Wyoming grow. (A parallel 100 years in the future would see Wyoming through an economic recession in the 1970's as a controlled mining boom helped keep Wyoming's unemployement figures of a low while unemployment soared elsewhere.)

The two decades saw the rise of the cattle and stock growers. Soon, a cattle based aristocracy emerged as more and more cattle were turned out on the vast ranges freed from Indian occupation as the result of Army campaigns.

Except for the Bates Battle which took place July 4, 1874 at the head of No Wood River at the southern end of the Big Horn Basin, no other fight ever took place between the Army and Indians in Northwest Wyoming. The huge Powder River east of the Big Horn Mountains country was the scene of a number of hard fought battles, skirmishes and fights, ending more or less, with the destruction of Dull Knife's village near Kaycee November 25, 1876. Other than troops being hauled from Forts Russell and Steele to help quell the Ute Indian uprising on the White River south of Rawlins in 1877, few reflections of the Indian with problems occured in Wyoming again.

Mining and Cattle

As a result, many Army posts were abandoned during that twenty year period. In 1890, Fort Laramie was sold at auction. Both Forts Fetterman and Sanders closed down in 1882 and Fort Steele saw its last troops in 1886. While Fort McKinney (what is now Buffalo) ceased as a military post in 1894, it was destined to become the Wyoming Solders' and Sailors' Home in June 1903. Camp Stambaugh, in Fremont County, was created in 1870 and abandoned in 1878.

One new post which was created during this period, however, when coal miners, following the leadership of the Knights of Labor in Rock Springs killed 27 Chinese and wounded 15 in labor riots. Maddened at the low wages being paid them, white miners were taking their fury out on the docile Chinese who were willing to accept the low wages. Troops called in to establish martial law were stationed at Camp Pilot Butte in 1885. That post was abandoned in 1899.

Near Lander a second new post, Fort Augur was established in 1869. The name of the post was later changed to Camp Brown and finally moved to the present site of Fort Washakie in the heart of the Wind River Indian Reservation. Actual military occupation of the post ended in 1909, but as Agency Headquarters for the Shoshone and Arapaho Indians, 'it is still called Fort Washakie.

During the period from 1870 to 1890, the Union Pacific Railroad was not only busy developing its coal mines, but the line was leasing hundreds of acres of land it had gained control of, through land grants, extended to support the building of the road to the booming cattle industry. Cattle raised in Wyoming had to be shipped to market and that was the business of the railroad.

Early Wyoming Industry

The Union Pacific was also re-locating sections of tracks, becoming involved in mining ventures, and helping to develop the territory as a whole. One example was the famous ''Rawlins Red'' paint mine which was located near Rawlins. By 1873, the paint, which was found to be an excellent rust preventative, was being used by the railroad on its own bridges, cars, and structures. A little later, ''Rawlins Red'' helped cover the world famous Brooklyn Bridge, thanks to the promotion by the Railroad.

Working closely with the Commissioner of Immigration, a Wyoming Territorial office created in 1872 to bring more traffic and investors to Wyoming, the Union Pacific joined hands with that early-day ''travel commissioner'' produced promotional maps. Those maps were widely circulated and encouraged travel in Wyoming to visit health spas, hunt for big game, fish the unlimited waters of the area, invest in the territorial agricultural, timber, mining, and business ventures. The railroad map issued in 1879 spoke directly to the subject: '' THE UNION PACIFIC,ITS BRANCHES AND CONNECTING LINES, The only lines across the Rocky Mountains, through the Great Mineral, Pastoral, and Agricultural Belts, to the finest Health and Pleasure, Hunting and Fishing Resorts on the Globe, and THE ONLY PERFECT ROUTE FOR TRAVEL ROUND THE WORLD.''

Early Scientists in Wyoming

Among those who used the railroad to Wyoming Territory in 1878 was a distinguished galaxy of famed world scientists led by Henry Draper, the well known American astronomer. It had been determined that a railroad stop only a few miles from Rawlins called Separation was the exact center of totality of the predicted 1878 solar eclipse. Draper led a collection of widely acclaimed scientists from Great Britain, France, Prussia, Russia and other nations to Wyoming to observe the celestial event. Thomas Alva Edison, the great American inventive genius, joined the expedition.

The U.S. Naval Observatory and U.S. Navy dispatched a naval officer, Captain W. T. Sampson, to help Draper and to take charge of the affair. A few years later Sampson would command the naval units at Santiago in a great U.S. sea victory.

When the eclipse was over, most of the scientists headed home, Edison, however, stayed on to take advantage of the hunting and fishing in the area. Edison hired Tom Sun, a rancher and big game outfitter who lived near Independence Rock to guide him on a fishing and hunting trip in the mountains south of Rawlins near Battle Lake. There, having snapped a bamboo fishing rod, Edison is supposed to have conceived the idea of using bamboo as part of his electric light, yet to be invented.

The growing cattle industry brought an unusual social development during this period. The wealth represented by the absentee ownership led to the development of a society quite unlike the Spartan life typical on most frontiers. Many of the absentee owners built huge homes on their holdings. Often these homes were used only during the summer and the fall hunting seasons— the only times the owners actually visited their holdings. All the trappings of great wealth accompanied them. Maids and butlers and extravagent entertainment became a part of the frontier. This style of life helped establish the name Cattle Kingdom as a popular press description of Wyoming.

Era of the "Cattle Barons"

Perhaps the most famous example of the opulent life style was exhibited by Moreton and Richard Frewin, who unlike many, at least spent most of their time in Wyoming. Englishmen by birth, they found themselves traveling over Wyoming in the fall of 1879, enjoying the hunting and fishing in the vicinity of Fort Washakie. Crossing the Big Horns late that fall, they saw the glory of the Powder River country and immediately made extensive plans to build a ranching operation there.

Richard stayed behind near modern Kaycee while Moreton, the best promoter of the two, traveled back to Great Britain to raise money to build the ranching empire the two brothers contemplated.

By 1880, the famous Powder River Ranch, Ltd., using the 76 brand had been established and named "Sussex" after the county the Frewins came from in England. The ranch was 30 miles wide and 90 miles long, By 1882 the Frewin brothers were running 40,000 head of cattle.

Moreton Frewin, in his many trips back and forth to Great Britain, had become well acquainted in New York. There he met and married into the financially powerful Jerome family. His wife's sister had married Lord Randolph Churchhill, the father of Winston Churchhill. Consequently, Moreton became the uncle of Winston Churchhill.

Eventually Moreton Frewin built his bride an English Tudor-styled ranch house at Sussex. The house, a mansion by any standards, was a local attraction for years. Fully staffed with butlers, maids, it even had a musicians' gallery above the main dining room so that soft dinner music could be played while Moreton and his bride entertained an international set of guests. The guests came to Wyoming to hunt and fish and enjoy the company of each other amidst the outstanding scenery that the ranch property afforded the visitors.

Atlas Theatre

158

The local people came to call the house "Frewin's Castle." When the cattle business suffered one bad piece of luck after another, the financial bubble burst not only for the Frewin estate but across the cattle kingdon. Today, not one vestige of "Frewin's Castle" remains. When the big building was vacated by the ruined family, local ranchers and people from small communities in the area came and stripped the "Castle" of its stairwells, door frames, doors, glass, floors and all the elegant components of the house that had been made as far away as Chicago, and hauled to Sussex. Many of the people bought portions of the house for use in furbishing their own ranch houses.

As a part of the cattle aristocracy, the story of the Frewin's rise and fall, while extraordianary in the size of the ranch, the people who built it, and the glitter of its guests, remains a classic example of the two decades in the cattle industry in the territory between 1870 and 1890.

More glitter was being added to Cheyenne as the "Kingdom" grew. Huge mansions were built on Ferguson (now Carey) avenue. Many cattlemen did as the Frewins did and built second homes in the city to accommodate them when business brought them to town. Reflecting the growing social sophistication was the swank Cheyenne Opera House built in 1882, which hosted many national and international artists. One of those entertaining artists was Lily Langtry. She played "Pygmalion" in Cheyenne before standing room only audiences. "The Jersey Lily" as she was known arrived in Cheyenne in her own special railroad car in 1884.

Cheyenne Club Formed

During this period the elegant Cheyenne Club, in the heart of the city, blossomed as a world famous operation. Serving cattle barons and travelers from around the world, the Club became internationally famous as a frontier outpost of cultured living. The wealthy patrons of the Club gathered periodically and it became well-known that the Cheyenne Club was the center of decision making for the "Cattle Kingdom." Discussions at the Club were soon echoed in the halls of the legislature and even on the floors of both houses of Congress.

Cheyenne also played host to many of the famed characters of Western lore. Wild Bill Hickcock married a world famous woman equestrian in Cheyenne March 5, 1876 at the Methodist Episcopal Church. Hickcock's bride was Agnes Lake Thatcher and she stayed in Cheyenne that spring and summer while her new husband went

Cheyenne Club, Cheyenne, WY 1880

William "Buffalo Bill" Cody

to Deadwood to seek his fortune. Instead, Hickcock met his death from a six shooter held by assasin Jack McCall. Before Hickcock left Cheyenne, he had a medical examination at Camp Carlin and found he was suffering from an advanced stage of glaucoma in the left eye, a fact which no doubt led to his limited gun play both in Cheyenne and in Deadwood.

Wyatt Earp and his brother Virgil witnessed a gun fight between Jim Levy and Charley Harrison in the spring of 1877 from the porch of the Dyer House Hotel on 16th Street. The two Earps had spent the winter in Deadwood, and that spring were hired to ride shotgun guard on a spring cleanup of gold coming to Cheyenne from Deadwood.

Buffalo Bill Cody's Wild West

A few years later Buffalo Bill Cody held his famous "Wild West" show in Cheyenne just prior to leaving for Europe. Cody was heading to England first where he would pay for the worldwide crowds coming to England to celebrate the Diamond Jubilee in honor of Queen Victoria. Buffalo Bill performed before most of the crowned heads of Europe and brought back priceless gem-encrusted watches and other personal gifts given him by the enthroned monarchs. Unfortunately he was paid very little cash for the expensive command performances and the show floundered financially.

CB&Q Railroad Pushes Cheyenne

Meanwhile, the Kansas Pacific Railroad came into Denver, and a subsidiary line called the Denver Pacific was built from Cheyenne to Denver in 1869-1870. Seven years later, the Union Pacific built another line from Cheyenne to Denver calling it the Colorado Central Railroad.

North of Cheyenne the Fremont-Elkhorn and Missouri Valley Railroad pushed through Douglas to Casper, being completed to that point May 15, 1888. This line picked up much of the cattle business in that area. The residents of Laramie County and Cheyenne, always on the alert for business, took a look at the future and decided to bond themselves to have a railroad built from Cheyenne north to connect with the FE & M.V.R.R. The Union Pacific joined in the venture, with the results culminating in the Cheyenne and Northern Railroad which ran to the North Platte

Valley in 1887, and later to Orin Junction just below Douglas.

A few years later the Cheyenne and Northern became known as the Colorado and Southern Railway and was later a part of the Chicago, Burlington and Quincy Railroad system. The CB&Q also built a new line from Cheyenne south to Fort Collins. The C.B.&Q.R.R. came into Cheyenne in 1887 from Sterling, Colorado building a fine railway station. Just the year before, the Union Pacific completed their huge Romanesque style sandstone station at the south end of Cheyenne's Capitol Avenue.

More Counties Created

County government was also growing during the two decades. In addition to Laramie, Sweetwater, Albany, Carbon and Unita counties, eight more counties were created. Those first five counties divided the new territory into long retangular slices of land running north and south in length.

The Fourth Territorial Legislative session created Pease and Crook counties in December of 1875. Crook was located in the far northeastern corner of the territory and was created from the northern portions of Albany and Laramie counties. Pease County (which became Johnson County on December 13, 1879) was created from the northern extremities of Sweetwater and Carbon counties. Uinta County gave up many acres to form Yellowstone Park in 1872.

In 1884, Sweetwater County relinquished a major share of its northern land area to Fremont County. Four years later in 1888 the Tenth Territorial Legislative Assembly created Converse, Natrona, and Sheridan counties. In 1890, just before Wyoming was admitted to the Union, two more counties were added, Big Horn and Weston, making a total of thirteen counties.

The lawmakers of the first nine territorial legislative sessions had been meeting in various Cheyenne buildings. When they convened in Cheyenne on January 10, 1888, for the Tenth Session, they were able to meet for the first time in their own Capitol Building built from an appropriation by the Ninth Legislative session in 1886. It was located at the north end of Capitol Avenue creating a broad vista from the imposing U.P. depot to the classic capitol building.

As was noted in Chapter 13, S.M. Curran of Carbon County was the only man who had previous legislative experience when the First Territorial Legislature met. Few delegates between 1869 and 1890 served at more than one session. An exception was W. H. Holliday of Albany County who served as a House member in the 1873 Third session and then was a Council member from Albany County in the 4th, 5th, 6th, 8th and 10th sessions. He served as President of the Council in the 1884, 8th session.

Most of the members of the Council or House seemed to be content to serve only one term. The long traveling distance to Cheyenne may have been one reason. Also, legislative duties were

Francis E. Warren

Territorial Governor following the death of William Hale. Warren held that post from February 28, 1885 until November 11, 1886. In 1889, President Harrison appointed him Governor and so, for a second time, Warren served as Territorial Governor. On October 11, 1890 Warren became Wyoming's first State Governor, but served only until November 24, 1890 when he served as second United States Senator from Wyoming.

This man was a rancher, banker, real estate broker, and merchant. He served in the United States Senate for 37 years and 4 days, the longest term of service in the U.S. Senate until 1964 when his record was surpassed by that of Arizona Senator Carl Hayden. Warren held tightly to the chairmanship reins of the vital Appropriations Committee from 1921 until the day he died and was also chairman at one time of the powerful Military Affairs Committee.

Wyoming Obtains Statehood

The Woman Suffrage Act was one of the most controversial bills passed by the Territorial Legislature. A repeal of the bill had passed the House and the Council, but by only one vote in the Council. That one vote margin gave the Territorial Governor the right to veto the repeal which Governor Campbell soon did and Wyoming retained the claim to be the first government in the world to extend the vote to women. Then when Wyoming applied for statehood it was Congressional Delegate Carey who summed up the virtures of the territory before the United States House of Representatives on March 26, 1890. Carey had a reputation for reliability among House members and they listened closely as Carey spoke on H.R. 982, the Bill for Wyoming Statehood.

Carey reeled off facts and figures relating to the population (which had barely passed the minimum of 60,000) and the mineral wealth of the area emphasizing coal resources. At one point, when discussing irrigation in Wyoming, Carey said, "That great irrigable lands in Wyoming, which become enourmously productive, are equal in extent to the combined irrigated areas of Egypt and Italy, which supports 10,000,000 people."

Whether that conjured up ideas of a Nile Valley or a Rome is doubtful, but it goes a long way to demonstrate the detailed research that Carey had undertaken in preparation for the speech. Carey made sure that the members understood Wyoming was the home of over 3,000,000 head of cattle, sheep, and horses, as well as bountiful timber and water resources.

tiring and dull and required more time than those men could give from their newly built business ventures. The fact that few ever served more than one session may have been good for Wyoming, since by the time Wyoming became a state well over 300 men from Wyoming Territory had served in either the House or Council. The State of Wyoming was able to draw upon many of these men for further service if not in the House or Senate as other elective office holders, or as members of boards and commissions.

One of those men, Willis Van Devanter, a lawyer from Cheyenne who had served in the Tenth Territorial Legislature had also served as Chief Justice of the Territorial Supreme Court. He served a brief term as Chief Justice of the Wyoming State Supreme Court and later became an Associate justice of the United States Supreme Court serving from December 16, 1910 until he resigned June 2, 1937.

Francis Warren Comes to Wyoming

Francis Emory Warren came to Wyoming Territory from Massàchusetts in 1868 and quickly made his mark as an astute businessman. Warren worked tirelessly on behalf of the new territory he adopted as his home. In 1873 Warren served as president of the Territorial Council, the beginning of a long and colorful career. In 1876 he was appointed Territorial Treasurer and held the office twice, served a second term in the Council and the next year was elected Mayor of Cheyenne. President Arthur appointed Warren as the 5th

He pointed out Wyoming's educational system was above average as the citizens held high the ideal of a sound education for all children.

Carey told the House about the new University of Wyoming, the insane asylum at Evanston, the new capitol building, mentioning that a new penitentiary was then under construction at Rawlins. (It opened its doors December 14, 1901.)

Carey told of the Territorial veterinary department, the water department, mineral department, fish hatchery, and the fact new counties were being born continually.

He stressed the stability of the economy pointing out that of the nine national banks in Wyoming, none had closed their doors in any financial crisis and only four of the eleven private banks had failed. He pointed out that in 1869 there was only $150,000 in banking capitol in Wyoming and that in 1890, that figure stood well over $5,000,000.

He pointed out that there was $230,000 in the treasury and the Territory had property valued at $2,000,000. "Open the books of some of the States and make a better showing," Carey challenged.

He noted that there was then 900 miles of railroad track in Wyoming mentioning the Union Pacific which crossed the state from East to West, and the Chicago, Burlington and Quincy, the Chicago Northwestern and, of course, the Laramie County-bonded Cheyenne and Northern with its new 125 miles of track.

Carey summed up his speech saying, "Many of yours are old and powerful states. Wyoming, young and enterprising, rich in resources, with Western ambition and strength, will hasten to overtake you and at your side bear a State's share of the burdens and responsibilities of the Republic. Wyoming, full of energy, full of hope, patient until well prepared with the constitution of her own making, now asks you, the Representatives of the American people, the choicest gift and blessing in your power to bestow, to be forever incorporated into the Union of States."

The Wyoming Statehood Bill, H.R. 982, 51st Congress, 1st Session passed the House on March 26, 1890. On June 27, 1890 the bill passed the Senate. On July 10, 1890 President Benjamin Harrison signed the bill admitting Wyoming as the 44th State in the Union. The "Harrison Connection" remained through the 1960's as his grandson, William Henry Harrison served as Wyoming's lone Congressman for six terms.

Joseph Maull Carey

VIGNETTE:

THE IRREPRESSIBLE CONFLICT:
"The Johnson County War"

The summer of 1886 in Wyoming was blistering hot and dry. The overstocked and overgrazed range had been burned under the hot summer sun.

The winter was going to be rough thought the members of the Wyoming Stock Growers Association. When the first blizzard blew in and was soon followed by a second titanic snow storm; their worst fears were confirmed.

The usual chinook arrived from the southwest and the warm wind sliced into the snowbanks, melting the drifted snow and ice, into runoff water. But the chinook did not last long enough to clear away all the snow and ice. Instead, another polar blast carried in more winter and more snow and that storm was succeeded by another equally paralyzing storm. The temperature sank lower, freezing streams, stockponds, and standing water into solid crusts of ice, clamping an icy lid down on any hope stock growers might have had of their cattle reaching what little feed had been left from the summer before.

When a very late spring did arrive, the C.Y. Ranch, owned by Territorial Congressional Delegate Joseph M. Carey found only 3,300 calves to brand. The year before they had branded 9,800. The 101 Ranch in Crook County reported they had lost 11,900 cattle of their 12,000 cattle. West of Cheyenne, in the Saratoga Valley, the losses reported to the WSGA offices in the capitol city amounted to 66 per cent. In the Powder River region, WSGA members found their losses as high as 50 percent. Even the WSGA members ranching in the Big Horn Basin took a beating and Otto Franc, reported that his huge German financed Pitchfork operation took looses upwards of 40 percent.

Ranchers Wiped Out

Many ranchers were completely wiped out, some were so badly hit they had to sell out, and the remaining members who stuck it out headed back to the wagon, taking up a notch in their belts, and hoping lenient bankers would help them over the crisis. The situation was complicated by changing economic conditions. Interest rates were at an all time high and cattle prices at an all time low. Many of the cattle lost in the violent winter had been purchased with borrowed money at 12 - 36%. Further the winter disaster brought a realization that the heavily grazed range would no longer support cattle through the winter. The experience of winter feeding forced many out of business in the years which followed.

Rustling Ran High

It was a bitter pill to swallow especially with the rustling that had evidently been going on. The rustling had not been the type where a herd is stampeded and taken to market, but rather, the kind where trusted ranch hands whittled daily at neighbors herds, taking only a few at a time. The WSGA hired range detectives for many years who apprehended many cattle and horse thieves. The threat of detection kept many would-be rustlers from casting a loop at cattle not his own.

There was little cash following the raging winter of 1886-1887, and membership in the WSGA dwindled. Dues where hard to collect and detectives could no longer be paid. Rustling continued even after the snows had decimated herds.

The vast cattle industry also faced another problem. With so much absentee ownership most ranch operations were entrusted to local foreman. Some of these foremen were dishonest and stole cattle. Others reported herd sizes on "book count," a usually inflated figure designed to make the operation appear more successful than in reality. Blaming rustlers and weather losses became a popular method of reconciling book counts with the smaller numbers actually reaching market. Combined with an increasingly less productive range, the appearance of increasing numbers of homesteaders who fenced the formerly open range, the unfavorable economic conditions, and the winter disaster, as well as actual rustling, it is not surprising that tension grew on the range.

The influx of settlers and farmers was changing the political climate. Impartial juries became difficult to find as growing resentment of the WSGA power appeared across the territory. The WSGA Secretary said in 1887, "In the present condition of the Association treasury, it is absolutely impossible for us to undertake any detective work, even if it were deemed advisable to do so. We have found from bitter experience that wherever evidence of cattle stealing is obtained through Association inspectors or detectives, it is almost impossible to obtain a conviction in the courts."

Cases against rustlers were hard to get into court and once there the rustlers were often turned loose by jurors sympathetic to the cause of the "little man" against the powerful WSGA. Association Secretary Thomas Sturgis wrote one WSGA rancher,

> It is very difficult to get an indictment from a grand jury with pretty definite evidence as to the guilt of the party charged with stealing cattle. Unfortunately, it is almost completely useless to bring matters to the court even after an indictment has been obtained and the evidence pretty well gathered. There seems to be a morbid sympathy with cattle thieves both on the bench and in the jury room...

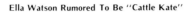
Ella Watson Rumored To Be "Cattle Kate"

Stock Thieves Stalked

That the WSGA may have had a legitimate complaint is illustrated by the story of Jack Cooper, a cowboy working on a ranch near the Searight Ranch at Alcova. Over a short time, less than a year, evidence and eye-witnesses reported that Cooper managed to change the "H" brand of the Searight's into a "Spear H," and the famed "Goose Egg oval" brand into connected ovals naming the brand "The Spectacles." Cooper was thought to have rustled 1,100 head of cattle, but when brought into court, after a two year wait, he was freed by Judge Samuel T. Corn for lack of evidence. Cooper lived only another year when he was mysteriously shot and killed.

Malcom Campbell, one of Wyoming's famed lawmen of the period, said in 1888, "We soon found that with jury packing, perjury, alibis and general rottenness encountered in cattle stealing cases it was impossible to convict a thief. In Johnson County alone, out of 180 indictments in four years, only one conviction had been secured." Sheriff Campbell went on to say that the Powder River country seemed to be filling up with bad men. Many of those bad men, the Sherifff pointed out, were going around in gangs threatening the small as well as the big ranchers. There were those WSGA members who figured that the bad men had probably drifted south out of Montana in 1884 on the heels of the wholesale roundup of bad men the Montana Stock Growers Association made that year. The cattlemen of Montana had hunted down and hanged 23 stock thieves in 1884.

While there was tension between the big cattlemen of the WSGA and the small cattlemen, this has been overplayed as a cause of the conflict. The WSGA did not always hate the homesteader or "squatter" as he was called. Many of the sons and daughters of the WSGA members were marrying into those homesteader families and a number of homesteaders had grown into full-fledged WSGA members themselves.

The Tragedy of Ella Watson

Not long after Cooper died on the Sweetwater range, six ranchers dropped in on Ella Watson and her boyfriend, Jim Averell. The six men took the woman and man in a buckboard to a canyon nearby and hanged them as cattle thieves.

For a long time, the hangmen claimed, Ella Watson, sometimes referred to as "Cattle Kate," had received stolen cattle in lieu of payment for liquor and entertainment. She and her partner, Averell, then branded them with Ella Watson's brand and sold them across the Wyoming borders or elsewhere.

Cattlemen, unsuccessful in trying to bring these two to court, eventually took justice into their own hands. Their brand of justice was commonly called "lynch law."

The WSGA members were unhappy about lack of convictions in the courts, but when those six hangmen stood before a grand jury in Rawlins for their deed, they also were turned loose for lack of evidence! Some claimed that Ella Watson was innocent and Jim Averell only owned a milk cow or two. But, by the time that side of the story had been told, Ella and Jim were dead and buried.

166

It was cause for lots of comment because a woman had been hanged, and above all else, she was hanged in the territory which had granted women the right to vote, sit on juries and hold office. One wag said he'd guessed if women had all those rights, they could be hanged too. The more concerned citizens did not like it though and some newspaperman took up the subject further fanning the flames of controversy across the state.

In Laramie, newspaperman J.H. Hayford reported that there was a war then in progress b' veen the cattle kings and the small ranchers pointing out that it looked like "an irrepressible conflict" was in the making.

Hayford's words were merely echoes of what WSGA members were saying at their annual convention that same year. "...Stealing of stock on the range are becoming so open and nortorious that concerted action of some kind must be taken. And strong measures resorted to, unless we are to give up the fight entirely and surrender to the 'rustlers'."

The next year Wyoming Territory was admitted to statehood, but little was done to relieve the tension. However, more and more stories sifting out of the Powder River area pointed an accusing finger at Sherriff "Red" Angus in Buffalo as being an accomplice to the rustler, if not actually a rustler himself. The Frewin brothers, Sir Horace Plunkett, an Irish lord with the NH and EK cattle ranches and the huge Bar C ranch also became targets of the bands of rustlers.

Sam Moore, Two Bar Range Foreman
Hackamore Rope Made By Tom Horn.

More Hangings Conducted

Tom Waggoner, who raised horses in Weston County, was known to be friendly with the large ranchers. In June 1891, a party of men rode up to his ranch, arrested him in the presence of his wife and three children and promptly hanged him from the limb of a cottonwood tree less than three miles from the ranchhouse. Sheriff Campbell claimed the rustler gangs used the Waggoner hanging as a warning to other small ranchers to stay away from the big ranchers.

In November 1891 two men, small ranchers, John Tisdale and O.E. "Ranger" Jones, were dry gulched, that is shot and killed by an assasin or assasins. The killings took place a few miles out of Buffalo in Johnson County and both killings were blamed on the big stockmen. That story was never proved nor did anyone ever confess to the dual murders, although strong tradition places the blame on Frank Canton held to be a hired gun for the big stockgrower interests. Emotional discriptions of the killings spread across the state.

Whatever the unknown truth, the killings inflamed the state as the newspapers took sides and letters to the editor carried accusations on both sides of the issue. As news editor Hayford had said, the "irrepressible conflict" was in progress.

In the spring of 1892, northern non-WSGA ranchers decided to hold their spring roundup, in defiance of the law, a month ahead of the legal roundup time. The news triggered firebrand members of the WSGA into action, led by a rancher named Major Frank Wolcott, a Kentuckian, who camed to Wyoming following the Civil War.

Wolcott was appointed Territorial Receiver of Lands in 1869 and from 1871 to 1873 had been the Territorial U.S. Marshall. By 1890, the peppery Wolcott had established the V R Ranch near Glenrock.

Another firebrand WSGA member was W.C. "Billy" Irvine, a pioneer cattleman of Wyoming, who had worked his way from cowboy to manager of several of the bigger Wyoming ranches. Billy Irvine was testy and heartily agreed when Major Wolcott suggested a "hanging tree."

Years later Irvine wrote Grace Raymond Hebard, Wyoming historian about his part in the Johnson County War. He said that after many cases of blantant cattle rustling had been taken to court but discharged for one reason or another,

"Something had to be done. We had resorted to the laws of our State time and time again, spending thousands and hundreds of thousands of dollars...It is the history of the world that where the laws of a country do not protect the citizens, they eventually arise and protect themselves. This was the condition of our State in 1892. Those of us who took part in said expedition have no apologies to make, never had, and never shall have the slightest remorse of conscience. On the contrary, we feel proud of our connection with it, and feel that we did the State a service."

Killing of Nate Champion

With those words, Billy Irvine summed up the feeling of WSGA members. The feeling that they did the "State a service" still can be found alive in Wyoming today.

On the other hand, there were many innocent small ranchers and businessmen who unwillingly got caught up in the range action.

Wolcott and Billy Irvine brought in twenty-five hired gunmen from Texas and organized the raid. Some of them had worn the tin stars of the Texas Rangers or had been other types of law officers. Another twenty-five men, all WSGA members, joined the hired guns from Texas. Not one working cowboy was asked to help. The owners and bosses felt it was their personal battle, not that of their hired hands.

Riding a train north from Cheyenne, the fifty men were joined by two newspapermen and several other interested men. The "regulators" as they called themselves de-trained in the Casper stockyards at dawn April 5, 1892. Unloading their horses and wagon, the invasion got underway shortly after dawn.

They had drawn up a list of 70 men who they meant to kill or drive out of Wyoming. Their plan was to sweep north to Buffalo cutting telegraph wires ahead, thus stopping any advance warning, and then descend upon Buffalo. There they were to take as many of the 70 as possible, assuring the citizens of Buffalo they meant no harm to the town, or their personal property.

It just did not work the way they planned it. Snow and sleet delayed them and discouraged the thin blooded Texans.

On April 9, the group surprised Nick Ray and Nate Champion in a cabin on the middle fork of the Powder River at the K C Ranch. Before the day ended, both Ray and Champion were killed. While the regulators were trying to pry Ray and Champion out into the open for a good shot at them, several Johnson County residents saw or heard what was going on, and raised the alarm in Buffalo. Sheriff Angus raised a posse and headed with all possible speed to the K C Ranch. But, by the time Angus and his posse arrived, the regulators had killed Ray and set fire to the cabin forcing Champion into the open and killing him. They had then moved on to the T A Ranch. They went by a different road than the one the posse was traveling, so the posse missed meeting the invaders. At the TA Ranch the invaders got word of the posse and hastily constructed fortifications.

Returning to Buffalo, Angus built up a bigger posse, mustered a defense force for Buffalo, and got on the trail for the T A Ranch where they found Wolcott, Irvine and Company. The Buffalo posse immediately besieged the ranch buildings and the invaders were pinned down by long range rifle fire. They did, however, get word out to Cheyenne friends.

In Cheyenne, Dr. Amos Barber, the Acting Governor found himself in a touchy situation. Barber first wired the President of the United States asking that Wolcott and Company be given aid from Colonel J. J. Van Horn, commandant of Fort McKinney located at Buffalo. He then wired Senator Warren, Senator Carey and Congressman Clarence D. Clark for advice.

Congress Acts to Halt Range War

The Wyoming Congressional Delegation in Washington followed up the Barber's wires to the President calling upon the Chief Executive personally to tell him as much of the tale of the invasion of Johnson County as they knew. The President then wired Colonel J. J. Van Horn, directing the colonel to proceed with all haste to the T A Ranch and stop the war.

Colonel Van Horn felt the Johnson County ranchers, not Wolcott and his men, were right, but he carried out his orders and arrived at the T A Ranch on April 13. There he ordered the attackers to abandon plans to fire the ranch buildings.

Regulators Arrested

The arrival of the troops stopped the spasmodic rifle fire that had been going on for several days. The relieved invaders were placed under arrest. On the basis that a fair trial was not possible in Johnson County, Colonel Van Horn saw them off to the closest railroad point at Douglas. Still under guard, the invaders arrived in Cheyenne a couple of days later.

There, the 44 invaders were indicted for first degree murder in the deaths of Ray and Champion. James Dudley and Alexander Lowther, both Texans, who traveled to Wyoming to fight in the Johnson County War, died from gangrene resulting from bullet wounds. Thus, both sides lost two men in the war.

Johnson County pressed the murder charges. That August the invaders entered a plea of not guilty and a date was set for the trial. Johnson County, however, found it could not pay the feed bill of the prisoners. So, the prisoners were released and a new trial date was set for January 2, 1893. That was changed later to January 21.

In the meantime, more than one thousand persons had been called into court in an effort to find twelve men who would serve as jurors without prejudice. By now the feed bill had reached $18,000 and the court still had not found enough jurors.

In the end, Johnson County could not pay the bill and withdrew the charges. All 44 men went free. The Johnson County citizens were enraged and refused to pay the $18,000 bill. In 1899, an act of the State Legislature appropriated the money to pay the 1893 bill.

On May 10, 1893 U.S. Deputy Marshall George Wellman was bushwacked and killed near Buffalo. The federal marshall had been helping serve injunctions ordered by the state against the holding of an early spring roundup in viloation of the state roundup law. In Washington, D.C. President Harrison and his Cabinet discussed the problem and as a result six companies of the all black crack 9th Cavalry Regiment were stationed in the Powder River country the summer of 1893. Officially the 9th Cavalry was on "maneuvers," but the citizens knew different. With five thousand federal soldiers roaming all around Natrona, Johnson, and Converse Counties, the bushwhacking came to an end.

An interesting sidelight to the Johnson County War was the tale of Asa Mercer, author of the book, *The Banditti of the Plains, or The Cattlemen's Invasion of Wyoming in 1892.* The author had been a Cheyenne publisher of a livestock-oriented newspaper and a staunch advocate of the WSGA and its members.

Following the abortive "war," E.H. Kimball, publisher of the *Douglas Graphic* wrote certain accusations about the big cattlemen. George W. Baxter, former short-term Territorial Covernor and large rancher, took offense at Kimball's story. He sued Kimball for criminal libel and the Douglas editor was jailed in Cheyenne. Mercer was a friend of Kimball and offered to provide his bail.

This action so upset cattlemen that they turned on Mercer breaking him by not buying advertising in his *Northwestern Live Stock Journal*, and cancelling their subscriptions to the paper. The surprise action so embittered Mercer that he wrote a book damning the invaders, revealing names and circumstances about the invasion which hitherto had been only guessed at.

When the book was published, copies of it were burned or otherwise destroyed, and each copy was systematically hunted down and destroyed. Even the Library of Congress copy disappeared. Mercer's press was destroyed in a mysterious raid.

Years later when the book was re-printed, those who had heard all about it rushed out to buy copies. It was, as several other writers have pointed out, the only book Americans have tried to destroy by burning.

Mercer, already had a colorful career before he came to Cheyenne to publish his livestock newspaper. He had been a founder of the University of Washington and had tried to populate the state of Washington and the University with more women by going to Boston and bringing back several shiploads of women to live in that state in the mid 1860's. He had been Commissioner of Immigration to Oregon and had edited and published newspapers all over the West.

Following the publication of his book, he moved to Hyattville, and died there in 1917. In re-printing the Mercer book, the publisher no doubt felt the Johnson County War was all over, and the time was safe for the re-print.

It is a fact that the Johnson County War brought a virtual end to the violence between large and small ranchers. Public opinons recoiled from the methods the large cattle interests had used. They pointed out Wyoming was now a state with legal procedures available to settle such issues peacefully. Perhaps more than anything, however, peace came to the range because even the largest cattle ranchers saw the futility of continuing the open range system—fences and the winter feeding of necessity along with a decline in foreign and eastern capital had changed the face of an industry!

The First Territorial Governor:
John Allen Campbell And Wife

Wyoming Governors 1869-1919"

Politics A Way Of Life

CHAPTER XVI

EPIC:

It took Wyoming fifty years to elect a native son to the office of governor. Robert D. Carey was born in Cheyenne in 1878 and in 1919 became governor on the Republican ticket. He also served as U.S. Senator and since he was the son of Joseph M. Carey they are so far the only father-son combination to have accomplished this. Bob Carey's election was doubly important to the Republican party because it healed a twenty-five year split in the party between a "Warren" faction and a "Carey" faction.

Ten men held the office of territorial governor— one of them being appointed twice (Warren) and one being acting governor twice (Morgan).

First Territorial Governor

The first territorial governor was John Allen Campbell, who served six years, supported Woman Suffrage and resigned to join the Department of State. The third governor, John Wesley Hoyt (1878-1882) later served as first president of the University of Wyoming. Governor Hale died in office, so Territorial Secretary S.N. Morgan served 46 days until Frances E. Warren was appointed Governor to finish the turn. Then President Cleveland appointed George W. Baxter, a prominent Wyoming rancher to the position. The public accused Baxter of misusing public lands and he resigned after 40 days. So Morgan again found himself acting governor. Next Cleveland appointed Thomas Moonlight the former commanding officer at Fort Laramie, but Moonlight was a granger and got along no better as governor than he had at Fort Laramie. Finally Benjamin Harrison appointed Frances E. Warren again in April 1889 and the people that fall elected Warren to the governorship of the newly organized state.

However, Frances E. Waren served only forty-four days when he resigned to become U.S. Senator leaving Amos Barber as acting governor. Warren's move set a precedent. Four more governors would resign their post as governor in favor of the U.S. Senate down through the years—Kendrick, 1917; Hunt, 1949; Barrett, 1953 and Hickey, 1961.

Dr. Barber unfortunately was acting governor during the Johnson County War so was defeated by the Democratic candidate, Dr. John Osborne at election. A heavy snowfall held up the official canvass from Converse and Fremont counties. Osborne came to Cheyenne and felt they were trying to cheat him of his position. He hired a notary public to swear him in. Then at night, had someone break into the governor's office, let him in and he barricaded himself inside. However, the canvassing board soon met and made it legal.

In 1905 Bryant Brooks was elected to fill out DeForest Richards unexpired term and then he was re-elected to a full term. During his term the governor's mansion was completed so they were the first family to occupy it.

In 1910, Joseph M. Carey ran on the Democratic ticket although a lifelong Republican. This was the only way he could combat the Warren machine"— he won a smashing victory and probably accomplished as many reform measures as any Wyoming governor. In spite of several governors being re-elected to a second term no one actually served the full eight years until Stanley Hathaway retired in January 1975 at the end of his full two terms. _____

Americans who listened closely to Wyoming at the close of the century would have heard the rising chorus of the many-throated bleats of thousands and thousands of sheep accompanied by the sharp whistle of the herder calling to his faithful sheep dog and horse.

They would have heard the thump, bump and grind of the cable tool rigs pounding and punching deeper and deeper into Wyoming's bossom searching for pay zones of oil so rich that not even the wildest promoter would have predicted their existence. The little central Wyoming town of Casper heard those sounds. When Natrona County organized, in 1890, the first assessed valuation produced a total of $449,151.28 which included 28,000 cattle and 28,900 sheep. By 1907 those figures had changed to 6 times the valuation with less that 25,000 cattle but 25 times as many sheep. The sheep boom had reached its height.

When World War I started, county valuation had multiplied another 6 times with half as many cattle, 350,000 sheep and the new figure of 2,284,843 barrels of oil.

Oil and Gas Wyoming

In 1921 Natrona County led all the counties of Wyoming with an assessed valuation of $61,070,426 — 220,000 cattle at about $800,000, 270,000 sheep over a million dollars, but 20 and a half million dollars in gas and oil. The oil boom had taken off.

With the largest oil and nearly the largest sheep valuation in the whole State of Wyoming in 1921, each industry had helped Natrona County leap from less than a half a million dollars to over sixty million in less than thirty years. Each industry brought a new way of life to the rangelands of Wyoming, to the small towns, and sent new breeds of politicians to Cheyenne and Washington to wrestle with problems.

The Herder and His Sheep

Sheep had been coming across the Wyoming on one trail or another since the first faint beginnings

CHAPTER XVI

WYOMING SHEEP-WYOMING OIL

of the Oregon Trail and the easy way West over South Pass. Sheepmen had their problems with Indians just as the cattlemen, but sheep crossing Wyoming at first were headed to some other area West of the State during the Oregon Trail period.

At one time it was noted that Jim Bridger had some sheep and goats at Fort Bridger in 1846.

Ten years later Judge W.A. Carter, post sutler at Fort Bridger for the Army who owned the post, had gathered a small flock together. North of Carter's herd, upon Fontenelle Creek where the Oregon Trail crosses it, "Sheep" Smith ran a flock of about 500 sheep, according to the tax rolls of Uinta County in 1872. Earlier, over 6,000 head of sheep appeared on the census rolls in 1870 in Albany County, although it was said they were on their way to some other point of destination in the West.

The Durbin Brothers in Cheyenne became interested in raising sheep for slaughter in 1870 and 1871. By 1875, a newspaper in Cheyenne listed sheepmen in that area and the approximate size of the flocks. Fourteen outfits, listed approximately 36,000 sheep.

Some cattlemen were beginning to take an interest in sheep raising, as evidenced by their partnerships or ownerships in which names like Warren, Searight, Whitcomb, and Sturgis were listed—all WSGA members who brought into the sheep business.

Sheep were about ten years behind the movement of cattle into Wyoming and they came in cautiously at first. One of the reasons was that the best sections of range had already been taken up by cattlemen.

General Brisbin, the retired soldier who wrote, *The Beef Bonanza or, How To Get Rich On The Plains,* in 1881 not only publicized the cattle business, but he also drafted a "get-rich" copy about the sheep industry. Brisbin pointed out that Willard Clark near Laramie in 1879 made an investment of $12,000 in a small sheep company. Clark got a small ranch house, some sheds, enough hay for two seasons, a number of rams and 2,100 head of native ewes. Since sheep produce two crops—wool in the spring and lambs in the fall—Brisbin said Clark produced a profit of $2,668 on his wool, $1,125 for 26 pureblood Merino ram lambs, and $4,545 on 1,515 lambs at an average of $3.00 each. The total profit on the $12,000 investment was $8,338 at the end of the first year! Brisbin noted, "The date is too imperfect to fix a ratio of profits, but Mr. Clark said in another year he would have his herd and establishment clear, and if in three years one can clear a herd and ranch worth $12,000, he would, I think, be doing very well."

It sounded so easy and the profits, according to Brisbin, were there for the taking. Not all men who came to Wyoming for the purpose of running a sheep ranch were taken in by the Brisbin "success story." They knew that range was hard to find and that the southwestern Red Desert area near Rawlins and on west to Rock Springs was about the only land left that cattlemen felt was not worth a fight.

Range, and the right to use it, was the biggest bone of contention between cattle and sheep operators.

Sheep cropped the range more closely to the ground than cattle, and in some cases, "tramp" sheepmen—those that had no range but chose to herd their flocks across established ranges of others—left a grazing scar in the heart of cattle ranges which infuriated cattlemen. It also infuriated the average self-respecting sheepman because he was accused of the act simply because he was a sheepman.

When the winter of 1886-1887 wrecked the hopes and the herds of many Wyoming cattlemen, the ranges they had used which were public domain in many cases, were left open. Sheep outfits moved onto those ranges. Since the law of open range seemed to be controlled by the man who got there first, and held it, the cattlemen who had used it began acts of violence upon the sheepmen.

A cow outfit normally hired many more hands than a sheep outfit. One herder could handle a flock or band of about 1,500 sheep with the aid of his dogs. On the other hand, a cow company with that many cattle used ten times that number of hands, and so the sheepman was nearly always at a disadvantage because he was out-numbered.

Cow companies saw more and more sheep flooding "their" range and so they drew "deadlines" over which no sheepman was allowed to pass. In some cases the deadlines were obeyed simply because the average sheepman did not want, nor encouraged violence. When the sheepman did cross the deadline, imaginary as they were and illegally drawn, sheep were attacked by masked men who clubbed them to death, ran off the herders, and then destroyed the sheep camp, wagons, or tepee used by the herder.

Poisoning of sheep food was also reported. Shooting sheep or rim-rocking them were also common ways of murdering the helpless animals. The instinct of a sheep is to follow one another and once they started moving it was easy to shove a whole band over a rimrock where they fell to their deaths.

Sometimes, masked riders would set fire to sheep, dousing them in coal oil and scorching them to death. In one case, the crew of riders also tied the sheep dogs to wagon wheels and ignited them as well.

Another variation of sheep killing was to run a herd into a stretch of quicksand and let them die there or find a boggy section and help the sheep mire themselves down.

Not all cowmen agreed with these acts even if they did not like sheep. One spoke up,

> "Most numerous are men that run their cattle on the open range; and have succeeded so far in keeping a reasonable amount of range for their cattle by drawing deadlines, making threats, writing anonymous letters to sheepmen signed with a skull and crossbones, wearing black masks when a crew of them visited a harmless Mexican to warn him to move his sheep, and once in awhile to enforce obedience when the sheepman and sheepherders were so misguided as to insist on getting some of the government grass(that was never intended by Nature for sheep) for their flocks. They have been obliged to shoot a few sheepherders, and club a few thousand harmless sheep to death with wagon spokes taken from the wheels of a sheep wagon...I am frank to confess that I lack the courage to look a sheep in the eye and hit it over the head with a wagon spoke. I will admit it has no business being a sheep and being a sheep I will admit that is has no business eating grass away from a steer, but I still could not club it to death with a wagon spoke. I can understand how, in order to strike terror into the hearts of other sheepherders, a lot of cowmen, if they are drunk enough, could shoot an unarmed defenseless sheepherder if he was slow getting over the hill with his sheep, because a herder has always had some kind of warning to leave, but the innocent dumb animal had no warning...This class of men has been able through these tactics to hold a certain amount of range for their cattle. But how much longer can they hold it? You may break the laws of the land for awhile...but finally you have all got to come to the feedrack of law and order, whether there is any fodder in it or not."

Seven years after Frank Benton spoke those words before the American Cattle Growers' Association national convention in Denver in 1902, a strange letter landed upon the desk of the French Ambassador Jean Adrian Aubin Jules Jusserand, the French dipolmat, who read the letter and sent it directly to P.C. Knox, the American Secretary of State. Knox read it and sent both letters and one of his own to Governor B.B. Brooks in Cheyenne, Wyoming.

Sheep Wagon, Two Bar Ranch Natrona, WY

SRING CREEK RAID TENSLEEP WYOMING MORNING OF APRIL 3, 1909 R. E. Carothers

What had happened to cause this international stir involving Wyoming? On the night of April 2, 1909 a band of masked riders had ridden up to a sheep camp in the No Wood River Valley and killed 25 sheep, wounded 25 sheep, destroyed the wagons and harness, and then shot and killed three sheep dogs. Three men were also killed. One was from Indiana, one was a naturalized American of French birth, and the third was a French citizen.

Involved now was far more than a few hundred head of sheep, some dogs, and a wagon or two. A French citizen had been killed. Not only that, he had been on his way home to perform his military service as a soldier of France.

The first letter, a translation copy of which is quoted as follows:

Bigtrails, Wyoming, April 16, 1909. The Ambassador of France at Washington. A heinous crime which cannot be paralleled even in the barbarian countries of Africa, Asia or Turkey has just been perpetrated in Bighorn County, State of Wyoming. During the night of April 2, at half past ten o'clock, a gang of 'cattlemen on horseback' attacked the 'sheep camps' of Joe Emgee and Joseph Allemand consisting of two camping wagons,

several dogs, a 'freight' wagon and a 'buckboard'. I heard of the crime at Joseph Allemand's house the next morning at 10 o'clock, I immediately proceeded to the spot about 6 miles distant. The sight was awful. There were some 25 sheep killed and 25 wounded, the remainder of the sheep scattered about. All the wagons and harness had been burned; three dogs had been killed, one burned; the two herds and the two wagons were about 300 metres apart, a small stream running between. There were two shepherds to a wagon; one, a Frenchman, was lying in the wagon; the other, an American, was lying at a distance of about 6 metres.

In the second wagon there were Joe Emgee, Joseph Allemand, and a young Frenchman 22 years old named Joseph Lagier of the Commune of Chabottes, in the Caton of Saint Bonnet or Orciers, Department of Hautes-Alpes. Joseph Lagier had been in Big Horn County about ten days; he had come to bid goodbye to his friends and was about to leave for France to perform his military services; he told his friends that he then had enough money to see him through his time in the ranks. Joe Emgee was an American. Joseph Allemand a naturalized American of French birth from Saint Bonnet (Hautes-Alpes). Joseph Allemand was killed in front of the wagon, a bullet perforating his abdomen near the liver and breaking his right arm; the murderers then put him to death with a shovel with which he was struck on his chest just where the neck begins. Joe Emgee and the young Frenchman were killed in the wagon; the murderers then poured kerosene on the wagon and Joe Emgee and Jules Lagier's bodies and set fire to them. There was but a part of the bodies of Joe Emgee and Jules Lagier left; they were almost completely burned and beyond recognition...

Crimes of this character have now been committed too often in this neighborhood in the State of Wyoming. It is absolutely necessary that the guilty be arrested so that there shall be no recurrence of such crimes and as it seems that the counties and the State of Wyoming have wholly neglected to arrest the offenders when such crimes were committed heretofore it seems to me that it behooves the Government at Washington to take the matter up and bring the guilty to justice. (signed) Virgile Chabot

The vetern diplomat Ambassador Jusserand, in turn, wrote to United States Secretary to State Knox on the 24th of April 1909:

According to the letter, they (Emgee, Allemand, and Lagier) were massacred by 'cattlemen' during the night of April 2; massacred is not putting it too strong; the body of one was pierced through by a bullet and the death blows dealt with a shovel. Their bodies were sprinkled with kerosene and partly burned; fire was set to their wagons; some of their sheep were killed, the remainder was scattered... I feel sure that Your Excellency will understand the extreme indignation felt by the writer (Chabot) at the crime under consideration and the earnestness with which he expresses the wish that it will not go unpunished. I am convinced that the Federal authorities and the authorities of the State of Wyoming will not neglect to take without delay every necessary step to bring punishment upon the guilty and secure for the victims' families every reparation they may be entitled to. It would seem that the case here reported is not an uncommon or solitary instance and impunity could not but further more crimes; Americans and Frenchmen alike are, as shown by this occurance, interested in having such cruelty brought to an end.

The Secretary of State wasted no time in sending copies of all correspondence to Governor Brooks along with a letter of his own. The criminals had to be brought to justice; this was not a local affair, it was international.

A young County Attorney in Basin by the name of P.C. Metz and the County Sheriff, Felix Alston were on the job. A grand jury was called in the latter part of April and seven indictments were handed down May 8, including three murder charges and one charge of arson.

Called the Spring Creek Raid by some and the Ten Sleep Raid by others, the crime was the sensation of the Rocky Mountains as the trial in Basin got underway. Not the least sensational was the total reward of $5,500 offered by the State of Wyoming and various associations including the newly formed Wyoming Woolgrowers' Association which had been organized in 1905.

At the trial, a young boy by the name of Bounce Helmer, and another Frenchman, Pete Cafferal, were star witnesses in the packed courtroom in November 1909. Of the seven men tried, George Saban and Milton A. Alexander were given 20 year sentences in the penitentiary at Rawlins. Thomas Dixon and Edward Eaton were tried for arson and received three year sentences. Herbert L. Brink, tried for murder in the first degree was sentenced to be hanged at the Rawlins penitentiary at Rawlins. Thomas Dixon and Edward Eaton were tried for arson and received three year sentences. Herbert L. Brink, tried for murder in the first degree was sentenced to be hanged at the Rawlins penitentiary. The other two men, Albert E. Keyes and Charles Farris, were granted immunity in exchange for their testimony.

Brink's sentence was soon changed to life, Saban escaped from a road gang and was never heard from again, Eaton died from a tick bite,

Dixon later killed himself in an oil field accident in Oklahoma, Alexander died later at Ten Sleep; Farris died in Montana, and Keyes vanished and was never heard from again.

Years later Mrs. Fred Bragg, whose husband owned a ranch a few miles from the scene of the Spring Creek Raid, said,

> Mr. Bragg ran both sheep and cattle and always tried to respect the rights of other stockmen. There was a deadline not far from our place on the Nowater . . . and my husband's attitude was that no herd of sheep was worth a man's life. His men were always under orders not to show resistance if they ran into overpowering forces. In the years that followed we built up large herds of good Hereford cattle at both No Wood under the Circle Dot brand and on Deep Creek where my husband and his partner, William Driscoll had the Hereford Cattle Company and branded with a Script A Bar . . . We were there when the terrible Spring Creek Raid took place . . . We knew many of those involved on both sides. It was a tragic affair, and, so far as I know, the last bitter fight between cattle and sheep interests in the war for open range.

Governor Brooks was able to relate to the Secretary of State that justice had been exercised in Wyoming.

> The French consul in Chicago obtained the complete court record and for a short period it was expected that France would ask indemnity for Lazair's (the name spelled Lagier, Lazier, and Lazair) death. This did not develop, however, but when the case was finally settled it was rumored that the United States Government paid the French Government twenty-five thousand dollars to indemnify the family of Lazair.

Arguments between cattle and sheep interests nearly vanished after the sentences were handed down, especially since summer grazing was partially controlled now by the newly created Forest Service. Policy was beginning to develop in both Agriculture and Interior Departments relative to helping both cattle and sheep owners lean their rights to grass and water on the public domain.

Dry Farmers and Reclamation Projects

Dry farmers came to Wyoming following the enlargment of the original Homestead Act when in 1909, more land was allowed the homesteader. Now not only cattlemen, but also sheepmen found grazing land increasingly scarce.

A number of reclamation projects had been started in Wyoming and it was hoped that thousands of acres of farmland would spring into lush irrigated lands as soon as the projects were completed.

The Shoshone Dam was started in 1905 and the intentions were to irrigate 200,000 acres of dry land. However, only 15,000 acres in Cody Country could be irrigated when the dam, now called Buffalo Bill Dam, was completed in 1910.

A second project was started near Casper in the form of Pathfinder Dam and a diversion dam at Whalen located near old Fort Laramie. Both dams were on the the North Platte River and it was predicted that 700,000 acres would receive the benefit of the waters of the Platte. Completed in 1911, a report said that less than 150,000 acres received water, and out of that, not quite 22,000 acres were in Wyoming; the rest of the irrigated land was in Nebraska.

Reclamation Projects Made Possible Irrigation

From Cattle To Sheep

Across the state in Jackson Hole the level of Jackson Lake was raised 17 feet in 1911 by a reclamation dam. But, that water too, went downriver, following the swift Snake River into Idaho. Wyoming water and reclamation was going to help someone, but not Wyoming ranchers and farmers.

In the meantime, the cosmopolitan aspects of Wyoming had taken another large leap forward as new people moved to the state. Notably they were English, Scotch and Irish and they came to Wyoming to take hold of the sheep business and make it bloom until by 1908 Wyoming was the top wool producer in the whole country. Whole families came from those sections of Great Britain and with them the Basque people from the high mountains between Spain and France and the Mexican people from New Mexico—even further south from Mexico they came.

Some of the old line cow outfits had felt the cattle pinch and turned to the business of having two crops a year, one which came from "woolies." Swan Land and Cattle Company, Ltd. showed they understood the change and entered the sheep business with a grand flourish in 1905. John Clay, manager of the ranch which embraced 308,541 acres and ran from central Wyoming into Nebraska said in 1912, "The advent of the sheep was the beginning of the end of the range business as far as the Swan Company was concerned...its (the open range) death rattle echoed over its broad acres in three words...the dry farmer..."

Swan told his Board of Directors that the dry farmer had found all the available range land, built fences, chased and dogged the Swan Company cattle and had caused so much trouble that it was better to sell the cattle and buy sheep. He said it was possible to herd sheep on obstructed range, but not cattle. In 1911 Swan Land had 112,365 sheep and had met a number of their financial obligations because of the sheep profits. Some of those obligations were still lingering from the terrible winter of 1886-1887— nearly a quarter of a century in the past!

Senator Frances E. Warren as well as being a politician in Washington, was also a fine stockman in Wyoming. Having incorporated the Warren Livestock Company in 1883, Warren supervised a number of activities which brought 284,000 acres under the ranch control, and by 1891 the huge company owned 110,000 sheep. His colleagues called him "The Greatest Shepard Since Abraham." Warren's reply to his fellow sheepmen when criticism was cast his way about being in the sheep business was,

Fellow sheepmen and what few other citizens there are in Wyoming, what's the matter with the sheep business? Have we deteriorated in the eyes of the world in the last two thousand years? Who writes poetry of the sheep and sheepherder at the present time? Why, fellow sheepmen, in ancient times all the poetry that was ever written was of the shepherd and his flock, and in every palace, in the most conspicious place, hung a picutre of a tall shepherd with venerable beard and flowing locks, his serape thrown carelessly over his shoulder, a long crook in his hand, leading his sheep over the hill to some fresher pasture. And when the people saw this painting (coming homeward) in the sunset glow, they cried, 'Lo! Behold the shepherd cometh.' Now what do they say? This is what you hear: 'Look at that lousy sheepherding scoundrel coming over the divide with his sheep. Boys get your black masks and the wagon spokes.'

Senator Warren would not have to worry about black masks anymore. A youthful country prosecutor, a tough old sheriff, a firm Governor, an inquisitive Secretary of State, and indignant French Ambassador, and a plumb mad French sheepman had helped set too high a price for black masks, kerosene, and wagon spokes used after dark.

The sheep industry had moved in beside the cattle industry. With the advent of farming on a larger and larger scale, it would not be too far into the future when Woolgrowers would hold memberhips in the Stock Growers and the Farm Bureau members would belong to one or the other association too. These three together would form a powerful political tool in Wyoming.

OIL BY THE BARREL

Many history books about Wyoming or the Rocky Mountains mentions that Oil seeps, or oil

Atlantic And Pacific Oil Company Drilling

180

springs, or some sort of oil traces were noticed by the earliest white men into the region. It was useful, as a rust preventitive, for softening up moccasins, keeping saddle leather pliable, gun patches, and any number of other trivial functions.

Jim Bridger and Kit Carson were supposed to have found some castoff barrels of flour left behind on the Oregon Trail by an already over-burdened emigrant train. The two mountain men mixed the flour with oil from a seep they found on Poison Spider Creek and sold it to passing emigrants as axle grease.

Bonanza Field Discovered

In 1889, according to one writer quoting the *Big Horn Rustler,* oil from the newly discovered Bonanza oil field was so powerful it could cure eye sores, smooth the skin, clear up sore throats, eradicate corns, relieve pain from burns and blisters, and detract from the pain of a bruise, cut scratch, or sprain. In addition, it cast a pretty arc of light when used in a lamp!

Oil At Glenrock

About the same time, the *Glenrock Graphic,* described how Gus Powell was making use of the oil found near Glenrock. The oil came from the Vernon Oil Field which later was incorporated into the bigger field to be named the Big Muddy. The editor said that Powell used the sticky black stuff to grease the flippers on his Fresno scrapper (a dirt mover pulled by horses), wipe his flapjack griddle with it, polish his tent floor, grease his beaver slides, and it was fine as gun grease. He even used it for gun patches. It was also useful for starting fires under Dutch Ovens, as oil for mowing machines, and the ladies in the area used to comb it through their hair since it hid any grey that might peep through their Victorian tresses.

The little weekly newspaper said Gus Powell sold out in favor of rattlesnakes since there were many in the area and that Powell sincerely hoped the Secretary of Interior would move the rattlers to another area so oil could be properly developed. The editor also said there was too much activity in Salt Creek and that oil prospectors ought to look closer at Glenrock.

First Oil Field

While the first oil well drilled in Wyoming was dug near Lander in the area now called the Dallas patch in 1883, the big pay off would come north of Casper in the Salt Creek area several years later.

Colonel Stephen W. Downey, an energetic Laramie lawyer who also served Wyoming as the Territorial Auditor, Treasurer, and Congressional Delegate as well as holding a number of other offices to which he was elected, had filed a number of claims in the Salt Creek region in 1883. Using the Mining Act of 1872, Downey located in the heart of what was to become one of the richest sections of Salt Creek, but for some unexplained reason allowed the claims to lapse, cutting himself out of a portion of 400,000,000 barrels of oil, according to Dr. T. A. Larson.

The next man with knowledge about oil and geology who took an interest in the region was Dr. Samuel Aughey, the Territorial Geologist in 1882. Before he became the geologist for the territory, he laid claim to several places, one of which he named "Jackass" an area which was to be fought over for ten years. This area provided the riches the Iba family derived from their work in the Salt Creek field.

Aughey's report to the Territorial Legislature in 1886 gave a description of Salt Creek and a fine drawing showing a cross section of the formations from which he believed oil would eventually be produced.

Piddling activity went on until 1887 when venerable old Cy Iba and his family of hardworking sons and daughters, dug placer claims all over Salt Creek. Iba, though really a gold miner, had passed through the region of the Seminoe Mountains noting oil seeps many years before, while on his way to California gold fields. He came back and prospected the Black Hills in 1875, settling near Casper to do his digging and establish placer claims in lieu of placer petroleum rights.

Over 14,000 acres were filed on by 1889 north of Casper. Phillip Martin Shannon, a fairly successfull Pennsylvannia oilman, drilled a 1,000 foot producing well on a claim he filed. The well produced about 10 barrels a day. Soon, Shannon was working in what became known as the Shannon Field. He drilled three more wells and sent his production in wooden barrels to Casper. There the oil was loaded onto freight cars on the Fremont, Elkhorn and Missouri Valley Railroad and shipped to the East.

By 1893 the head of the Geology Department at the University of Wyoming, Wilbur C. Knight, issued a bulletin in cooperation with Professor E. E. Slosson of the Department of Chemistry which described the potential of the oil field and amended and expanded the original Aughey report.

In the meantime, the Bonanza Oil Field was drilling wells at the north end of the Big Horn Basin. The Big Horn Oil Company headed up by Captain J.N. Cassell had found oil there in 1888 in a 900 foot well and by 1889 more companies moved into the area.

If Shannon and his associates in the Shannon oil field thought they were isolated from a market because of the lack of good transportation, the Bonanza field was in even worse position. Shannon was able to get his product to a railroad but in Bonanza, those early day drillers and promoters were not only isolated from a railroad and consequently a market, but they were also a long way from a source of oil field supplies. Still they financed, re-financed, drilled and drilled again. They knew there was oil and those feverish oil field optimists could not be stopped.

By 1902 Cody had been established and a well was drilled two miles from Cody on Cottonwood Creek. This well produced enough oil that promoter George T. Beck was forced to build a small refinery near Cody.

The same thing was happening in Casper. Shannon had built a 100 barrel per day refinery where Center Street and the Chicago Northwestern Railroad tracks intersect today. Shannon meant to be near transportation when he got his crude into Casper via the long strings of horses and mules pulling freight wagons over the sagebrush covered hills each day. The refinery produced 15 grades of lubricants "varying in type, and from light cylinder to a heavy 'Visco' axle grease."

Twentieth century uses of oil were being multiplied every day in America and across the world. Whole naval units were converted to the use of oil as well as were the merchant fleets. It was however, the invention of the "horseless" carriage that revolutionized the use of oil.

Mrs. Fred Bragg said in 1893 she and her husband had gone to see the Chicago's World Fair and rode the ancestor of the present automobile. She noted that everyone waved at them. So, she said, they gaily waved back, only to discover that the coattails of one of the men in the car had caught fire and that the people had been waving to warn them.

In Laramie, Frank Lovejoy built a "horseless carriage" which ran on gasoline. He also brought the first automobile, known as a Locomobile Steamer in Wyoming in 1898.

In Casper in 1908, a Pope-Toledo auto appeared owned by J.P. Chantillion. It was a twenty horse power five passenger car. That same year the citizens of Cheyenne saw the famous New York to Paris drivers pass through the city. Five years later in 1913 the State Legislature adopted metal license plates for automobiles.

The problem of interchangeable parts slowed the purchase of automobiles until Henry Ford developed the Model T which solved that problem. Fords were cheap, consequently the gasoline business boomed as did its parent, the crude oil business.

Conservation became an issue under President Teddy Roosevelt and his friend, Gifford Pinchot, under whose supervision forests were being handled in the Department of Agriculture.

Teapot Dome

A few years later, huge sections of oil-bearing lands called "Naval Reserves" were set aside, held against the future need of the United States Navy and its vast fleets which were dependent upon oil as fuel. This action from President Taft in 1909 caused much land in Salt Creek to be withdrawn leaving little room for exploration, filing placer claims and drilling. It led to the Teapot Dome investigation a few years later as unscrupulous oil promoters, including some high placed politicians, tried to use the Naval Reserves in an illegal manner.

In the meantime however, American, English, French, Belgian, and Dutch oil interests came to Wyoming to invest in Salt Creek and elsewhere in Wyoming. A more modern oil refinery came into being in 1910-1911 as the Franco-American Wyoming Oil Company built a six-inch pipeline to Casper and constructed the refinery near Oil City (as Casper was now being called).

The investors re-named the Franco-American company, calling it the Midwest Oil Company and soon after that changing it to the Midwest Refining Company. By 1913, Standard of Indiana had moved into the picture in Casper and added a cracking plant. Cracking was a more scientific way to refine and produce gasoline as well as crude by-products.

Once again, Wyoming was absorbing more of the cosmopolitan atmosphere as natives of France and Spain worked the sheep ranges. Texans drove their cattle northward to market; Scotch, Irish and English built both herds of cattle and sheep into fine ranches and the influence of oil field drillers, promoters, and financiers from all over the world added to the main bloodstream of the Equality State.

Meanwhile, Wyoming had been sending men to fight in the Spanish American War and would do the same as World War I darkened the horizon of Europe in 1914. _____

"Wyoming in foreign wars"

CHAPTER XVI

VIGNETTE:

On the night of February 15, 1898 the battleship *Maine* was blown up and sunk in Havana harbor in Cuba with the loss of 260 American lives. Public opinion in America reached crescendo heights calling for war with Spain, at once, and Wyoming citizens flocked to the colors to back up their words.

President McKinley acted fast, and so did Congress, providing $50 million dollars to spend for a war with Spain. Americans set out on their first venture as a liberty and freedom loving people intent on seeing that countries not so fortunate, seeking freedom from the yoke of tyranny, would receive help from a strong America.

Declaring on April 25, 1898 that a war had existed since April 21, Congress allowed the Secretary of War to wire the various states asking that elements of their National Guard units be mobilized, sworn into the service of the United States and prepared for foreign duty.

Governor W.A. Richard was informed that Wyoming's share of the war would be four companies of infantry and one company of artillery. Company C of Buffalo, Company G of Sheridan, Company F of Douglas, Company H of Evanston and a part of Company A of Laramie were mustered in Cheyenne and sworn into the federal service. They left for San Francisco May 18. On August 13, the Wyoming Battalion was the first to raise the American flag over Manila; and until July 6, 1899, the battalion fought in small skirmishes and patrol actions in the steaming Philippine jungles. Returning home, they were met at San Francisco by Governor DeForest Richards and his staff.

Colonel Jay L. Torrey, a former Missourian with national guard experience, then living in Wyoming, raised a volunteer cavalry regiment. Two-thirds of the regiment were Wyoming men. Called "Torrey's Rough Riders," this Second United States Volunteer Regiment, never saw action in the Spanish American War, suffering casualites when their train headed for Florida rammed both sections together causing five Wyoming soldiers to die. They were mustered out of the service and returned to their homes in October 1899.

The Alger Light Artillery, another volunteer unit made up of 125 Cheyenne men, went to the Philippine Islands and landed there December 7, 1898. This unit saw extensive action and returned home in August 1899.

War Declared— "Flu" Sweeps Wyoming

The "splendid little war" Secretary of State John Hay wrote about to his personal friend, Teddy Roosevelt, was over. A monument was raised in Cheyenne to the men from Wyoming who had served and sacrificed their lives. In 1901, the legislature appropriated money for bronze medals to be struck and presented to the men who served in the Philippine Islands. In the final accounting, Wyoming had sent 1,054 volunteers when only several hundred were needed. Sixteen of those volunteers died as war casualties.

When World War I broke out in Europe, friends and relatives watched Canadians, Basque, English, French, Irish, Scotch, Welsh, and others of foreign birth, depart to serve their nations. These men, who had worked on the ranges of Wyoming, bid their employers and families goodbye to cross the Atlantic Ocean to be swallowed up in the nightmare of trench warfare in France. Within weeks the folks back in Wyoming heard from Scotch wearing kilts and called "Ladies From Hell" by the Hun; or read about Verdun from an Irish or Welsh lad that had worked for them; were shocked by an Englishman's description of gas and gas masks; and felt terribly sorry for the French "Poilu", or French soldier living in a sea of mud and slime churned each day by heavy artillery barrages.

It was a sad time for many Wyoming people as they watched those young men go, leaving them with an empty feeling.

Still, oil had to be drilled for, sheep had to be sheared; coal had to be dug; and cattle had to be raised. All these products became more scarce as the months of war devoured wool, meat, oil, coal and the lives of young men.

Grudgingly America edged into the war as a ship was torpedoed, or some particular action angered the Americans. It came as no surprise to the nation when President Woodrow Wilson, at last, gave his war message to Congress and asked for a Declaration of War.

When Ex-Governor Brooks read the message to a large crowd that evening in the lobby of the Henning Hotel in Casper, the crowd of two thousand Wyoming citizens began to sing "America" and then the National Anthem.

On April 6, 1917 war was officially declared. The enemy was the Imperial German Government. Five weeks later on May 18 the Selective Service Act became law and America had the draft.

Dr. T.A. Larson related, "Approximately 12,000 Wyoming men entered the military service—about 6 percent of the population. This was above the national average, which was to be expected since the state had more men than women. Washakie County, with more than 10 percent of its population in uniform, claimed to lead the nation, and similar claims were made for Natrona County. Of 8,279 Wyoming draftees who were examined, 78.85 percent were accepted for active service. Only Oklahoma and Arkansas had higher percentages. The state was credited with having 3,978 volunteers in service in addition to the draftees."

Only a few short years before, Wyoming women had knitted and sewed numerous items for their men in the Spanish American War. Now, they redoubled their efforts and stepped into help sell Liberty Bonds, worked in the sugar beet fields and in many cases did the man's work around the farm, ranch, or house while the men were in Europe.

Just before the war ended, Spanish flu swept the nation and nearly 800 Wyoming citizens died from it. Almost every kind of public gathering was curtailed. The election that fall re-elected Frances E. Warren, the 75-year-old patriarch of Wyoming politics, to the U.S. Senate again. Warren's son-in-law was General "Black Jack" Pershing, commander of the American Expeditionary Forces.

Everywhere in Wyoming production zoomed higher and higher. Sugar factories, helping meet the increased demand for sugar, were built in Lovell and Worland. Farmers fed pulp from the beets to cattle and sheep adding to the growing understanding among the cattle, sheep and farming interests.

America went wild as they learned that the Kaiser, Imperial head of the German government, had abdictated and the armistice was signed on November 11, 1918.

The nineteen-month war was over for America. Once again the Nation had shored up the bulwarks of democracy and had stood resolute against enemies of freedom and liberty, but the cost was staggering. In dollars, America had spent nearly $22 billion and America mourned her 115,000 killed and 206,000 wounded.

In Wyoming the figure for World War I was 468 killed and nearly twice that number who were wounded. Today names of those who died are inscribed on a bronze table in the capitol building in Cheyenne. Returning home, veterans organized into the American Legion and the Veterans of Foreign Wars and for many years the veterans have been a formidable political entity on the state and national level.

When the soldiers did return home, they found Prohibition in force, a fast-moving economy expanding rapidly on all fronts, and a warm and typically Wyoming welcome from their friends, neighbors, employers and families. It was good to be back home.

EPIC:

YELLOWSTONE REPORT

Ever since John Colter had mentioned the geyser action, mud pots, and other natural phenomena in the Yellowstone area of the Rocky Mountains, it has been known as "Colter's Hell." And stories reaching Saint Louis or the Eastern seaboard about this area had been either discounted or denounced as lies.

But in August 1826 Jedediah Smith, David E. Jackson, William L. Sublette, Jim Bridger, and others traveled from Sweet Lake, now called Bear Lake, into the Jackson Hole region, and on into Yellowstone Park and saw for themselves these strange phenomena.

And we still have a copy of an interesting letter which Daniel T. Potts wrote back to his brother—a written record of the first known visit to the geyser region around Yellowstone Lake. (The original letter is now a part of the fine collection at the Yellowstone Park museum.)

"...that of the Yellow-stone has a large fresh water Lake near its head on the very top of the Mountain which is about one hundred by fourty Miles in diameter and as clear as Crystal. on the South borders of the Lake is a number of hot and boiling springs some of the water and others of most beautiful fine clay and resembles that of a mush pot and throws its particles to the immense height of from twenty

to thirty feet in height. The Clay is white and of Pink and water appear fathomless as it appears to be entirely hollow under neath. There is also a number of places where the pure sulphor is sent forth in abundance. One of our men visited one of these whilst taking his recreation there. At an (instant) the earth began a tremendous trembling and he with difficulty made his escape when an explosion took place resembling that of thunder. During our stay I heard it every day…"

Of course, Potts was describing the familiar Yellowstone Lake, the largest in North America above 7,500 feet in elevation. His estimate of the lake size was close, as Yellowstone Lake has about 100 shoreline miles. It covers about 138 square miles.

One other popular geyser was the Fishing Cone. It was located off-shore, and continual hot water boiled to the surface mixing with the ice cold lake water. This may have been the geyser that Bridger spoke of, saying that the hot water rose to the top, leaving colder water below so that a fish caught here was *cooked* as it was being pulled to the surface!

From that time on, the fur trappers and mountain men moved in and out of the area at will (though hampered by various difficulties such as climate, terrain, and Indians.) However, their descriptions of the physical features were still received with a great deal of skepticism. Some of the men—like Jim Bridger, with his marvelous sense of humor—responded by really *embroidering* their tales, while others avoided any discussion of the Yellowstone because they resented having doubts cast on their honesty.

In the East, almost all people in authority were unwilling to accept at face value the stories of geysers, mud pots, and hot springs. Although Governor William Clark attempted to add John Colter's discoveries to his map in 1815, nothing further was done officially until 1859 when the Raynolds-Maynadier Expedition, ordered to the Canadian border to observe an eclipse of the sun, were also ordered to explore the tributaries of the Yellowstone and the mountains of the area and the Madison and Gallatin rivers. They split the expedition; Raynolds went up the Wind River until the deep snows of the mountains turned him back to the valley and he went on to Montana, while Maynadier moved along the foothills of the

Absarakas—neither one really entered the Yellowstone area. Raynolds reported that he found two men, Jim Bridger and Robert Mildrum, who had visited that part of the Yellowstone.

Finally, in September-October 1869, David E. Folsom, C.W. Cook, and William Peterson, three curious Montanans, set out to determine for themselves the truth of the rumors. In 36 days they saw the Grand Canyon and Falls, Yellowstone Lake, the mud area, and the lower geyser basin. They claimed to have gotten the feeling that the area must be protected in some way from exploitation. When they returned to Helena, their tales were so vivid as to convince people of the realities of Yellowstone, especially Montana's Surveyor General, Henry D. Washburn.

Yellowstone named National Park

The Washburn-Doane Expedition left Montana on August 23, 1873. Among others in the group were Cornelius Hedges, who later urged that the area become a National Park, and Nathaniel Longford, who published the notes of the expedition and went on a lecture tour, assuring his incredulous audience that these wonders did truly exist. This group seriously explored—climbing and naming Mt. Washburn, descending the Grand Canyon, and naming many of the physical features. Doane made an official report to the government, Lanford and Hedges spent the winter advertising the region and discussed setting it up as a national park—a new and novel concept.

Dr. F.V. Hayden, a geologist who had been with Maynadier Expedition in 1859, had always intended to return to the Yellowstone. The expedition of 1871 had been set up as a Geological Survey and was accompanied by two well-known men, the photographer William Henry Jackson and the artist Thomas Moran. This group explored Mammonth Hot Springs, Lower Geyser Basin, and over to the Yellowstone River.

. After the Washburn-Doane Expedition returned, a bill was introduced into Congress to establish the Yellowstone area as a National Park. Through the efforts of Hayden, Langford, and Hedges and the help of some knowledgeable Congressmen the bill was pushed through in two months.

An act to set apart a certain tract of land lying near the headwaters of the Yellowstone River as a Public Park.

Be it enacted by the Senate and House of Representatives of the United States of America, in congress assembled. That the tract of land in the Territories of Montana and Wyoming lying near the headwaters of the Yellowstone River....is hereby reserved and withdrawn from settlement, occupancy, or sale...and dedicated and set apart as a public park or pleasuring ground for the benefit and enjoyment of the people; and all persons who shall locate or settle upon or occupy the same or any part thereof, except as hereinafter provided, shall be considered trespassers and removed therefrom.

Section 2—said public park shall be under the exclusive control of the Secretary of the Interior...whose.. rules and regulations...shall provide for the preservation from injury or spoilation of all timber, mineral deposits, natural curiosities, or wonders with said park, and their retention in their natural condition...

Approved, March 1, 1872
Signed by President U.S. Grant

Two Million Visit Yellowstone

During the first few years, administration of the Park was difficult. Funds were short or even non-existent, people felt the park belonged to them and they could do as they wished, and the staff was inadequate. In 1886, it was placed under the jurisdiction of the army which continued to administer it for thirty years. During that period many of the policies and regulations were laid down and enforced until they became acceptable and reasonable to the people.

The volcanic origins of the Park were brought violently to people's attention again in August 1959: a great earthquake at Hebgen Lake caused considerable damage and some loss of life. Areas of the Park had to be closed while repairs were made, or new walks laid for safety reasons before the public was allowed free access again.

Although Yellowstone Park is a place of heavy mountain snows, more than two million visitors come to Yellowstone Park annually: and each year the wintertime visitors increase by great numbers as accommodations for them are improved. Eventually, our very first National Park may become a year round facility.

INDIAN LEGEND——

Coyote's Prophecy Concerning Yellowstone Park

According to an ancient story, Coyote came into the area, subdued Grizzly Bear, who was the chief of the inhabitants, and appointed Golden Eagle to be the commander.

Coyote is supposed to have said, "In generations to come, this place around here will be a treasure of the people. They will be proud of it and of all the curious things in it—flint rocks, hot springs, and cold springs. Springs will bubble out and steam will shoot out. Hot springs, and cold spring will be side by side. Hot water will fly into the air in this place and that place. No one knows how long this will continue. And voices will be heard here, in different languages, in the generations to come."

The river was called Yellow Rock by the Indians because of the color of the formations along the shoreline, especially in the canyon. The Frenchmen and trappers called it Roche Jaun. David Thompson, the British explorer, in 1797 used the term "Yellow Stone" to refer to the river, and Lewis & Clark used it in their Journals and map. Colter's Hell was associated with the mouth of the YellowStone and so, eventually, the whole area took on the name of the river.

By 1923 all twenty-three Wyoming counties had been organized. When Wyoming became a state only ten were organized so they could send delegates to the Constitutional Convention. A county is created by an act of the legislature. Each county is formed from a sub-division of an older county. The State Constitution originally said that in order to form a new county it must have $2,000,000 valuation within its boundaries and must leave the older county with a valuation of $3,000,000. The new area must also have 1,500 bona fide residents and the voters must be in favor of organizing the new county. As time went on these figures were increased until in 1929 the population was set at 5,000 residents in the new county and the valuation at least 9 million dollars. This law has never been used as no new counties have been established since then.

The State Constituion also provided that each county shall be governed by an elected board of county commissioners—three in number and the county government shall be located in a community known as the county seat and most offices housed in the county owned building called the court house. This is also the depository of all county records.

The county fair was a means of getting together with friends. Most women entered the various contests with their baking, their garden products, or products of their sewing or crocheting. Prize animals and crops were also judged. Manufacturers of new ranch and farm equipment displayed their wares, horse races and early forms of rodeos took place and all were followed by dances and big meals.

State Flag and Seal Adopted

Wyoming's pride in itself grew right along with the growth of cities and counties. By 1921 the State Seal had been settled upon; the State Flag design of Mrs. A.C. Keyes of Casper, having been accepted earlier in 1917. That same year Wyoming adopted the Indian Paint Brush as its official flower. Ten years later in 1927. the Meadow Lark was approved as the State Bird and in 1935, on December 10th, Wyoming Day was proclaimed commemorating forever the day that Territorial Governor Campbell signed into law, the Woman Suffrage Act.

"Cowboy" Insignia

A top-notch bronc rider from Lander, Albert "Stub" Farlow, became the likeness of all cowboys riding a bucking horse as it is Farlow's silhouette implated on Wyoming license plates. The bucking horse insignia had been used by the 148th Field Artillery in World War I. Later, an updating of the insignia was done by Allen True of Denver and it was reduced to fit the license plate where it has been ever since 1936. Thus, "The Cowboy State" is well advertised wherever a Wyoming-licensed automobile travels.

CHAPTER XVII

WONDERFUL GROWING WYOMING

Cottonwood Tree

Cottonwood Official Tree

In 1947 a giant cottonwood tree was located on a Hot Springs County ranch measuring 29 feet in circumference and 76 feet 11 inches in height. The Legislature named that tree the official Wyoming tree. Lyrics by C.E. Winter and music by G.E. Knapp provided Wyoming with an official State Song in 1955 and a month later "Equal Rights" was adopted as the official State Motto. Finally, in 1967, Jade (Nephrite) was adopted as the Wyoming State Gemstone.

Along the way, as Wyoming grew out of being a Territory and into Statehood, the state began to collect a number of "firsts." For instance, Wyoming was the first U.S. area to grant women the right to hold office, to vote, and to sit on juries. This gave it the widely recognized name of "Equality State." That was in 1869 and it was called the Woman Suffrage Act, passing on December 10th the date later declared officially as Wyoming Day. Then, in 1870 Easther Hobart Morris was the first woman in the United States to be appointed a justice of the peace. That same year on September 6, Mrs. Louisa Swain of Laramie marked her ballot and voted, the first woman to ever do so.

Earlier in 1870 women were empaneled to serve on a jury and Mrs. I.N. Hartsough of Laramie was named foreman of the jury and Mrs. Martha Boies of Laramie was named bailiff, the first women anywhere to hold these titles and offices.

The Territorial Legislature, took great pride in passage of the Free County Library Law, in 1886 the first such act ever produced in America. Five years later Yellowstone Reserve, the first timber reserve in the United States was created, under the administration of President Harrison.

The first woman ever elected to a state office was Estelle Reel who in 1894, was elected State Superintendent of Public Instruction. Four years later, President McKinley appointed her Superintendent for all Indian schools.

First Ranger Station

Buffalo Bill Cody's dream of irrigation in the Cody area came to pass in 1902 when the Shoshone Reclamation Project was started, the first of its kind in the United States. That same year Shoshone National Forest was established and it is the oldest national forest so designated as such in the United States.

The next year 1903, the Wapiti Ranger Station

192

was named and it then became the first ranger station in the United States.

Devil's Tower National Monument

Three years after that, Devil's Tower National Monument was established in 1906, becoming the first national monument created in the United States.

In 1910, Mrs. Mary G. Bellamy of Laramie was elected to a seat in the Wyoming State House of Representatives. She was the first woman in Wyoming to hold a seat in either the House or Senate in Wyoming. In 1931 Mrs. Dora McGrath of Thermopolis became the first woman in Wyoming to be elected to the State Senate.

After Governor Ross died in office, his wife, Mrs. Nellie Taylor Ross was elected in 1925 to serve out the two years left of her late husband's term. Following that term in office as the first woman in America to be elected Governor of a state, Mrs. Ross was appointed Director of the U.S. Mint in 1932 and she held that position for twenty years.

The population continued to climb in Wyoming so that by 1900 the census revealed a population of 92,531. Ten years later, the population rose to 145, 965 and in 1920, there were 194,402 people counted by the Census as living in Wyoming. Not many people moved to Wyoming during the next ten years as the population moved to 225,565 in 1930.

Following World War II, the 1950 Census proved Wyoming had made the substantial move ahead as 290,529 people were listed as inhabitants of Wyoming. Still, the Wyoming populace was crying for more of everything—people, industry, agriculture, business. Faintly in the background, however, a number of other Wyoming people were thinking differently. Dude ranchers, a few cattle and sheep ranchers, a few farmers, some outfitters and once in a while a very courageous individual were quietly saying that perhaps Wyoming could go too far. Fishermen reported fishing just as good, due to the increased efforts of the hard-working Game and Fish Commission, but there were lots more out-of-state fishermen, notably those from Colorado and Nebraska, using Wyoming streams and lakes in the 1950's.

The soft and hardly discordant voices were beginnings of the faint stirring of enviromental issues that would be taken up at much of the legislative sessions in the 1970's.

Devil's Tower

Mining in Wyoming

Wyoming had been living close to history as it was being made during the first fifty years of the twentieth century. Copper mining had boomed in the green and fertile Saratoga Valley with the discovery of the Rudefeha Mine in 1897, when James Haggerty staked the most important find of his long and meager prospecting career. After naming the mine for the men who had grubstaked him, Haggerty was able to go back to his home in England and retire. The "Ru" in Rudefeha came from the first two letters of J.M. Rumsey's name. The succeeding letters represented Haggerty's other partners, thus *Ru*msey, George *De*al, George *Fe*rris, and *Ha*ggerty, when put together spelled the name of the multi-million dollar copper find.

Thousands of tons of copper ore were shipped from the area and finally a smelter was built at Grand Encampment in 1903. Much the ore arrived via a giant overhead aerial tramway which started 16 miles away high in the Sierra Madre mountains. The tramway brought the ore in big buckets down cables stretched between 304 towers.

One of the promoters of the area and a man who certainly helped to oversell the area, was George W. Emerson, who, at one time, proposed to build a new state capitol somewhere equidistant between Casper, Lander, and Rawlings. Emerson's plans failed and voters decided to keep the capitol in Cheyenne in 1904. At the same time they made permanent the site of the state university at Laramie, the penitentiary at Rawlins, and the insane asylum at Evanston. The new capitol, which would have been named after Emerson, never surfaced in the legislature as the zealous promoter moved onto greener pastures in California.

Coal Mining Booms

Coal mining employed a large number of people in Wyoming in those days at Hanna, Carbon, Rock Springs, Kemmerer, and other coal camps and mines along the Union Pacific Railroad in the southern half of the state. In the northeastern section of Wyoming near where Newcastle is today, the town of Cambria in 1889 boasted 550 anthracite coal miners who lived and worked, in a

Number Seven Mine And Dump Located In Rock Springs, WY

194

Pictured Above Is The Famous "Hole-In-The-Wall Gang": Left To Right—William Carver, Harvey Logan [Kid Curry] Sitting—Harry Longbough [The Sundance Kid], Ben Kirpatrick [The Tall Texan] And Robert Leroy Parker [Butch Cassidy].

narrow little valley. The B&M (Burlington and Missouri Railroad) pushed its iron rails into that small valley where Cambria was located to carry coal dug by the Austrian, Swedish, and Italian miners to smelters and iron foundaries in the East.

At Gebo, near Thermpoplis, more coal miners were at work. In the Sheridan area, a coal town called Acme was thriving. In 1910 there were nearly 10,000 men digging coal in Wyoming. Along with the good times and hard work these industrious people introduced, mine disasters created a pall over the Wyoming coal mining communities. At Hanna in 1903 an underground mine explosion killed 171 men. Five years later, another underground explosion at Hanna took the lives of 58 miners.

While people were still talking about the terrible loss of lives in 1903 at Hanna, Tom Horn stood on the gallows in Cheyenne and was dropped to his death. Horn, called a range detective by some and called a hired assasin by others had shot and killed a 14 year old boy named Willie Nickell in July 1901 at the Iron Mountain ranch of the boy's father, Kes Nickell. Deputy U.S. Marshall Joe LeFors had managed to get a confession from Horn and jail him. Nearly two years later, Horn was hanged for the death of the boy. Up to that time, Horn's reputation as a killer from one end of Wyoming to the other end of the state was well-known and it was believed but never documented that he had killed a considerable number of cattle thieves over the years. His reputation did not die with him in Cheyenne in 1903.

Six years after Horn was hanged, word drifted back to Wyoming from South America that the famed train and bank robber "Butch" Cassidy and his sidekick, "The Sundance Kid", or Harry Lonabaugh, had died before the rifles of the Federales, South American soldiers. Cassidy and his Hole-in-the-Wall gang had played havoc all along the Union Pacific line for a number of years. The outlaw and his cohorts were believed to have ranged as far north as Malta, Montana where they held up the Great Northern, west into Idaho and Nevada where Cassidy and his crew had held up banks; and, in Utah and Colorado where they made off with bank money and mining payrolls.

Outlaws in Wyoming

George LeRoy Parker was the given name of Cassidy. He got the "Butch" part of his name when he worked as a butcher in Rock Springs. But after serving time in the Territorial penitentiary in Laramie, young Cassidy formed a gang and there is little doubt that he had held up banks and express cars along the southern end of Wyoming.

195

He was not a badman in the strictest sense of the word in that he was not a killer. Since he only held up banks and railroads both of which represented great wealth, Cassidy was looked upon as a sort of "Robin Hood" character by many citizens in Wyoming and the West.

Generally speaking, Cassidy was well liked by those that knew him. He had worked at being a cowboy in the Big Horn Basin country and those who knew him, spoke only of the nice kind of easy going cowboy he usually was. He was heartily disliked by railroad and bank detectives who could not catch up with him. Local citizens told and re-told the stories until "Butch" became a legend in certain areas, especially the Little Snake River country, Brown's Hole south of Rock Springs and Rawlins along the Wyoming-Colorado border.

Lynch law, that is where mob rule took over from legitimate law officers and gave a killer, outlaw or holdup man a "necktie party"—as a hanging was then referred to—had pretty nearly disappeared from Wyoming by the turn of the century. One of the most famous lynchings other than the Ella Watson and Jim Averell affair in 1889, was the Parrot lynching in Rawlings on April 2, 1881.

George "Big Nose" Parrot— The Famous Holdup Man On The Cheyenne to Deadwood Stage Route.

Railroad Detectives

George Parrot, who because of his large nose was dubbed "Big Nose George," had been a holdup man on the Cheyenne to Deadwood route. In 1878 he, "Dutch Charlie" Burris and several other cutthroats had tried to derail a Union Pacific train near Medicine Bow. Frustrated in their efforts, they were observed trying to pry a section of track from the cross-ties and were reported to Tip Vincent, a railroad detective and Carbon County Deputy Sheriff Bob Widdowfield.

The two popular young lawmen tried to sneak up on Big Nose George· and his gang, but were ambushed and killed. One of the gang members was called Sin Wan, but was said to be Frank James, a well-known outlaw. A posse failed to turn up any of the gang following the discovery of the bodies of Vincent and Widdowfield. Parrot's gang drifted north into the Powder River country. A reward of $7,000 was posted for the killers, dead or alive. A big reward like that, The Union Pacific and County Commissioners of Carbon County who had put the money up said, would certainly turn up some evidence.

The effect of the reward proved right when "Dutch" Charles was caught, handcuffed to a seat in a passenger car on the Union Pacific at

Rock River, and hauled back to Rawlins to be tried. When the train stopped at the small coal mining community of Carbon, located near Hanna, a mob took the handcuffed culprit from the Carbon County Sheriff and lynched him from the nearest telegraph pole.

Shortly after that Big Nose George was apprehended at Miles City, Montana. Again, the Carbon County Sheriff brought back the criminal handcuffed to a seat on a passenger car to Rawlins. Again the train stopped at Carbon and again the same lynch mob took the prisoner away from the Sheriff. Only this time, after placing the noose around Parrot's neck and hearing his abject confession they relented, feeling Parrot would die on the scaffold once judge and jury heard the story of the killing from Parrot. They let Sheriff take Parrot to jail in Rawlins. Parrot was tried for murder in the first degree and the verdict was guilty. The legal hanging was set for April 2, 1881. During his stay in jail, Big Nose George made an attempt to escape which failed. Then Rawlins citizens still sore over the killings of the popular young lawmen began to fear the Executive Clemency (a stay of execution from the Governor) might prevail since Big Nose George had become part of a psalm singing group holding daily meetings at the jail. So, on the morning of the same day Parrot was to officially be hanged, a lynch mob overpowered the legitimate law officers and took Parrot to the nearest telegraph pole and lynched him. They failed in their first attempt because the rope broke, but they forced Parrot back up a ladder and made him jump off.

One of the last lynchings that took place in Wyoming happened in Casper in 1902. Early on the morning of March 28, 1902, twenty-four masked men overpowered acting Sheriff Warren E. Tubbs and lynched Charles F. Woodward. Woodward had killed the popular Sheriff Charles Ricker of Natrona County. The killing took place on Woodward's ranch West of Casper. Woodward escaped to Montana, but later was captured and brought back to Casper where he was jailed.

Alfred J. Mokler, Natrona County newspaperman wrote in his book, *History of Natrona County*, "Numerous coldblooded murders had been committed in Natrona County and not once had an assassin been required to pay adequate punishment and in a number of cases they were turned scot-free."

District Judge Charles W. Bramel sentenced Woodward to be hanged on March 28, 1902. A gallows was constructed to do the job. However,

citizens fearing Executive Clemency, stormed the jail and took the prisoner from Tubbs. It was only a few minutes after midnight when the lynch mob hanged Woodward on the day set for the hanging and they used the official gallows built for the job.

Billy Nye, the Laramie newspaperman and humorist linked woman suffrage with the "Midnight justice" handed down by lynch mobs as he wrote the following:

> So far as Wyoming is concerned, the Territory is prosperous and happy. I see, also, that a murderer was hung by the process of law the other day. That looks like the onward march of reform, whether female suffrage had anything to do with it or not. And they're going to hang another in March if the weather is favorable and executive clemency remains dormant, as I think it will.
>
> All these things look hopeful. We can't tell what the Territory would have been without female suffrage, but when they began to hang men by law instead of moonlight, the future begins to brighten up. When you have to get up in the night to hang a man every little while and don't get any per diem for it, you feel as though you were a good way from home!

One last outlaw gave lawmen a chase in Wyoming, but it happened many years after Woodward was lynched. Bill Carlisle, called the "The Lone Bandit" held up a Union Pacific train with a toy glass revolver in 1916. He held up U.P. trains several more times and finally after being sent to Rawlins to the penitentiary, escaped but was captured again. For the three holdups he confessed to, his total loot only amounted to $936.82. It was small pay for the chances he took and the wounds he accrued near Wheatland when he was captured. Years later he was paroled in 1936, ran a tourist shop and gasoline station in Laramie and then finally died in 1964 in Pennsylvania.

First Woman Mayor

Mrs. Susan Wissler of Dayton became the elected mayor of Dayton in 1911. She was the first woman to hold such a position in Wyoming. In the same year the *U.S.S. Wyoming* was christened and an airplane also made an appearance in Gillette.

Liberty Train

Railroads were continuing to be built in Wyoming. In 1905 rails moved West from Casper to Shoshoni, Riverton and Lander. On July 3, 1906 the Chicago Northwestern reached to Shoshoni and on October 17, in the same year, the railroad reached Lander.

The railroad could not have arrived at a better time since almost 1-1/2 million acres on the Wind River Indian Reservation was opened up for settlement under the Homestead Act in 1905. Five years earlier Chief Washakie, at the age of 102 years had died and was buried with full military honors. The same year, Arapahoe Chief, Sharp Nose passed away. The Riverton Project at a cost of $25,000,000 was started and reclamation engineers said at least 265,000 acres would receive irrigation. Only 50,000 acres were irrigated, however, once the diversion of the Wind River was completed and the canals and ditches were put into use. But it was reclamation, no matter how much it cost or who proposed it. Arid lands were being irrigated and reclaimed.

Several sections of the Big Horn Basin were being reclaimed, too, at far less the cost and under private enterprise. Iowa bankers R.E. Coburn and W.L. Culbertson joined with Loveland, Colorado promoter D.T. Pulliam and built the Upper and Lower Hanover Canal system near Worland diverting water from the Big Horn River. It took several years to accomplish, but in 1912 some 20,000 acres of land were being fed life-giving water from the canals that had been built with giant steamshovels and horsedrawn equipment.

A little north, the Big Horn County Irrigation Company did nearly the same thing as the company dug over 50 miles of canals through the county. Both irrigation projects were financed privately and today the area represents one of the real garden spots in the entire state of Wyoming. Goshen Hole in the southeastern section of Wyoming went through a similar experience.

Following the efforts of the private irrigation companies, both Holly Sugar and Great Western Sugar companies built sugar factories in the Big Horn Basin and elsewhere in Wyoming. Today sugar factories are found at Lovell, Worland, Sheridan, and Torrington. The sugar factory built at Wheatland is now engaged in mineral production and the sugar factory at Sheridan has been used in several capacities, one of which was as a flour mill.

Fishing and hunting in Wyoming has always been a popular outdoor sport and activity. As far back as 1869, Wyoming citizens had been careful of the herds of animals, the fine bird hunting, and the fishing they inherited. One of the first acts of the Territorial Legislature in 1869 had been to close the season on upland birds, making it unlawful for big game to be slaughtered and then sold in meat markets.

Hunting Seasons

Six years later a big game hunting season was set from August 15 through January 15. This unheard-of practice was initiated by Wyoming, alarmed at the wanton slaughter of its big game.

In 1884, a fishing season was established running from June 1 through November 1, and two years later a bag limit for big game hunters was established. By 1889 a State Game Warden had been named, a closed season on moose ordered, a fee set up for non-resident hunters for guides, and citizens were required to pay $1.00 as a gun license, a sort of big game hunting permit.

From time-to-time stories had reached Cheyenne about the terrible slaughter of elk going on in the Yellowstone-Jackson Hole region by a gang of "Tuskers." These men had found out that certain members of the Benevolent and Protective Order of the Elks of America would pay as high as $50 per pair of elk tusks, which would then be set as cufflinks, settings for rings, or watch-fobs.

The elk is the only ivory bearing animal within the continental limits of the United States and Wyoming has been blessed with many of the noble looking animals. BPOE officers as well as game wardens were incensed with the gang of killers, who were methodically killing elk of either sex. In addition to the ivory tusks, the gang would scalp and sell the skins to saloon keepers for stuffing and mounting. They also smoked the meat and sold it. A good six-year-old bull elk would bring as much as $75.00 including teeth, skin, and smoked meat! With so much attention focused on this situation and a national and state law, passed on scalping and selling the hide of a big game, the slaughter fell off. But it took many years to get the practice of killing elk for tusks halted. In the meantime, a winter feeding program for snowstranded elk in that region of Jackson Hole where elk migrate each winter was established. Later the winter feeding station became a national elk refuge. But for a time indignant Wyoming citizens, a firm Game and Fish Commission and outraged big game hunters were definitely on the prowl for tuskers and all three forces joined to bring the disgusting crime against elk to a halt.

Fish and Game Commission

By 1925 a Wyoming State Game and Fish Commission was established and six "lay" members were to be appointed by the Governor. This Commission is considered as one of the outstanding examples of game, bird, and fish conservation agencies the world over. Today, Wyoming basks in magnificent hunting and boasts of the world's largest North American Pronghorn Antelope herds. Wyoming also had the largest elk herds in all of America. Extraordinary white tail deer and mule deer hunting brings thousands of hunters to Wyoming each fall to help harvest the deer, antelope and elk.

Bighorn sheep and moose hunting are considered excellent sports in Wyoming. Fishing is great and with thousands of miles of streams and many natural lakes and man-made reservoirs, the fishing for all varieties of trout and other species of game fish draws fishermen in great amounts to Wyoming all year round. Upland bird hunting is also very good. So, Wyoming can say that its laws made by its citizens regarding fishing and hunting have maintained one of the best outdoor recreational and sporting climates in any of the states of the nation.

Radio was being experimented with in Wyoming in 1922. In Casper, N.R. Hood built a home operated station on which he broadcast Victrola records over the air, as far away, he said, as 1,000 miles! Occasionally Hood added a stock market

report or the weather news. Down in Laramie, KFBU was also going on the air in 1922. It was an Episcopal station and after a couple of false starts, it ran from December 10, 1925 through the spring of 1927.

At the same time, flappers were the rage as Clara Bow became the "It" girl in the motion pictures. Casper had five motion picture theaters in 1922 and three of them were showing pictures based on "whizz-bang," "jazz," and "flappers."

The oil boom was well underway in 1922. U.S. Senator John B. Kendrick was quoted as saying that he did not believe Wyoming had anything to fear from a Senate investigation into Teapot Dome but the investigation did produce a scandal left over from the President Warren Harding Administration.

Briefly, the Naval Reserve area embracing the Teapot Dome had been set aside for years. When complaints about that area being leased and without competitive bidding, were directed to Senator Kendrick, he went to work on it. Through investigation and probing questions to the Interior and Navy Departments, it was found that there were, in fact, leases being prepared for the Sinclair Oil Corporation.

Out in California, the Elk Hills Naval Reserve came under the same type of questioning. As a result, Secretary of Interior Albert B. Fall and Harry F. Sinclair received sentences and were sent to prison. Also, Fall resigned and so did Navy Secretary Edwin Denby. The leases in both naval reserves in Wyoming and California were cancelled.

Oil and a severance tax were on the minds of Wyoming citizens in the 1924 election. A one percent tax was suggested. Since the Teapot Dome affair, the oil industry had received a black eye and proponents of a severence tax felt it the right time to hang the tax on the oil industry. Party lines meant nothing as members and leaders of the Democratic and Republican parties shifted back and forth trying to find a safe position while the red hot issue commanded the attention of the people and press of Wyoming. Finally, the idea was offered to the citizens in the form of an amendment and when the final vote was tallied, the tax missed becoming law by only the narrowest margins. The idea of a severance tax did not die. It would be used as a political hammer on the oil industry for years to come until it finally passed in the 1970s.

Governor William B. Ross held office during those stormy days, but died in office just before the election of 1924. Mrs. Ross was elected to her late husband's office.

Frank C. Emerson faced Mrs. Ross in the fall election of 1926 for the office of Governor. He won with a close margin of 1,365 votes. Emerson had come to Wyoming from Michigan. He worked in the mercantile business near Pinedale; and then moved into the Worland area and served as a water and canal superintendent for the irrigation companies in the Big Horn Basin.

Governor Emerson faced another tough foe when he stood for second term. Leslie A. Miller has served in both the House and Senate and when the vote was counted, Governor Emerson pulled into the lead and won 38,058 votes to 37,188 for Miller—less than he had won over Mrs. Ross. He died 44 days later of influenza. Emerson served from January 3, 1927 until February 18, 1931, the day of his death.

Alonzo M. Clark, Secretary of State in the Emerson administrations now became Acting Governor until the next regular election. Clark was a native of Indiana, educated in Nebraska, and had been a homesteader, rancher, teacher, and county political officer in the Lusk-Gillette area for a number of years when he ran for and won the office of Secretary of State. Yet, when the Republicans met in 1932 to pick a successor to Emerson, they overlooked Clark and chose Harry R. Weston of Jackson, a relatively unknown candidate.

In the other political camp, Leslie A. Miller and Thomas D. O'Neil of Big Piney faced each other in the primary. Miller won and then continued on into the fall election and emerged a winner with a clear cut win of 3,500 votes over Weston.

That same year Franklin Delano Roosevelt swept Herbert Hoover out of office. A former Wyoming visitor in 1878, Thomas Alva Edison died at age 84, America's greatest and most honored inventor. Just before the election, Colonel Charles Lindberg and his wife had landed at Rock Springs and spent the night there. They were on their way back from a flight to the Orient. They filled their airplane at the Rock Springs airport the next with enough gasoline for a non-stop flight to Des Moines.

Depression Wyoming

As the depression crept into Wyoming, Governor Miller resorted to more centralized controls in state government and reduced state expenditures by 30%. In 1934, the Governor helped his party to win enough seats in both the Senate and House so the Democratic Party controlled them.

In 1935, Miller ran for re-election and won

against Alonzo M. Clark. It was to be one of the greatest victories for the Democratic Party since the first Territorial Legislature in 1869.

Franklin D. Roosevelt won a second term as President winning every state except Vermont and Main. Miller won in Wyoming and every state elective office held a Democratic winner too. Joseph C. O'Mahoney won the Senate seat over challenger Congressman Vincent Carter, Paul R. Greever won the seat vacated by Carter as he defeated former Congressman Charles Winter and both the House and Senate on the State level were safely in the hands of the Democratic Party. Two years later, Harry Schwartz of Casper ousted the only remaining Republican in winning over U.S. Senator Bob Carey.

1936 was the best year the Democrats had in the modern history of Wyoming. The only trouble was a deepening depression was paralyzing the nation and beginning to choke Wyoming too.

Taylor Grazing Act

The Taylor Grazing Act passed that same year. It called a halt on homesteading. All land not used or restricted as well as otherwise vacant land was to be leased for grazing. The federal lands under this act amounted to well over 16,000,000 acres.

According to Dr. Larson, up to 1935, "...almost ten million acres of land were patented under the homestead laws in the decade of the twenties, and another one and one half million acres passed to patent in the 1930's." The act put a stop to speculating; established a definite pattern for federal grazing; and separated serious ranching elements from the get-rich-quick wartime land speculators, who had filed on many homesteads trying to produce needed World War I commodities on a strictly short-term basis. From now on the only homesteading that would occur would be on reclamation areas or projects and the rest of the federal lands would be classified and grazing permits would be issued upon payment of a fee.

Oil and Gas Leasing Act

Another act creating an impact upon Wyoming was the Oil and Gas Leasing Act of 1920. Once the act went into effect, federal lands could be bid upon by oil companies for drilling purposes. If an oil strike was made royalties were to be paid to both federal and state governments. The Congressional delegation in Washington from Wyoming worked hard on this act. At home, Governor Robert Carey also put a lot of effort into the act.

They wanted an even larger return of royalty payments to the states than the 37-1/2 percent royalty Wyoming finally got which was to be taken from the base payment the federal government received. The money that Wyoming received from this oil and gas payment was spent upon education and highways. Half of it went to the public schools; 41 percent went to highways and roads; and nine percent went to the University of Wyoming for capital improvements.

Because of the Oil and Gas Leasing Act and the payments Wyoming received from the act, education and highways in Wyoming have had a substantial source of income for years.

Wyoming amply repaid the federal government the money expended on reclamation. Payments into the federal treasury from the Reclamation Fund between 1920 and 1930 amounted to well over 200 million dollars. Just about the same amount or about 200 million dollars had been spent by the federal government on reclamation in Wyoming. So—Wyoming was paying its way. Few other states could make the claim.

As the American public became addicted to the use of automobiles, gasoline was the high priority item. In Wyoming in 1920 there were 24,000 auto licenses issued. Ten years later the figure had jumped three-fold to 64,000 automobiles using Wyoming Highways and carrying license plates.

A one cent per gallon of gas tax was enacted in 1923 in Wyoming to help build and maintain highways and roads. By 1929, nearly 100 miles of oiled highways appeared in Wyoming. The Wyoming Highway Department, another of those unsung but excellent commissions found in Wyoming, said in 1926 that tourists had produced six to seven million dollars worth of tourist business. By 1935, while Wyoming citizens were learning how to live with the new 2 cents sales tax, the State Highway Patrol was created. The same year the State Liquor Commission was created, and the whole state recognized the Woman Suffrage Act of 1869 by proclaiming December 10 as "Wyoming Day."

Early Automobile

Two years later in 1937, the ruins of old Fort Laramie was purchased by the Wyoming Landmark Commission. The next year, after it was given to the federal government and placed in the National Park Service, Fort Laramie became the 74th national monument to be administered by the Park Service.

When World War I was over, the soldiers came home to a nation that was dry. The Volstead Act had passed and the 18th Amendment to the Constitution prohibited the sale and distribution of alcoholic beverages anywhere among the states. For ten years federal, state county, and city law officers tried their best to enforce the Prohibition Law but found themselves paying out millions for enforcement, arresting half the public, and spending their time in futile efforts trying to keep outside liquor from Canada, Great Britain and other nations from being "run" from ship-to-shore along the vast coastline of the nation or across the Canadian or Mexican borders into the states.

War Ends Depression

In addition, a whole new style of entertainment grew out of the prohibition era including night clubs and speakeasies (illegal night clubs). Chicago-New York style gangsters moved in and rapidly gained control of the liquor and beer markets. Bootleggers and moonshiners all figured in Wyoming history.

By 1933 the 18th Amendment was repealed by the 21st Amendment and the nation and Wyoming were both "wet" once more. Several states or sections of states chose to remain "dry."

About that same time veterans began to wonder if they should not receive some sort of bonus for their efforts in World War I. They felt they deserved something more than compensation for disabling wounds or service connected disabilities. Even though a number of presidents had vetoed a bonus, Congress passed the Bonus Bill in 1936 which pumped one and a half billion dollars into the economy of America which was still staggering along under the heavy load of the depression. Veterans promptly put their bonus checks into new cars, down payments on homes, and paid off old bills and taxes. The Bonus Bill not only satisfied veterans, but gave the economy a shot in the arm.

By 1937 the depression seemed to be slowing down a bit and the citizens saw in newsreels in theaters and heard on overseas radio reports of Benito Mussolini's crack Italian air force bombing helpless Abyssinian ground forces armed with spears in Ethiopia. They got the same look at Adolph Hitler's Wermacht, the Austrian corporal's slick ponderous war machine forcing a union between the Third Reich and Austria. The complete Austrian takeover came in 1938. The Rome-Berlin Axis was forming and countries normally considered as allies of America such as France and England were in need of strategic materials such as oil and gas, tanks and airplanes, arms and ammunition, and medical supplies.

One solution to the terrible depression was found in the great wartime production American industry plunged into. Strategic materials were produced in America and sent overseas, putting thousands of unemployed Americans back to work. That was the magic that solved the depression. Any governmental programs were merely tactics designed to keep America going until the machinery of capitalism in this great republic could get fired up again.

VIGNETTE:

"World War II in Wyoming"

In 1940 Wyoming celebrated its 50th anniversary and an appropriate commemorative stamp, depicting the Great Seal of Wyoming, was issued by the U.S. Postal Department. At Laramie, the University of Wyoming was getting ready to top the 2,000 enrollment figure. The highest it had yet reached.

Elsewhere in Wyoming, a young Cody attorney and veteran of World War I was launching his first political campaign of a long and colorful career. Milward L. Simpson was running against dapper Irish U.S. Senator Joseph C. O'Mahoney. Simpson lost by a large margin, but he came back twenty-three years later to capture a seat in the United States Senate.

For two full sessions Democrats had been in control of the State Legislature, owning a majority in both the House and Senate. That ended in 1938 when Nels H. Smith, a Weston County rancher, was elected Governor. Governor Smith did not know it then, but he was to serve as Wyoming's war-time Governor during World War II. As a

matter of fact, the Burke-Wadsworth Bill passed in the national legislature in 1940 and it should have been a tip-off for the registration of all American men between the ages of 21 and 35 for possible induction into the Army. Six years before General MacArthur had told the President that the Army was not big enough or strong enough to defend America in case of war. The government knew America was heading toward war even if the public did not know it.

Even with the first peace-time conscription of 800,000 in America taking place, Americans were finding it hard to put the idea of isolationism behind them. Ever since World War I the idea that America was isolated from the rest of the world, had no need to get involved in other problems in the world, and, if left alone, could remain neutral, had been the national theme.

Then in 1941 President Franklin D. Roosevelt initiated the Lend-Lease plan to sell, transfer, exchange, lease, and lend any articles of defense to any country deemed vital to America's well-being. In mid-1941, the momentum of the draft picked up. Ages were lowered to 18 and extended to 45. By now Hitler had swept into the Dutch and Belgian lowlands, knocked out Paris and half of France, kicked the British off the continent at Dunkirk and was bombing London on a 24-hour a day basis. Mussolini was still trying to administer a sound defeat to the Ethiopians in Africa and the Japanese were whittling away at Manchuria.

By mid-October 1940 in Natrona County some 2,500 young men had registered for the draft. All that winter and the following spring Wyoming men, like many in America who had suffered from the depression and were out of work, found steady employment in coal mines, iron mines, oil fields, on the railroads, and in far away defense plants, building ships, tanks, guns, airplanes, and explosives. The nation slowly came to the realization that war was imminent. Women also went to work in defense plants, ship yards, and other war time installations.

Some of these Wyoming men hired on with Morrison-Knudsen, a worldwide naval contractor who was fulfilling contracts at Wake Island, Midway Island, and many other small coral atolls in the Pacific Ocean. When the Pearl Harbor attack was launched, a number of them died or were captured at Wake Island. Wake fell December 22, 1941 and those prisoners-of-war were finally released late in 1945.

In 1941 the dire warnings of Gabriel Heater and Fulton Lewis, Jr. on the late night radio shows went almost unheeded as people tuned their radios in on more popular shows. They laughed with Fred Allen, Blondie and Dagwood, The Great Gildersleeve, and hummed along with Fred Waring. Lowell Thomas reported the war, but most folks listened to the Yanks and Dodgers battle it out in the fall World Series.

Wyoming chuckled when they heard about the part time auto mechanic from Rapid City by the name of George Hopkins who bailed out of a rickety old biplane and parachuted to the top of Devil's Tower. Hopkins was stranded there because he was afraid to climb down the 1,220 foot slick rock. The daring mechanic-parachutist had to spend the next six nights on top of the tower before a team of mountain Alpinists climbed up and brought him down—blindfolded!

World War II Declared

The event was hardly over when Americans heard an excited voice over their radios Sunday morning, December 7, 1941 announce that an

WYO. NAT. GUARD CAM

attack on Pearl Harbor, Territory of Hawaii was then in progress.

On December 8 President Roosevelt gave his war message to America calling the attack "unprovoked and dastardly." As he was speaking recruiting stations for all branches of the service were jammed with men and women too, all eager to serve their nation in time of war.

Then Wake Island fell later on in December, Bataan surrendered in the spring of 1942, and everywhere, the war news was bad. The only good news came when General Jimmy Doolittle led an aircraft carrier based bombing attack on Tokyo, a reminder to the Japanese that the Americans would be back, sooner or later.

During the summer of 1942 it seemed as if most of the young men in Wyoming were in uniform, as well as many middle aged men. V-Mail, short for Victory Mail, was being recieved from all over the nation and from Ireland, England, the Pacific, as American troops began their long distance effort to win the war. Even World Heavyweight Boxing Champion, Joe Louis, put on a uniform. He only took it off to defend his title against massive Abe Simon and then contributed his $100,000 purse to the Army Emergency Relief.

Military Installation in Wyoming

When 1943 rolled around, Wyoming had four military installations located within its borders. Fort Frances E. Warren at Cheyenne had been turned into a Quartermaster Replacement Training Command. An Air Base had been built at Casper where final four engine bomber training was finished just prior to shipment overseas. In Douglas, a Prisoner of War camp was built in 1943. Heart Mountain, a few miles out of Cody and Powell was a Japanese Relocation Camp and 10,000 Japanese-Americans were forced to work and live there.

On the homefront gasoline rationing had been instituted in 1943 with only four gallons allowed for ordinary purposes each week. At one time during 1944 gasoline rationing dropped down to 2 gallons a week as precious gasoline was being used to fly airplanes, drive trucks, and oil by-products powered the ships of the U.S. Navy.

Food was also rationed as a system of points was devised for issuing stamps and coupons to each family depending upon its size.

With the Allies landing in Europe in June 1944, the Americans and their Allies had turned the corner and moved from defensive tactics into a full-fledged offensive. The vaunted German Army reeled back across France, fell by the thousands before Russian guns in central Europe, and retreated from the toe of the boot in Italy before the military juggernaut of the Anglo-American armies.

In the Pacific Theater of Operations, General MacArthur and Admiral Nimitz island-hopped their way from Guadalcanal to New Guinea to Saipan and Guam on their way to Japan.

The Union Pacific Railroad in Wyoming provided an idea of what was needed for war during those days. Every conceivable kind of railroad car was seen carrying troops, tanks, food supplies, artillery, coal, gasoline and other vital and strategic materials both East and West 24-hours a day, every day of the week. The almost endless lines of trains hurrying back and forth, criss-crossing America, underscored the tenacity, the purpose, and the unswerving intent of the Americans as they went on to finish off the war in Europe on May 7, 1945 and the war in the Pacific on September 2, 1945.

Nearly 17,000,000 men had been examined for the service, and of that figure approximately 10,000,000 were drafted; volunteers counted almost 6,000,000 including 216,000 women.

Out of a population of 250,742 Wyoming listed about 35,000 men and women in uniform during the war. Of that figure, 1,095 paid the supreme price, having been killed or died during World War II.

Once again Wyoming had shouldered a proportionate share of a war the nation was engaged in and could feel justly proud of the part men and women, both in and out of the uniform, had played in helping win the war.

Wyoming had done its share, right down to high school students taking time out of classrooms in the Lovell, Worland, and Torrington areas to top sugar beets. Now that the war was over, everyone was glad to come home from the service or defense plants. Hitler, Mussolini, and Hirohito had been soundly defeated and after those atomic bombs dropped at Nagasaki and Hiroshima, the Americans felt there would not be any more wars. A dictator or war mongering nation would think twice after seeing the awful destruction caused by just one atomic bomb.

The political office most sought by Wyoming politicians has been the post of United States Senator. Among the reasons for this are the longer term of six years, the prestige of the office and greater challenge and opportunity to serve ones country.

In the history of Wyoming there have only been seventeen Senators—4 of whom were appointed to the office. Eleven have been Republicans and six Democrats, but the Democrats largely served longer terms and during most of the time there has been one from each party serving.

Until the passage of the Seventeenth Amendment in 1916 Senators were elected by the state legislature, so John B. Kendrick was the first Senator elected by the people.

Men who served several terms and built up seniority unil they held important committe assignments include: Clarence Don Clark—22 years; John B. Kendrick—16 years; Francis E. Warren—37 years; Joseph C. O'Mahoney—24 years; Gale McGee—17 years.

Of the men who have served or are at the present time serving from Wyoming, eight of the seventeen have been attorneys and six were ranchers. One was a professor, one a businessman and one a dentist.

The Wyoming State Legislature in 1893 elected 23 Republicans to the Senate and House while the Democrats elected 21 of their members to the Senate and House to serve in Cheyenne. The Populist party turned up in the House holding 5 seats. Thus, the total members in the upper and lower houses in the legislative session was 49 meaning it would take a vote of at least 25 to win the Senate office.

Warren could not muster enough votes, nor could anyone else. In fact, it has been pointed out that over thirty ballots were taken during the session. No one was a winner. Five days after the session had concluded its business, Governor Osborne simply appointed a man to the office.

Governor Osborne and his advisors sent Ashel C. Beckwith, an Evanston merchant-banker-stockman to Washington, D.C. in March to present his credentials to the Senate. He was hopeful of taking a seat in the Senate alongside Senator Carey.

After the Senate Committee on Privileges and Elections considered the credentials of Beckwith, they passed them on to the Senate with a resolution recommending Beckwith be properly seated. Two weeks had been consumed during this committee action.

The resolution was tabled until August 7 when Vice President Adlai Stevenson offered for acceptance Beckwith's credentials along with the resolution from the Senate Committee. That date was August 7, the day the Fifty-third Congress convened.

Five full months had gone by, and, saying his business committments demanded his time, Beckwith sent in his resignation. This left the post wide open once more. Governor Osborne toyed with the idea of appointing someone else, but waited until he saw what was going to happen to

EPIC:

"Wyoming Senators 1890-1975"

Wyoming's sister state to the north. Montana Legislature wished to hold a special legislative assembly and elect a Senator, then the Senate would accept his credentials. This would assure that he was seated properly in the Senate.

Governor Osborne and his advisors knew Wyoming would never hold a special assembly just to elect a Senator. If the whole Legislature in 1893 could not make up their mind in over thirty ballots, it was unlikely they would be able to make up their collective minds again.

Thus, Senator Carey was Wyoming's only Senator for a two year period in 1893 and 1894. While Carey was serving, Warren was building up a political machine whose energies would be directed by Willis VanDevanter, a Cheyenne attorney and close personal friend of Warren's. The "Warren Machine" smoothly ground out victory after victory for Warren, helping him win the post at the next election and to hold that post for 37 years.

Cheyenne, WY

Clarence Don Clark from Evanston was serving as Wyoming's Congressman while the single Senator problems were causing political headaches. He had come to Evanston from his native state, New York, and settled in Wyoming in 1881. He was an attorney and soon became involved in local and state politics serving as county attorney and also as a member of the State Constitutional Convention.

It was Clark who won the election of 1895 for the vacant Senate post. He then held the Senate seat continuously until the fall of 1916 when he was defeated by Governor John B. Kendrick. Clark served 22 years. He held the chairmanship of the Senate Judiciary Committee and other important posts and committee assignments.

John B. Kendrick was 53 years old when he decided his business and ranch could get along without him as he entered the political arena. Kendrick served from March 4, 1917 until November 3, 1933. His terms in office are marked by hard work and today the Kendrick Project near Casper still carries his name. His home town of Sheridan honored him by naming Kendrick Park in his memory.

When Senator Warren died, Republican Governor Frank Emerson named Casper sheepman Patrick J. Sullivan, an Irishman, as the man to fill the post until the next regular election. He entered the sheep business near Casper in 1888 and became a naturalized citizen in 1894. He served two times in the State House from Natrona County and then moved to the Senate and served four terms. His appointment to the U.S. Senate came December 9, 1929. He served until December 1, 1930. He did not run for re-election.

Former Governor Robert D. Carey ran for the vacant post against Casper attorney Harry H. Schwartz in the fall of 1930 and won. He took office in March 1931.

Depression Politics

Schwartz was not to be denied. Although Carey defeated him 43,626 to 30,259 for the Senate seat in 1930, he ran a second time against Carey in 1936 and won. This time Schwartz polled 53,919 votes to 45,483 votes cast for Carey.

Harry Schwartz came to Wyoming from Ohio where he had already served a term in the Ohio State Legislature. Following his political work in Ohio, Schwartz had held a number of important posts in the General Land Office in Washington, D.C. In Wyoming he served in the State Senate from Natrona County from 1933 to 1935 and then ran a second and successful campaign against Robert Carey.

Schwartz was defeated in his bid for re-election by E. V. Robertson of Cody in 1942. Robertson was born in Wales, immigrated to the United States and won his citizenship in 1925. At Cody, Robertson was engaged in the ranching business. At the time of his election he had held important posts with the Wyoming Stock Growers Association, the Wyoming Woolgrowers Association, and the Wyoming Farm Bureau.

With all three farm and stock organizations supporting Robertson's campaign for the Senate, the campaign paints a picture of the merging of the three, who only a few years before had been at each other's throats. However, Robertson was not the only man the three organizations supported in a political campaign.

When Senator Kendrick died in office in 1933, Joseph C.O'Mahoney a native of Massachusetts had come to Wyoming as a newspaperman in 1916. Within a year he went to Washington to work for Senator Kendrick as secretary to the Sheridan Senator. While in Washington, O'Mahoney went to night school at Georgetown University and by 1920 had won a degree in law from that institution. He won an appointment as First Assistant Postmaster General in March of 1933 and served until December 31, 1933 in that position. He resigned because he had been appointed to fill the vacant Kendrick seat in the Senate by Governor Leslie A. Miller.

O'Mahoney was sworn into the Senate office January 1, 1934 and immediately began his campaign for the office that year and was elected. He won again in 1940 and a second time in 1946. Frank Barrett defeated O'Mahoney in 1952, but proved Wyoming voters do not count a man out with one loss as he ran and won the Senate again

in 1954 to fill the unexpired term caused by the untimely death of Senator Hunt. Senator O'Mahoney chose not to run in 1960 and retired from office in 1961.

Edward David "Ted" Crippa from Rock Springs was appointed to fill the Senate office following Senator Hunt's death. Crippa served from June 24, 1954 until November 24, 1954 when he vacated the post in favor of O'Mahoney's successful election. Crippa did not choose to run for the post.

Lester C. Hunt came to Wyoming from his native state, Illinois in 1917. As a dentist, he lived in Lander where he practiced his profession. In 1933 he ran for and won a seat in the State House of Representatives from Fremont County. Two years later, Les Hunt was elected Secretary of State. After serving four years as Secretary of State he won the post of Governor in 1943. Hunt ran for the U.S. Senate half way through his second term as Governor. His life ended June 19, 1954, a few months short of the full six year term to which he had been elected.

Frank A. Barrett, Lusk attorney and native of Nebraska had already served four terms in the United States House of Representatives and was half way through his four year term as Governor of Wyoming when he won a seat in the Senate from incumbent Senator O'Mahoney in 1952. Barrett's record of having served as United States Representative, Governor, and United States Senator has not yet been equaled.

While Barrett seemed to have achieved the impossible in defeating O'Mahoney, a young University of Wyoming history professor won a nip and tuck contest over Barrett six years later. Dr. Gale W. McGee had served in a number of

U.S. Senator Joseph C. O'Mahoney

colleges and universities after leaving his home in Nebraska before coming to teach history at the University in Laramie. A keen student of politics, McGee gained valuable practical experience serving as a legislative assistant to Senator O'Mahoney. McGee was one of the most popular professors on the campus at the University of Wyoming when he served notice that he would be a candidate for the office then held by Senator Barrett.

It was a formidable task McGee took on, considering Barrett's political career and record of successful campaigns and victories. Following a bitter struggle fraught with recriminations, McGee squeaked by Barrett winning by 2,200 votes.

In 1964 Senator McGee faced John Wold, Casper geologist and former State Republican Party chairman. McGee won that year and six years later, Wold faced McGee once more. This time Wold had won the Wyoming seat in the United States House of Representatives. However, Senator McGee won that race too.

At present, Senator McGee is the senior U.S. Senator from Wyoming. He is a member of the Senate's two most powerful committees—Appropriations and Foreign Relations—and, he is the chairman of a third committee, Post Office and Civil Service. One of his key assignments on the Appropriations Committee is chairman of the Subcommittee on Agriculture which is important to Wyoming's rural residents.

As mentioned previously, Congressman Thomson ran for the Senate in 1960 against Raymond Whitaker of Casper and won. He died December 9, 1960 just prior to taking office.

Governor J.J. Hickey stepped down and Acting Governor and Secretary of State Jack Gage appointed Governor Hickey to fill out the term vacated by Thomson's death. It would only be a two year term as it would have to be voted on at the next regular election. Even then, two years from then, the post would only carry a four year term—thus filling out the full six year term of office in the Senate.

Following his appointment to the U.S. Senate in 1961, Hickey faced his old political rival, Milward L. Simpson whom he had defeated for Governor. Once again the two attorney-native sons faced each other and this time Simpson won. Hickey was appointed Judge of the U.S. 10th Circuit Court of Appeals in 1966. He died September 22, 1970.

Milward L. Simpson was born in Jackson Hole and was a third generation native son of a pioneer family. Simpson was the first graduate of the

Milward L. Simpson

University of Wyoming to become Governor. Simpson had served as President of the Board of Trustees of the Universtiy of Wyoming and had run for the Senate once before, but was defeated by Senator O'Mahoney. Calling Cody his home, the place he practiced law, Simpson was elected governor of Wyoming in 1954 and served in that post from 1955 until 1959.

While he was in the Senate, Simpson was a member of the Senate Interior and Insular Affairs Committee and the Government Operations Committee. He did not choose to run for re-election in 1966. He is presently retired and living in Cody and in Arizona

Two political heavyweights squared off against each other in the election for the Governor's office in 1966. One was Teno Roncalio, then serving his first term in the United States House of Representatives. The other was Governor Clifford P. Hansen. It was a close race, but Governor Hansen won it. Once again the Congressional seat had proved, as Dr. Larson said, to be "a slippery seat" as Roncalio not only lost the Senate race, but his Congressional seat as well.

Hansen was a native of Jackson and from a pioneer Wyoming family. He had gone to the University of Wyoming and years later came back as the President of the Board of Trustees. Hansen was a cattleman and was strongly backed by the Wyoming Stock Growers as well as the Wyoming Woolgrowers and the Wyoming Farm Bureau.

In 1972, Senator Hansen ran for re-election and defeated Mike Vinich of Lander in a landslide victory. Presently Senator Hansen is the ranking Republican of the Committee on Veteran's Affairs and is a member of the Senate Finance Committee, the Interior and Insular Affairs Committee, and the Select Committee on Aging.

The G. I. Bill to veterans of World War II gave those ex-servicemen and ex-servicewomen returning to their homes following the end of World War II the opportunity to further their education, and better prepare themselves for whatever profession they might choose to follow. The terrific impact of hundreds of thousands of young men and women enrolling at colleges and universities all over America caught the high institutions short-handed, short of classrooms, short of money, and short of teachers.

The University of Wyoming was no different. Enrollment had reached about 2,000 for a high just prior to World War II. By 1946, the enrollment was more than 4,000 students.

In addition, the Board of Trustees went out and hired a new president, Dr. George Duke Humphrey from Mississippi. "The Duke," as he was familiarly called by everyone—students, teachers, and citizens, set about to correct deficiencies he found *at the University of Wyoming. He boldly informed the State Legislature, budget increases and new buildings were needed all over the campus.

Then, "The Duke" got Wyoming a football coach. The school had done exceptionally well in basketball under Coach Ev Shelton. A mythical world championship had been won in 1942, and all through the 1940's Shelton coached teams, took top honors on the hardwood floors in their conference, and usually found their way to the NCAA regional playoffs. But, it was football where the school lacked spirit. When Coach Bowden Wyatt arrived, he brought with him a talented array of assistant coaches who were tough, hard working, and affable.

Wyatt taught his players if they tackled harder, blocked harder, ran harder, passed harder, and had the desire to win they would win, but it would take work, and lots of it. The formula paid off. By 1950, Wyoming had been invited to a major post-season bowl, the Gator Bowl in Jacksonville, Florida. The upstart band of underweight Cowboys ripped Washington and Lee apart, and won the game, 20 to 7.

CHAPTER XVIII

EXPANDING WYOMING 1945-1976

Wyoming was on its way to becoming a major football power. Within the next few years, the Brown and Gold colors of Wyoming pulled rabid Wyoming fans to Laramie, and other cities in the nation to see the Cowboys haul in victory after victory, and win a number of bowl games under Wyatt's successor, Phil Dickens, then Bob Devaney, and finally, Lloyd Eaton.

On the campus, it was noticeable to veterans that if they had a lot to learn, so did the professors. The older teachers could not always cope with the mixed lot of students who had held ranks ranging from colonel to private, and had been all the way round the world a time or two. Some of them seemed stunned by the onslaught, but adjusted.

In the fall of 1945, Governor Lester C. Hunt went to Casper to re-enact the signing of the Wyoming Junior College Bill. President Dean Morgan of the newly established Casper College said that when they opened the doors to Casper College in September, some 56-full time students would be ready to enter Wyoming's first junior college. The Junior College Act simply stated that any school district which supported an accreditied four year high school could levy a two mill tax on itself, and thus create a junior or community college.

By 1946 Nortwestern Community College in Powell had been established. Two years later in 1948, both Eastern Wyoming College in Torrington and Northern Wyoming Community College in Sheridan had been established. Western Wyoming Community College at Rock Springs made its appearance in 1958 followed by Central Wyoming College at Riverton in 1966. The last junior or community college to be established in Wyoming was the Laramie County Community College at Cheyenne, which opened its doors in 1968.

Each of these colleges has been a boon to students not leaving home the first year or two of their planned college education. Many of them could afford to go on to finish their college educations because of the money they saved by going first to a junior college close to home. The schools have also been a boon to local businessmen and industry as many vocational, technical

and career education courses have been implemented and tailored to solve industrial and business employment problems.

Part time students and night schools at these seven junior colleges have helped many to augment their earning power by increasing their knowledge in their work. Night courses offering no college credit have usually been the product of the demand by local citizens and courses such as fly tying, camera courses, cooking, and any number of hobbies and fields of interest have evolved. Junior college night school classes have become an important aspect of the educational and social life of these seven communities once the dishes are done and the meal is over. They have offered an intellectual and social as well as educational escape for many persons, a great many of whom have started their educations all over again once their children have left home.

Many of the veterans coming back from the war set out to build new homes or re-model their old homes. The Office of Price Administration was still in control of building materials and had not let go of their war-time restrictions as late as the spring of 1946. Lumber merchants and building contractors became angry and called for the end of the OPA, and restrictions which were hampering the mild building boom Wyoming enjoyed in the late 1940's. The OPA was nullified and in mid-summer, 1946 new construction began all over Wyoming, putting to work a large number of men and women engaged in the building trades.

The only soft spot in Wyoming's economy in the first few years following the war was the coal industry. Railroads converted from coal-energized steam locomotives to the more modern diesel fuel engines, resulting in layoffs in the coal mines along the southern end of the state. Some of the unemployed coal miners found work in the new trona mine at Westvaco, and in the Rock Springs-Green River area. Trona, from which soda ash is derived, is used in laundry detergents, soaps, bicarbonate of soda and is so pure that it needs little processing to produce baking soda from the ore. By 1952, the trona mines and trona mining possibilities were attracting the interest of multi-national corporations which began to move slowly into the area.

The oil wells around the Worland-Manderson area were carrying a high concentration of sulphur. The field was new and as it began to be developed, major sulphur corporations entered crude oil. The Texas Gulf Sulphur plant was the pilot plant in commercial production in the world. plant in commerical production in the world.

The Office Of Price Administration (OPA) Hampered Lumber Industry Until Repealed in 1946.

Far across the state, the Campbell County area was experiencing a uranium boom. Ranchers found their fences torn down by Gieger counter-carrying prospectors. In 1955, both Johnson and Campbell counties were subject to the argument raging as to whether the uranium bearing areas were under the control of the federal government or the ranchers. Eventually, the differences were settled, as the uranium boom moved south to the Sweetwater Valley along the old Oregon Trail. Halfway between Muddy Gap and Sweetwater Station a new town was built, called Jeffrey City. There a uranium mine and mill went to work while north of there, the Gas Hills began to produce uranium too. Not long after that, several other corporations built uranium mills in the heart of Shirley Basin.

All this helped Wyoming achieve national ranking as the second largest producer of uranium in America. Only New Mexico, so far, has mined and produced more of the energy ore.

Even with the surge into the mining efforts following World War II, the Sunrise iron ore mine kept right on producing thousands of tons of hematitie iron ore which in turn, was shipped to smelters in Pueblo, Colorado. Since 1900, the Sunrise mine has provided payrolls to literally thousands of employees and had been a steady taxpayer.

Blowing Copper Encampment Smelter
Encampment, WY

Minerals Abound In Wyoming

While iron has not reached the proportions of coal mining in Wyoming, in the 1950's extensive surveying was being carried on by engineers of United States Steel Corporation in the Atlantic City area near South Pass. By 1961, a huge mine was opened producing taconite iron ore, and some 600 miners went on company payrolls. In addition to the taconite, the mining company also made wide use of bentonite to bind the taconite pellets together so that resource was useable.

Bentonite had been mined in Wyoming for over fifty years, mostly in the Crook and Weston county area. There are, however, other mines now. By 1973, over a million and a half tons of the fine clay was mined. It is used in the building industry and for oil field drilling mud. Bentonite is shipped as far away as Australia and in the domestic American market is often referred to as the ''ore with a million uses.''

Gypsum and phosphate are other minerals that are mined and used in Wyoming. Several gypsum plants are located in the Cody and Lovell sections of the Big Horn Basin. Stauffer Chemical Company in southwestern Wyoming is involved in phosphate rock mining.

Coal began to make a comeback as Pacific Power and Light Company and Utah Power and Light Company began using coal in their new coal-fired power plants. Pacific Power and Light Company built their $25 million dollar plant near Glenrock on the North Platte River and developed a coal mine north of the plant. Utah Power and Light used coal, mined by Kemmerer Coal company, already one of Wyoming's oldest continuous operating mining companies.

Since those two power plants were built in the 1960's, Wyoming coal mining has steadily increased each year. By 1972, the production figure for coal in Wyoming stood at an all time high of 11 million tons.

Oil and gas production continued to rise after World War II, helping meet the demands made upon both from automobiles, factories, and industrial enterprises. The citizens of Wyoming can thank the heavy taxes oil and gas production have paid over the years resulting in low personal property taxes and money to run the fine educational programs Wyoming enjoys.

By 1960, nearly 14,000 people in Wyoming derived their income from the oil and gas industry. $68,000,000 was paid to those 14,000 people in wages in 1960.

Wyoming's basic economic strength was begin-

214

ning to flex its muscle of natural resources. Natural resources were on the rise and would soon overtake agriculture.

In 1972, cash receipts from agriculture reached $282,445,000, but figures released by the *Casper Star Tribune* in 1974 pointed out mineral production in 1973 exceeded $820,000,000.

A third industry that increased markedly after World War II was the tourist industry. In 1927, the state legislature created the Department of Commerce and Industry. The task of this department was to promote agriculture, minerals, industrial, scenic, recreation and wildlife development in Wyoming. The promotion was to be carried on with the use of brochures and maps. Twenty-eight years later, the department divided, becoming the Wyoming Travel Commission and the Natural Resources Board.

Tourism as an Industry

In 1955, ten years after World War II was over, Wyoming decided to cultivate the third largest industry in the state—tourism. The booming tourist business demanded help, and they were to get it as the Travel Commission produced brochures, took advertising in major national publications, helped produce films about the state, and displayed Wyoming at recreation and outdoor shows in the areas in the United States where Wyoming visitors came from.

As soon as the war was over, Americans filled up their gasoline tanks on point-free and ration-free gasoline and took long trips. New cars were being built, rationing was over and all America needed a vacation. Tens of thousands of these tourists headed for the Yellowstone National Park. Few even knew there was a Grand Teton National Park, but they soon found out and went home, encouraging friends and relatives to go to Wyoming! Actually, the mass exodus of travelers caught tourist court and hotel operators off-guard in Wyoming and elsewhere in the West.

Tourism was a new and mighty source of cash, and since so many people were using automobiles, a combination hotel and tourist court emerged which we now call a motel. It was easier to park a car and handle you own luggage at these new motels.

Camp grounds took on new dimensions as trailers, then campers and mobile homes, helped swell the tourist traffic to the Cowboy State. The results were new campgrounds, new trailer parks, and an over-all highway building program that has done a good job of keeping pace with increased traffic.

State Fish Hatchery
Laramie, WY

215

Millions Of Visitors Admire The Wildlife Which
Abounds At the Many Parks And Reserves
Throughout The State

Chambers of Commerce, and great attractions such as Frontier Days in Cheyenne, the tourist business was estimated in 1963 to be well over $100,000,000.

Cheyenne Frontier Days
Shoshone Indians

Tourists were now coming to see the Big Horn mountains, the Whitney Gallery of Western Art at Cody, the Green River Rendezvous at Pinedale, the Devil's Tower, and the old Fort Laramie, as well as over 50 different rodeos, pageants and parades all over Wyoming. Frontier Days, Lander's Pioneer Days, the Cody Stampede, the State Fair at Douglas, and the Central Wyoming Fair at Casper were drawing hundreds of thousands of visitors, while in the countryside, rock hounds and artifact collectors were scouring Wyoming for arrowheads and semi-precious gems and stone.

Over the years the Wyoming Game and Fish Commission had come to realize that the best way to manage Wyoming's magnificent herds of big game and to keep those herds young and vigorous was with a successful fall hunt each year. By the same token, the Game and Fish Commission knew the population of Wyoming was not sufficient to maintain a steady and healthy harvest. In the decades following World War II, the Commission did much out-of-state promoting, publicizing, and helping non-resident hunters learn that Wyoming hunter success stood in high percentage figures.

In 1951, the Natural Resources Board was created by act of the state legislature. The objective of the new commission was to search for and locate new industry for Wyoming. The new Commission worked in agricultural fields, helped find and develop water, traveled all over the country visiting potential industrial organizations who indicated an interest in Wyoming, and fully explained Wyoming's corporation taxes and personal taxes.

Of course, Yellowstone Park was the singular attraction. Grand Teton Park soon caught up, and in the meantime the "gateway" towns like Cody and Jackson and Dubois began to build more and more motels, lodges, and other businesses directly tied to the tourist businesses such as curio stores, western clothing stores, photograph shops, cafes, and gasoline stations. These gateway towns publicized the fact that it was easier to stay in their towns and then drive in to Yellowstone or Grand Teton Parks, and return to the gateway town each night.

Rodeos, Fairs, and Pageants

The idea of a "point of destination" grew, and as historic and scenic locales were developed, many tourists found a growing number of attractions Wyoming can offer the visitor.

In 1948, it was estimated that $40,000,000 was spent in Wyoming by tourists. Because of the added work of the Travel Commission, the many

Actually, the Natural Resources Board was echoing the worry, most of Wyoming had in those days about out-migration of its young people. It was felt that if more industry came to Wyoming, it would follow that Wyoming's youth would find better employment opportunities resulting in less out-migration. It was a good theory, and the people worked hard at it, as did the Natural Resources Board.

In the meantime, Wyoming went through one of the worst blizzards in memory in the winter of 1949. Snow piled up so deep that Air Force cargo airplanes flew low level missions over the worst blizzard swept areas on "Operation Haylift" bombing, as it were, stranded stock with bales of hay. Road crews worked around the clock to break through huge drifts of snow isolating oil drilling crews, stranded motorists, and small farms.

Population on Up Swing

The Census in 1950 showed Wyoming had just 10,000 people less than 300,000. That was the year Bowden Wyatt took his trim Cowboy football team to the Gator Bowl. Business was good, tourist business was crashing ahead and winter sports were taking hold little-by-little so the tourist dollar could be spread more evenly throughout the year instead of just during the summer. Things never looked better.

For the first time, Wyoming citizens could see the Korean War as television sets brought the war into their livingrooms every night on the news. Up to now, radio, newsreels in theaters, magazines, and newspapers had been the source of information, generally speaking, to America. In 1954 KFBC-TV in Cheyenne was established although

Indian Chief On Train Enroute To Crow Agency.
Sheridan, WY

a Denver television station had been seen in Cheyenne as early as 1952 and in 1957 Casper had television of its own with KTWO-TV.

It was not uncommon during those early days of television for the people on the block who had television to have "T.V. parties" and neighbors came to see the fights, wrestling matches, or to watch Jackie Gleason and Art Carney perform.

Space-Age Wyoming

Following World War II, the Casper Air Base became a county airport, and soon various units of the Air National Guard from other states came to Casper for their summer training programs.

Regardless of the heavy National Guard use of the field, air travel in Wyoming picked up considerably during the 1960's as both Frontier and Western airlines provided good service and scheduling in and out of Wyoming.

Dude ranches that used to receive their guests on trains were now going to airports to meet them. Travel by air meant a quicker way to get to Wyoming, and in turn, a longer stay on the dude ranch, or guest lodge. Wyoming had a number of bona fide dude ranches where adults could be a

cowboy and really get away from it all for a period of time. Many of the dude ranchers outfitted and packed guests in the summer to high country lakes where the fishing and sightseeing were superb. In the fall, the same dude rancher outfitted and was a big game guide. Some outfitters only worked at packing in the summer and guiding for big game in the fall. Whatever the case, the visitor who could take advantage of these deluxe hunting and fishing trips were treated to the best there was in the hunting and fishing fields in America.

The Christmas Tree contest in 1957 produced a 103 foot tall tree in Lander. According to Chamber of Commerce President Bill Nightingale, Governor Simpson and Vice President Richard Nixon would turn on the 350 forty-five watt bulbs in a long distance ceremony the night of December 3rd at 6 pm, Mountain Standard Time.

On October 4, Soviet scientists announced they had launched Sputnik I, a 184 lb. space satellite that was then in orbit around the world. Sputnik I orbited at 140 miles to 560 miles above earth and made a complete circuit every 1-1/2 hours. The American reaction was to roll up their sleeves and

218

go to work as crash engineering programs got under way to do the same and then pass the Soviets. Explorer I went into orbit on January 31, 1958 and Americans cheered.

Then on February 20, 1962 John Glenn, Jr. riding in space craft Mercury-Atlas 6 orbited the earth three times in four hours and fifty-five minutes and returned safely to earth! Glenn was the first American to orbit the earth even though Alan Shepard, Jr. had been the first American in space in May 1961.

In 1959 Warren Air Base at Cheyenne became the first Atlas Intercontinental Ballistic Missile Base in the world. Warren was now a part of the Strategic Air Command.

In August, a death-dealing earthquake hit Yellowstone National Park. At 11:37 pm, August 17, 1959 an earthquake, one of the most severe to be recorded in North America, shook the west side of the great national park so badly that it sent a 20 foot wall of water down Hebgen Lake over Hebgen Dam and down Madison Canyon which was packed with overnight campers.

Elsewhere earth fell in, cracks appeared, geyser action was upset, and the level of hundreds of geysers, springs, lakes, streams, and ponds rose or fell. When the death toll was taken, it was reported that at least 26 tourists were killed. Millions of dollars of damage was done. Concentrated action by state and federal agencies quickly restored facilities.

Nothing like this had occured since the Gros Ventre Slide above the little town of Kelly in Jackson Hole in 1925. Tons of earth from Sheep Mountain slid off forming a dam backing up Gros Ventre River and creating what was referred to as Slide Lake. Two years later, the dam of earth dissolved allowing a wall of water to sweep away the town of Kelly killing six people.

Sculptor Robert Russin from the University of Wyoming had been commissioned to do a large bronze bust of Abraham Lincoln. The heroic monument was to be placed high on the Summit, half way between Cheyenne and Laramie on what used to be called the Lincoln Highway, but is now noted at Interstate 80. The statue was cast in Mexico and when it was placed on its granite base in 1959, the statue stood forty feet high and weight over three and a half tons.

Wyoming had gained another 40,000 people, according to the 1960 Census. (That December, after having won the race in the primary against Frank Barrett, and the fall race for the U.S. Senate, personable young Congressman Keith Thomson died before he could take the oath for office. Governor Hicky resigned in January 1961 and Acting Governor Jack Gage appointed Hickey to fill out the unexpired term caused by Thomson's death.)

That same year Utah sculptor Avard Fairbanks finished his statue of Esther Hobart Morris and that statue was placed in Statuary Hall in Washington, D.C. The next year, a duplicate of the statue was mounted and placed in front of the state capitol in Cheyenne.

In 1962, Mrs. Keith Thomson ran for and was elected as Wyoming's first woman Secretary of State. Eight years before, Mrs. Minnie Mitchell had been elected the first woman in Wyoming to serve as State Auditor. Mrs. Mitchell has also been the first woman in Wyoming to serve as State Treasurer in 1952 when she was appointed to fill the post vacated by the death of her husband, J.R. Mitchell, who had been elected State Treasurer in 1950. He died May 6, 1952.

Two significant measures passed in the 1963 legislature under Governor Hansen: first, the legislature reappointed itself raising the House membership from 56 to 61, and decreasing the Senate membership from 27 to 25 seats. The second important issue was the passing of the Right to Work Bill. This act said essentially that any person could hold a job even if that person did not belong to a labor organization or union.

The last measure was the most controversial of the two and even today the Right to Work Act in Wyoming is the subject of political campaigning and constant efforts to dislodge it by organized labor.

VIGNETTE:

"Education Wyoming"

Nearly every person who describes the history of education in Wyoming says it began in 1852 at Fort Laramie when Army Chaplain Richard Vaux opened a school for the children of the army personnel. Dr. Larson points out that the school may not have started until 1856, basing his opinion upon an MA thesis written by Mrs. Lodisa Watson, who found the actual date to be 1856.

Education actually got a much earlier start. Many wagon trains crossing on the Oregon Trail included a "school wagon" where some man or woman held classes each day as they moved across the continent.

Education came in other ways too. Jim Bridger, who could not read or write, once hired a young German lad to teach him Shakespeare. Bridger committed long sections of Shakespeare to memory, but it was in German. Other mountain men, who were proficient on the trail and trapping but could not read or write, sought the help of Father DeSmet and other early religious men.

The Mormons helped their youngsters to keep up their writing and reading as they traveled West to their Zion. Some learning went on outside of any formal confines. White mountain men taught Indians how to use firearms, how to trap, the value of beaver skins and the like. By the same token, the Indians taught white men many things about prairie and mountain life, much of which could save a man's life in an emergency.

The second school in Wyoming began in 1860 at Fort Bridger when post sutler, "Judge" William A. Carter imported a school teacher to see that his own children had a proper education. Miss Fannie Foote came all the way from Saint Louis to teach and could be called the first "schoolmarm" in Wyoming.

In Miss Foote's classroom, all the children at Fort Bridger including Indians and Mexicans joined the classes she taught. She taught elementary mathematics, ancient and modern literature, reading and writing. School started promptly at 8 a.m. everyday except Sunday Classes were not dismissed until every single student had finished the day's assignment. The teacher stayed behind in those days to make certain the slowest student in the class completed the entire assignment. The older youngsters quickly realized that the faster the little ones and slower ones learned, the quicker school was out. It was a good system and worked well.

In 1867, a letter to the editor of the *Cheyenne Daily Leader* complained about children running around loose upon the streets of Cheyenne. The author of the letter wanted to know why there was not a public school in Cheyenne? The question helped trigger action in Cheyenne so that by January 6, 1868 the first public school with free education in Wyoming opened its doors in Cheyenne. A "Standing room only" crowd filled the 18th Street schoolhouse that frigid January night when the school was officially dedicated. It was built to accomodate 125 children who were instructed by the principal, superintendent and three or four teachers.

The next year Wyoming became a territory. Education got an official place in the hearts and minds of the citizens as the territorial legislature passed various acts relating to public education in Wyoming.

Benjamin Gallagher became Wyoming's first Territorial Auditor December 10, 1869, consequently becoming the first Territorial Superintendent of Public Instruction. Auditor-Superintendent James H. Hayford held the office next taking office June 4, 1870. Hayford was extremely well educated having graduated from medical school in Michigan, then studying law, and being admitted to the bar. He owned the *Laramie Sentinel*. He returned to the newspaper profession after two years in public office.

In 1873, the Superintendent of Public Instruction moved to the office of State Librarian. Thus, the two jobs were held by one man. John Slaughter, who took office on December 12, 1873.

For the next seventeen years Slaughter held the dual post. He stepped aside on March 14, 1890 due to illness, but his daughter, Minnie Slaughter was appointed to the post and held it until October 11, 1890.

In the annals of Wyoming, woman suffrage Minnie Slaughter has been largely overlooked. She was the only woman to hold any Territorial office of any stature during the years before statehood. At the time she succeeded her father, Minnie Slaughter had lived in Cheyenne since 1868 and certainly was well acquainted with the office her father had held. She only lived a few years longer, passing away in 1892 in Denver. She is buried in Cheyenne.

With the writing of the State Constitution, the office of State Superintendent of Public Instruction became an elective position with a four year term. Stephen Farwell was the first person elected to the position. He was followed by Estelle Reel, who had the distinction of being the first woman in the United States elected to a state office. Within a short time President McKinely appointed her National Superintendent of Indian Schools.

Early School Class

Upon her resignation from the state office, Carrol Parmelie was appointed. He is remembered for pushing through the measure providing for free textbooks in public schools. He also obtained a Carnegie Library for Johnson County.

Katharine Morton, holding the office for four terms, was the first one to serve for an extended period of time although several have served two terms.

Today Wyoming faces the impact of many new citizens who have school-age children. One of the most important aspects of this mineral and industrial impact is the continuance of good schools, which Wyoming now has and is working on every day, in the State Office of Education in Cheyenne.

Nineteen people have served as chief school executive in Wyoming's history as a territory and a state. Two were appointed to the post. So far, only two have worked for and received doctoral degrees in their fields of education.

Out of the nineteen persons who have served in the Office of the State Superintendent of Public Instruction, eight were women, eleven were men. Two were foreign born, but later became naturalized citizens. Two were lawyers, one studied medicine, two owned or worked for newspapers. Four were merchants, and one was a rancher. Ten of those persons were educators. Only one, Velma Linford was born in Wyoming.

For a more detailed look at the history of the office, and its history, read the booklet produced by Dorris L. Sander for the State Department of Education. It covers the entire period from July 25, 1868 through 1973. It is a careful research of the Biennial Reports submitted by the various State Superintendents of Public Instruction.

EPIC:

"Media Wyoming"

The history of media—newspapers, radio and television—in Wyoming holds several interesting surprises, even if they weren't always financial successes. For, as the reader checks back through the early history of newspapers, it is amazing to note that since the first newspaper, the *Daily Telegraph*, was published at Fort Bridger in 1863 by Hiram Brundage there has been an approximate total of nearly 500 newspapers published and printed in Wyoming.

Many ot those early-day newspapers no longer exist. For the record, the following table shows how many have been published in each of the twenty-three counties.

Albany	32
Big Horn	20
Campbell	10
Carbon	32
Converse	21
Crook	28
Fremont	45
Goshen	20
Hot Springs	12
Johnson	70
Lincoln	10
Natrona	32
Niobrara	13
Park	22
Platte	17
Sheridan	12
Sublette	4
Sweetwater	19
Teton	4
Uinta	17
Washakie	5
Weston	19
Migratory	2

The last term, is "migrator," means they were not always printed in any one place or town, since they moved from time to time.

Traveling along the Union Pacific Railroad as it was being constructed, the *Frontier Index* was published at Fort Sanders, Laramie City, Green River City, and Bear River City in the spring, summer, and fall of 1869. Actually, from March through July, the little one-page sheet was being published while Wyoming was still called Dakota Territory. After that, it was published in Wyoming Territory.

At about the same time, the *Sweetwater Mines* was coming off the press in the spring in 1868 at Fort Bridger, in South Pass City in the summer, and at Bryan City in the fall.

These two newspapers, which really did print news, looked more like what we call handbills now, but they are known in the preceeding table as migratory newspapers.

Three early-day Wyoming newspapermen earned wide recognition by their style of writing, and in the first two cases, their own particular brand of wit.

Famous Columnists

Edgard Wilson Nye, better known as Bill Nye, worked in Laramie on the *Laramie Daily Sentinel* and the *Laramie Boomerang*. Nye's dry humor and the ability he used to put that wit into his editorials and stories caught the fancy of the new territory in which he worked. People liked his keen sense of humor—not only in Wyoming Territory, but also all over the nation, and later around the world as he toured, speaking on syndicated touring engagements with James Whitcomb Riley. For a time, Nye was the best paid humorist in the country.

The second humorist-writer was Norris C.

Barrow, the publisher and owner of *Bill Barlow's Budget*, later known as the *Douglas Budget*. Barrow used the pen name of Barlow. He published several leather-bound books which he called *SAGEBRUSH PHILOSOPHY*, stating in the foreword that they were "Pure Stuph Written to Read." In Barrow's books and in his editorials in his newspaper, he dealt with the issues of the times in a humorous but very cynical manner. He coined phrases about the newly-arrived automobile; called it a "Benzine bronk" and said if you, as a man, wanted to be a member of the New York Stock Exchange, you would have to own an automobile since it became, "...a badge of bankable respectability—a splendid, if evil-smelling, snyonym of billy-goat distinction among the ultra-swell."

The sort of humor may be lost in our present society, but when it was written in 1907 Barrow was taking a direct swipe at New York Society and was applauded for doing so by his readers. Barrow also took swipes with searing editorials at the leading figures of that day and age, such as Teddy Roosevelt and the Vanderbilts and Rockefellers. He was less than kind to the "Swells" as he called them, but always amusing.

The third man was a tragic figure in many ways. He was Asa Shinn Mercer, the newspaperman who fell afoul of the Wyoming Stock Growers Association and became a victim of his own times. Up to 1892, Mercer was a dedicated and hardworking member of the press having published newspapers all over the West and finally winding up in Cheyenne publishing the *Northwest Livestock Journal*. He went to the aid of a newspaper friend of his, E.H. Kimball, editor of the *Douglas Graphic*, who was languishing in a Cheyenne jail charged with criminal libel by George Baxter, the former Territorial Governor who had been removed for illegally fencing public lands for his own benefit. Baxter was also a powerful member of the Wyoming Stock Growers Association.

When Mercer tried to go bail for Kimbal, a friendly and professional gesture, Baxter and his cohorts boycotted Mercer's weekly newspaper and broke Mercer, financially. That so embittered Mercer that he wrote the damning book, *THE BANDITTI OF THE PLAINS*, exposing to all the world his version of the Johnson County War. The book was destroyed—or at least every copy that could be found was burned, and the book printing plates were destroyed. Mercer finally moved to Hyattville and the Mercer family still ranches in that area in northern Wyoming.

The Wyoming press had produced many fine writers who have gone on to work for the wire services, other large newspapers, or become independent free-lance writers. Lest we forget, the early day newspaperman was just as much a pioneer as any gun-toting frontier marshall, or leather-clad mountain man. We should hail these men who not only went out and got the news, wrote it, and then had to hand-set the type to print it in a press they labored over—and generally, delivered the paper themselves. If Jim Bridger, General Dodge, Esther Hobart Morris, and Francis E. Warren helped build Wyoming and were pioneers, then in the same spirit, we should hail Nye, Barrow, and Mercer.

As you look back over the history of newspapers in Wyoming various names that appeared on the mastheads of those papers catch the imagination—such as: *Platinum City News*, a Centennial weekly published in 1924; *Missing Link*, published in 1882 in Laramie; *Semper Fidelis*, a Shermain publication in 1878; *Dillion Doublejack*, from 1902 to 1909, a weekly in the copper fields near Enterprise; *Platte Valley Lyre*, a weekly which enjoyed a 13-year life at Saratoga from 1888 to 1901; *The Rowdy West*; published first at Fort Fetterman in 1886, it died at Douglas in 1887; *Glenrock Graphic*, a weekly at Glenrock, lasted from 1887 until 1889. Then there were *Lost Springs Times*, a weekly that held the attention of those hardy folks living in the Lost Springs area between Douglas and Lusk while it was published from 1914 until 1932; *Colony Coyote*, a weekly published from 1914 until 1926; *Lightning Flat Flash*, a weekly that started out in 1907 at Hulett as the *Intermountain Globe*, and continued publication at Lightning Flat until 1926. In Dubois the *Courier* which started in 1919 became the *Dubois Frontier* in 1929, and changed names once more as the *Dubois Mountaineer* in 1939 before folding in 1941. *Cheyenne Daily Argus* was both a daily and a weekly and lasted from 1867 until 1869. *Black diamond*, a weekly started in 1898 at Diamondville, was succeeded by the *Diamondville News*, but it folded in 1900. *Flock Master*, a Natrona county weekly at Arminto lasted only one year in 1915. *Guernsey Iron Gazette*, a weekly that started at Guernsey in 1901, became the *Guernsey Gazette*, in 1905, whose forerunner was really *The Iron Gazette*, organized and started in Hartville in 1899. *Vita Nuova*, published in 1908 in Rock Springs in Italian, was Wyoming's only foreign language newspaper. The *Wyoming Watchman* was published as a weekly in Evanston for one year in 1908.

Some of those early newspapers have lasted over the years, using different names born with each new owner. Look at the *Worland Grit*, published as a weekly first in 1905. Thirty-three years later, in 1938, *The Grit* was merged with the *Wyoming News*, another Worland weekly started in 1935. For a little over a year the weekly came out under the title of the *Worland Grit & Wyoming News*. In 1939 that weekly became a five-times a week daily under the title of the *Northern Wyoming Daily News*, the name it still bears today. Along the way, the daily newspaper also merged with the *Washakie Signal Fire*, a weekly in Worland that printed its first paper in 1939, but was merged with the daily in 1943.

In Wyoming now, there are 30 weekly newspapers found over all Wyoming except in Albany, Natrona, Sheridan, and Washakie counties. In addition, there are 9 daily newspapers in Wyoming now, and 1 monthly, the *WYOMING STOCKMAN FARMER.*

The Territorial and early day Wyoming newspaperman was known to write fearless editorials. His stories reeked with cynicism and his pen dripped with acid as he took free-wheeling swipes at his competitors and all things in general, but more often at the politicians of that day and age. They were, those reporters of the early days, the very spirit of the freedom of the press. The papers they owned, or worked for also displayed that spirit as they named their papers to reflect what they stood for: *The Wyoming Blade* (Hulett), *The Worland Grit* (Worland), *The People's Voice* (Buffalo), *The Optimist* (Kaycee), *The Lower Valley Live Wire* (Thayne), *The Laborette* (Rawlins), *The Kemmerer Camera* (Kemmerer), and *The Apex*(Sundance). It doesn't take too much imagination to see that those publishers not only believed in the freedom of the press, they proclaimed it from their very mastheads.

They were the first to criticize their own home towns. *The Laramie Daily Sentinel* on May 11, 1871 called upon the Albany County Commissioners to do something about the loose hogs rooting in every city street gutter. Hundreds of hogs were causing general havoc, chasing kids, spooking horsemen, upsetting mothers pushing permabulators down the board sidewalks, and the like. Something *was* done about it, thanks to the reminder by the newspaper. A fine of $100 for every pig found downtown was levied, if the hog owners didn't corral the owners of their ham and bacon.

E. H. Kimball was the same editor that took a trip to a Cheyenne jail in 1892 thanks to ex-Territorial Governor Baxter, also published the *Glenrock graphic* in 1889 in Glenrock. He was a sort of early Chamber of Commerce, as were most of the newspapers. Kimball wrote in 1889, ''Come on Ye Capitalists and Speculators, and parties desirous of a good business location! Glenrock has the inducements to offer, and room for thousands of people!'' Kimball hoped Glenrock would grow. It would take a power company and a coal mine and a good sized oil strike to make Glenrock grow, as it has now, almost 100 years after Kimball tried to promote the town.

There was one thing for certain: any public officer in any public office had better do the job to which he was elected or appointed. If not, or even if there was the slightest suspicion that the officer was doing less than the job called for, it was a safe bet the offender would become the subject of a red hot editorial. Look at what Bill Nye said on January 8, 1880 as he literally dismembered Wyoming Territorial Secretary Albertis Worth Spates.

Spates had just been relieved from his duties,

and it is evident that Nye was glad he was leaving Wyoming. Nye said that Spates would "Be remembered as the champion intellectual light weight of all time. He will stand out on the pages of some future cyclopedia as the go-as-you-please appetite and the angle worm legs..." Nye felt he had helped Wyoming grow, and that Spates was a hindrance. "...No man, single-handed, can pave the way for wealth and enlightment, when every two weeks a reclaimed lunatic or star idiot is sent here to get a square meal and give away the affairs of State to all eternity. At times I am free to say that I am discouraged and disheartened." Finally Nye said, "...Dealing with a particular class of fools is easy enough, because you get used to their ways, but when a minister plenipotentiary is busy at all seasons of the year ransacking the globe to secure rare and costly specimens of new and unique fools, it becomes a difficult task to catalogue and arrange them."

All media in Wyoming over the years have worked hard for the public as they aired politician's view points so a voter could get a clear idea of just who was running for office. Because of this, it goes without saying that politicians did not always like the media, but they certainly respected it.

The demand for truth rules the press today in Wyoming. With 9 daily newspapers, 30 weeklies, and a host of trade publications being written, printed, and delivered to Wyoming's citizens, there can be little question that Wyoming people are having an opportunity to find out what is going on in their State.

If they feel they don't get enough news, then the electronic media surely fills the gap. There are 34 radio stations in Wyoming now including 5 FM stations, one of which is the University of Wyoming radio station on the campus of Laramie. In 1930, KDFN radio station took to the air waves as an officially recognized radio entity with the right to carry on broadcasts on an assigned frequency. Later on the call letters were changed to KSPR. Now, that same station is called KTWO in Casper. KTWO has the distinction of not only

being the oldest radio station in Wyoming, but in August 1975 the station went to an assigned 50,000 watt power signal, making it by far the most powerful station in the State. That means that radio broadcasts heard from Casper will also be heard in the western half of the United States. "K 2" as they call themselves at KTWO, may well become the largest broadcast and news medium in Wyoming.

At present, Wyoming has three television stations which include KTCU-TV, Cheyenne; KTWO-tv, Casper; and, KWRB-TV in Thermopolis. In addition, Wyoming citizens are given the opportunity to view television broadcasts from TV stations in Montana, Idaho, Utah, Colorado, South Dakota, and Nebraska.

Usually, out-of-sate broadcasts are handled by cable television. Even so, the local cable television stations sometimes carry local programs which they originate.

NET, the National Education Television, is now being seen in a number of Wyoming cities, and in one case, one television channel carries a county library program on a regularly weekly basis (Natrona County Library, Casper, Channel 12).

Another aspect of electronic media is the wire services. The Associated Press and the United Press International both have their headquarters in Cheyenne close to the state capitol where much state news happens. Managers of these news services which gather news from the nation and internal news off their own wires, in turn, send out stories covering Wyoming events to various members of the media in Wyoming who subscribe to their service. The wire services also send out-of-Wyoming news of various events taking place in the Cowboy State.

In addition to the wire services, the AP or UPI, radio and television stations can be, if they wish, affiliated with ABC (American Broadcasing Company), NBC(National Broadcasting Company), or CBS(Columbia Broadcasting System). Entertainment, news, and informative programs originate over these systems for which the local radio or television stations pays a fee.

CHAPTER IXX

CHANGING WYOMING

The Democratic landslide sweeping President Lyndon B. Johnson into office in the fall of 1964 had its effects on the Wyoming election too. Geologist John Wold of Casper was defeated by incumbent Senator Gale McGee, and newcomer Teno Roncalio norrowly defeated incumbent Republican Congressman William Henry Harrison. Also, the Wyoming State House of Representatives was to be controlled by Democrats, the first time since 1958. All facts considered, the election of 1964 was a super election for the Democratic Party in Wyoming.

Missiles in Wyoming

In 1965 the citizens of Cheyenne were dismayed when the 389th Strategic Atlas Missle Wing was shut down. On the heels of that notice it was learned that the 389th was to be replaced by the 90th Strategic Missile Wing and some 200 Minutemen missiles were to be installed near Cheyenne. The change represented the first and largest intercontinental ballistic missile base in America.

During the 1965 legislative session, the state sales tax crept up from 2% to 2-1/2% by act of the State Legislature. The minimum wage took a jump to 75 cents per hour by legislative act, too.

Wyoming also celebrated its 75th birthday in 1965. All over the state, a number of celebrations and pageants were put on, and in Casper, the 75th Anniversary of Statehood was celebrated with Casper's 100th birthday!

A New Type Transportation

During the winter of 1965-66, there was a marked increase in the use of snowmobiles. Up to that point ranchers and stockmen had found it tough going in the heavy snow in some sections of Wyoming, as they bucked deep drifts and wide fields of snow, isolating herds of cattle and other stock needing feed. The use of power wagons, sno-cats, snow plows, and an occasional snow-plane had been the rancher's means of transportation in their winter feeding program. Now, they had the relatively easy, if noisy, snowmobile.

Others finding the snowmobile not only fun but economical were the hunters, ice fishermen, and other recreation-minded people. These soon found that an all-day trek from Jackson to Yellowstone and back was virtual winter wonderland trip, filled with sights of trees decorated with ice necklaces, deep blue skies, and sparkling snow. It was a whole new way to visit Yellowstone. As time went by, other trips or snowmobile treks were blazed from Dubois to Pinedale over the Continental

Divide, from Casper to Medicine Bow, and from just about anywhere a snowmobile could travel with its long endless rubber tracks to carry sightseers, fishermen, and photographers into a Wyoming winter wonderland.

On the mineral front uranium, trona, and oil production figures rose in 1965, while natural gas and coal stayed the same. In Cheyenne, a new chemical plant was built. The $3-1/2 million-dollar Wycon Plant produced urea, a chemical compound used as a fertilizer.

The 1967 Legislature officially named the Casper Troopers as ''Wyoming's Musical Ambassadors.'' It was a title justly and honestly won, as the Troopers had carried off many drum corps titles: the World Open Championship, the Veterans of Foreign Wars national championship, and the Color Guard (restricted to girls only) of the Troopers had won five consecutive national championships.

The Troopers were dressed in Civil War era uniforms, which were replicas of the 11th Ohio Volunteer Cavalry Regiment. This regiment had served the length of the Oregon Trail through Wyoming during the Civil War years, and everyone who saw and heard the Troopers thrilled to their stirring music.

In 1967 Governor Hathaway instituted a series of out-of-state trips to encourage business from other areas to come to Wyoming. Publicized were the low taxes, vast natural resources, excellent educational opportunities, and unlimited recreational opportunities. By 1968, trips to New York City, Los Angeles, Houston, and San Fransisco had been made.

On the 4th of July, Glenn Ford, a popular Hollywood actor led the parade at the Cody Stampede, and helped in the dedication of the new million dollar addition to the Whitney Art Gallery. From now on the historic art center would be called the Buffalo Bill Historical Center. Winchester Western, a firearms company reproduced their famed Model 1873 lever action rifle and sold it as a commemorative firearm. A royalty from the sales was presented to the art center. Dr. Harold McCracken, the best known authority on Frederic Remington and Charles M. Russell headed up the Buffalo Bill Historical Center.

The winter of 1968-1969 saw hundreds of motorists stranded on the new Interstate 80 stretch of highway between Wolcott Junction and Laramie. The highway there was dubiously dubbed ''The Sno-Chi Minh Trail.'' Residents of by-passed towns like Medicine Bow and Rock River had tried to tell federal highway engineers they were laying out the new road too close to the shoulders of brooding Elk Mountain. The by-passed townsmen said the snow would fall to depths of ten to twenty feet, and that the blowing snow was fierce. But, now one listened to them, and the result was, and still is, a terrible stretch of road in the winter, though a lovely stretch of road in the summer.

In 1969 the Department of Natural Resources had been re-named and new duties assigned it. From now on, the new branch of executive government would be called DEPAD, the Department of Economic Planning and Development, Four divisions called Industrial, Mineral, Water Development, and Planning would work under the

U.S. Senator Gale McGee

director, Roy Peck, a former Riverton newspaperman. The department pursued the theory of "Quality Growth," a plan to help Wyoming grow, but keep its great living standards intact at the same time.

The summer of 1969 a commemorative stamp was issued by the U.S. Postal Department honoring John Wesley Powell and his courageous crew for their early explorations of the Green River and the Colorado River.

In 1967 the State Legislature took advantage of the Land, Water and Conservation Act which triggered an outdoor recreation plan for Wyoming. By 1969-1970, the Legislature funded an outdoor recreation program, and also created the Wyoming Recreation Commission. This organization, long needed in Wyoming, was to be responsible for the planning, acquisition, development, and management of all state parks, historical and archeological sites.

In Sheridan, when the famed Sheridan Inn was about to be torn down, Mrs. Neltje Kings stepped in and purchased the historic old Inn and slowly brought it back to its days of elegance when Buffalo Bill stopped there along with other famed characters of yester-year.

An interesting fact surfaced in the 1970 Census. Wyoming had only gained 2,350 people since 1960! The State had enjoyed 46% population increase between 1930 and 1970, but after checking the 1970 figures it was determined that fifteen Wyoming counties had lost population. The only counties making gains were Albany, Campbell, Fremont, Johnson, Natrona, Park, Sweetwater, and Teton. As a matter of fact, half of Wyoming's population resided in Laramie, Natrona, Albany and Fremont counties.

An out-migration of young people had been occuring between 1960 and 1970, and Wyoming was not able to compensate for it. Not even the net increase due to birth rates was able to offset the loss of job seeking young people leaving Wyoming, or the younger set in Wyoming seeking more urban way of life.

Added to that, there was more white collar jobs being offered in Wyoming than farm-ranch jobs, and right along with the national decline in the rural-related jobs, Wyoming had the same experience.

It was with these facts in mind that Governor Hathaway and his economic advisors were worried about Wyoming's lack in population growth, and the out-migration of Wyoming's richest natural resource—the young people of Wyoming.

The Quality Growth Plan offered by the DEPAD

Governor Stan Hathaway

unit of government and the Recreation Projection from the Recreation Commission carried the promise of more jobs and a good future for a good many young folks as each commission, under the leadership of the Governor, dug in and went to work backing up these progressive plans.

J.D. Brunk, a former state senator from Hot Springs County replaced Roy Peck as head of DEPAD in 1970, and in the Annual Report of DEPAD for 1970 Brunk discussed water project loans and sprinkler irrigation and outlined a number of water projects DEPAD had been involved in during the year. The report pointed out that because Wyoming's payrolls were tied 13.6% to the minerals industry which did not experience a downturn like the national economy, Wyoming was able to show not only an increase in its per capita income, but also had been able to maintain an exceptionally low set of unemployment figures. The DEPAD report did note that because Wyoming failed to produce consumer goods, cost of living was high because those consumer goods had to be transported to the state thus commanding higher prices.

The way was certainly clear, but how to do it was another problem. Mineral production was, even then, on the upswing, and from now on, the new corporations so dearly sought in Wyoming were now beginning to arrive.

18 Year Olds Right to Vote

The 1972 legislature gave 18-year-old persons the right to vote in Wyoming, and also produced a new formula for the minimum wage. It was a rising minimum wage scaled to go from a $1.40 per hour on June 1, 1971 to $1.50 in January 1972, and up to $1.60 on December 31, 1972. Up to that time the minimum wage was $1.10 per hour.

The state legislature in 1971 also created DAFC, the Department of Administration and Fiscal Control; a Bureau of Criminal Indentification and Investigation; the Legislative Service Agency-Management Council; and, the Community College Commission.

The year 1972 proved to be a good one for the whole state and for the first time in Wyoming's history total bank deposits exceeded one billion dollars. That was a far cry from the speech Congressional Delegate Carey had made in March 1890, stressing that there was hardly $150,000 banking capital in all of Wyoming when the state became a Territory in 1869.

The billion dollar bank deposit figure in Wyoming represented a 19% increase over 1971

which meant deposits were increasing at a steady rate. This is considered by economists as a dynamic economy and usually called for increased investments in Wyoming's economic future.

DEPAD reported in 1972 that the oncoming energy shortage would increase Wyoming's financial future.

No one in their right mind could argue against that. Certainly not those who lived in Gillette or Rock Springs, both of whom were riding the big splurges of digging, drilling, mining, and transporting minerals found virtually in their backyards.

When the election of 1972 wound itself up, there were many who wanted men and women standing for office to cry out against mineral development, or at least to say they would work for reclamation, re-seeding, site location lag time, and anti-pollution controls of every description for noise, land, water, and wildlife.

Oddly enough, those issues didn't really stand out in the election in the Senate races as Senator Hansen faced Mike Vinich, a Lander businessman. Neither did those issues get a full round of discussion in the race for Congress as incumbent Congressman, Roncalio faced Bill Kidd, a Casper businessman.

The issues talked about were the drug problems, crime, the war in Vietnam, national defense, inflation, unemployment, and above all else, deficit spending in Washington, D.C. All four candidates said they would work closely with the Department of Interior underwhose broad guidelines much of Wyoming's surface and sub-surface minerals were being mined.

The incumbents won their races, and Wyoming stepped into 1973 with happiness as the cease-fire in Vietnam was announced January 28. It took three more years before the longest and costliest war in which the United States was involved would actually cease.

Wyoming men and women — 12,241 of them — had worn the uniform of one of the branches of the services in that unpopular war. That figure represents a period of time reaching back to January 31, 1955 and stretching ahead to May 7, 1975. In that time frame 130 Wyoming men lost their lives while another 699 were wounded in Vietnam, or suffered service-connected disabilities. Not documented, were 3 Wyoming Prisoners of War.

At the urging of Governor Hathaway, the 1973 State Legislature passed the Enviromental Quality Act which created the Department of Environmental Quality Act which created the Department of

Environmental Quality. The organization of the department took effect July 1, 1973 with Robert Sundin as department head. This new executive department was charged with the responsibility of maintaining the quality of Wyoming's environment as industrial development occurred. In other words, as each mineral was developed in Wyoming, the effect upon land and water quality was to be examined with the utmost of care.

Even with the gasoline shortage in 1973, and many dire predictions that the tourist industry would suffer, Wyoming's travel business was still strong. In fact, a good fall hunting season coupled with a really fine skiing and snowmobile winter season helped defeat any real serious deficit caused by a summertime decline.

Traffic was certainly up along the Union Pacific Railroad as 100-car unit-trains traveled from the Hanna and Rock Springs areas hauling coal to Wisconsin and Iowa. Strict air quality regulations in the midwest forced power plants in those states to seek a coal which contained a low sulphur content. That meant, at least for them, Wyoming low sulphur coal.

"Coal—Wyoming's coal," said Ernest K. Thurlow, manager of mineral development for Burlington Northern Railroad," is the name of the game." Thurlow foresaw a huge development for more energy coming from coal when he spoke those words in November 1970. He was dead right.

While Thurlow was making his speech, Governor Hathaway was speaking at the dedication of the new 212 mile pipeline, the dedication of the $7 million dollar gas plant built by Mc Culloch Oil, and the completion of an Inexco oil well in the fabulous Hilight Oil Field south of Gillette. At the tri-ceremony, Hathaway said that Hilight, "...was the biggest oil patch in the Rocky mountains." He noted that the triple operation signalled Wyoming's debut as a major producer of natural gas."

The Forty-Second Legislature created the Wyoming Conservation and Land Use Study Commission in 1974, stating that the commission's responsibilities would be to make recommendations to the Governor and the Legislature concerning existing land use controls, additional controls, and necessary or appropriate constitutional amendments and legislation regarding statewide land use policy and planning.

Also, the Slurry Pipeline Bill passed the Forty-Second Legislature. This bill, signed into law, conditionally guaranteed the transportation of coal from Campbell County to an Arkansas steam generated power plant fired by coal. After the coal had been mined, and then reduced to a fine sand-like substance, it would then be entered into the thousand-mile long pipeline carrying water which inturn would transport the coal slurry to its destination.

The problem yet to be solved is where the water is to come from? Pipeline officials have said it could come from ground water supplies of which, they have claimed, Wyoming has a large surplus. It might also come from a far away South Dakota reservoir on the Missouri River. Since there has not been enough really hard evidence that the ground water Wyoming has would not affect other water tables, or that it can be recharged sufficiently enough to allow the amount the pipeline officials have said they'll need, the pipeline remains to be built. Also, pipeline officials have many crossings they will need to secure from railroad lines scattered between Wyoming and Arkansas.

Governor-elect Ed Herschler was administered the oath of office on January 6, 1975 as retiring Governor Stanley K. Hathaway looked on. Hathaway had just completed two full terms amounting to 8 years and 4 days, the longest time any one man had ever served the people of Wyoming as their Governor. He had served from January 2, 1967 until January 6, 1975.

VIGNETTE:

"Where away Wyoming?"

Three things gripped the attention of Wyoming citizens up to mid-July 1975 other than rising prices, gasoline price hikes, and inflation: first, the Vietnam War was officially declared over May 7; second, the continuing story of former Governor Stanley K. Hathaway; and, third, the National Bicentennial year was getting ready to celebrate the Nation's 200th birthday.

No one liked the Vietnam War; not even from the very beginning was it ever popular. For twenty long years America had been sending her young men to slup their way in and out of the humid jungles and rice paddies in the war-torn tiny nation half a world away while the politicians in Washington stumbled around trying to figure a way to get out of the way with honor.

The act was now finished, and the most unpopular was ever fought by Americans was over. Everyone sincerely hoped that Congress could get to work on the pressing domestic issues of the energy shortage, inflation, rising unemployment, crime, drugs, and a dozen or more other issues considered far more important than a "no-win" war which is what the Vietnam fiasco became in the long run.

Hathaway Named To Interior

Curious as to what their former governor, Stan Hathaway, was going to do now, Wyoming citizens finally got their curiosity bump scratched when Hathaway reported that President Jerry Ford had nominated him as Secretary of Interior. While most people applauded the President's choice, it was not a popular nor unanimous nomination by any stretch of the imagination.

Environmentalists joined forces to testify before the Senate Interior Committee headed up by Senator Henry Jackson of Washington. Their message was that because of the energy impact and rapid development of energy-related minerals in Wyoming, Hathaway might not be prudent and conservative enough with the Nation's mineral resources to serve as Interior Secretary, the caretaker of 540 million acres of federal land.

For nine long, grueling weeks the confirmation of Hathaway was tested before the Senate Interior Committee; each year, each phase, and each decision Hathaway had made in his eight years of Governor of Wyoming was spotlighted. Not only that, private investigations were intensely and thoroughly checked out on Hathaway's personal life.

Finally, the Interior Committee in the Senate hung a tag of "do pass" on Hathaway's nomination and sent it to the Senate floor to be voted on by the Senate. On June 12, 1975, the United States Senate confirmed President Jerry Ford's choice for Secretary of the Interior by a vote of 60 to 36. On June 13, 1975 the first man in Wyoming history to be nominated and confirmed to Cabinet level, former Governor Stanley K. Hathaway, was sworn into office by Supreme Court Justice William H. Rehnquist as the President joined Mrs. Hathaway at the ceremony as spectators.

Six weeks later, to the day, Interior Secretary Hathaway resigned from the post citing ill health as the reason. At first, when Hathaway went to the President and offered to resign because of ill health, the President asked his personal physician to see to it that Hathaway go to Bethesda Naval Hospital. There a mild case of diabetes was discovered, a loss of weight, and extreme fatigue contributed to Hathaway's illness. After a week, and with a predicted stay of a month or more, Hathaway resigned saying he felt he ought to step down in view of the fact he could not function properly at the head of the vital post from a hospital. Reluctantly, the President accepted the resignation.

The unspoken fact of all of this nomination, confirmation, and resignation was the culmination of Wyoming undergoing a transition from an agricultural economy to a mineral economy and Hathaway became the target for frustrated environmentalists trying to halt the move. Oil had been the mainstay for many years as Wyoming's most prolific mineral. Coal production had been up, and then, down. But now coal, oil, trona, uranium, bentonite, sand and gravel, gypsum, iron, copper, and oil shale had moved into first place in the Wyoming economy. About the only thing Wyoming could do was to guide the development of its minerals.

Hathaway had worked hard at the task of guiding development, but environmentalists didn't think he went far enough. So, they fought Hathaway, and called in all the help they could get to fight the nomination.

In the meantime, the third event happening in Wyoming in 1975 were the many kick-off plans for the Bicentennial Year, 1976. All across the nation Bicentennial Commissions were meeting and helping groups organize for the presentation of pageants and plays for the preservation of history commemorating America's 200th birthday.

Wyoming's Bicentennial Commission was headed up by well-known author Peggy Simson Curry of Casper. Among other events planned were the arrival of the Freedom Train in Casper in the fall of 1975; a wagon train made up of replica Conestoga prairie schooners, one from each state, passing through Wyoming on its way to Philadelphia for the July 4, 1976 celebration; the dedication of Independence Rock as a state park; and a host of other events of local and state interest.

All summer long in 1975 out-of-state fishermen, mostly from Colorado and Nebraska, streamed into Wyoming to enjoy the great fishing in the state. At the same time, new arrivals were coming into Wyoming to take up homes and jobs as new citizens due to the mineral development impact. While the rest of the Nation suffered an economic setback, Wyoming continued to move ahead and keep unemployment figures below the national average.

The face of Wyoming is changed even as this book was being written. Less encouragement to out-of-state fishermen, hunters, and visitors was now being heard by old and new residents of the state. At the same time, all residents were demanding extreme caution in mineral development and cautious treatment of the land, air, and water.

Transition is not easy. Wyoming was losing her identity as a "bridge" state. While vast multitudes still use Wyoming as a bridge to go from here to there, or vice versa, more and more people are stopping to stay and live in Wyoming than ever before in the state's history. Wyoming is now a point of destination.

The day and age of the Oregon Trail is past. Territorial days are gone. Wyoming, for better or worse, is growing up. Growth is hard on everyone, including the ardent enviromentalists, the public office holders, ranchers and farmers, town builders, frustrated educators, miners, oil field workers, and the old-timers who remember Wyoming as it was. But everyone can agree, generally speaking: Wyoming is a great place to live, yet, and everyone is going to work to keep Wyoming that way.

The effort of it all, and the beauty of it all, and the history of it all is Wyoming's Wealth.

INDEX